Doing Social Work Research

Doing Social Work Research

Louise Hardwick and Aidan Worsley

Los Angeles | London | New Delhi
Singapore | Washington DC

SAGE Publications Ltd
1 Oliver's Yard
55 City Road
London EC1Y 1SP

SAGE Publications Inc.
2455 Teller Road
Thousand Oaks, California 91320

SAGE Publications India Pvt Ltd
B 1/I 1 Mohan Cooperative Industrial Area
Mathura Road
New Delhi 110 044

SAGE Publications Asia-Pacific Pte Ltd
33 Pekin Street #02-01
Far East Square
Singapore 048763

Library of Congress Control Number: 2009943560

British Library Cataloguing in Publication data

**A catalogue record for this book is available from
the British Library**

ISBN 978-1-84787-912-7
ISBN 978-1-84787-913-4 (pbk)

Typeset by C&M Digitals (P) Chennai, India
Printed and bound in Great Britain by TJ International Ltd, Padstow, Cornwall
Printed on paper from sustainable resources

Mixed Sources
Product group from well-managed
forests and other controlled sources
www.fsc.org Cert no. SGS-COC-2482
© 1996 Forest Stewardship Council
FSC

Aidan Worsley would like to dedicate this book to his mother and father, Bill and Olive Worsley. Dad, I think of you every day.

Louise Hardwick would like to dedicate this book to Monica, Tom, Ursula, Molly and Leo.

CONTENTS

ACKNOWLEDGEMENTS

This book could not have been written without the contributions made by all the service users, carers, students and practitioners we have met and worked with over the years. Their imagination, commitment and determination are applauded. We would also like to thank our colleagues at the universities of Liverpool, Central Lancashire and Chester for their comments, observations and insights that have also helped shape this book and move it towards completion.

INTRODUCTION

It's a little perplexing that relatively few social workers appear to be doing research into practice. Who better to interview service users or run a focus group of carers for the purposes of research than social workers? Who better to analyse complex situations and make a sound assessment based on the evidence? Surely social workers know more about social work than anyone else, possess the right value base and an enviable range of transferable skills for research that equip them commendably. And yet, research appears to be in its infancy for practitioners in the social care workforce. We would argue that research involving social workers (and service users) tends to be done *to* us rather than *with* us. Even less often is research actually done *by* us. This is perhaps even more surprising when we start to think more globally about the nature of social work.

'The social work profession promotes social change' (International Federation of Social Work, 2000). These are the very first words of an important definition of our vocation and they beg the question – in what ways do we really promote social change? Similarly, the (UK) Code of Practice has, as its first line: 'Social Care Workers must protect the rights and promote the interests of service users and carers' (General Social Care Council, 2004). The question of how we might respond to these fundamental challenges to our professional practice is given an answer: practitioner research. This book is written especially for every social worker, whether on a qualifying training course, post qualifying programme or simply a practitioner in the field. This book will also provide help to those throughout the social care workforce who are interested in learning more about doing research. It is a book designed to help people research their practice and roots itself in the kinds of research that a typical social worker might consider doing. It's a very practical guide, using examples drawn from practice throughout. But its main emphasis – and main hope – is that it is about *doing* social work research. We aim to inspire, enable and encourage the reader to engage in research because we think that is what is best for the profession and, more importantly, the many millions of service users and carers that social workers support, challenge and empower throughout their careers.

HOW THE BOOK WORKS

The whole point of this book is to encourage research by talking about it in a clear, uncluttered way, avoiding unnecessary jargon. It tells social workers what they need to know to begin doing research and, in that sense, should be seen as an introductory text – although it will suit experienced as well as beginning practitioners. It is important that the reader is aware that a vast array of research methods texts exist which look in considerable detail at many of the areas we discuss. We therefore advise the reader to use this book in conjunction with others to deepen their understanding of key issues. Our focus is social work research. This book aims to demystify the research process by helping people engaged in social work practice learn about it. Case studies will help the reader examine the concepts, theories and methods than underpin research. The book has an abundance of activities that are based in real life practice, each one of which aims to bring alive important aspects of learning to be a practitioner researcher. In this way, reflection is encouraged and we hope the reader will become an active participant in the book. Each chapter ends with 'key points' that underline what one needs to take on board and suggestions for further reading. This is also a book for the many students – on qualifying and post qualifying courses and throughout the canon of social care awards – who are looking to learn about or begin research, perhaps as part of a dissertation or project. Each chapter has a section that specifically looks at how the activities it will go on to describe relate to the National Occupational Standards for Social Work. We felt this was important because it underlines that research is a core part of the practitioner's role but may also help in relating research activity to competency structures.

HOW TO USE THIS BOOK

This isn't a book that is necessarily meant to be read from the beginning to the end. Rather, it presents the reader with self contained chapters that focus on specific aspects of research that will be especially pertinent to different people at different times, dependent upon their own approach to research. Having said that, the sequencing of the chapters follows a logical path through the areas that the practitioner researcher needs to understand in order to engage in research. The book has two main sections. The first section contains the first three chapters of the book. They cover the underpinning ideas that, as practitioner researchers, we need to understand so that we can appropriately contextualize our research – seeing it in the broader context of other research. They consider such questions as, 'what is special about social work research'? There have been many debates on this matter and we all need to arrive at an understanding of where social work research sits in relation to, for example, healthcare research. We also make the argument for the practitioner researcher – the challenging notion that as busy practitioners we should, to some extent, be researchers as well. It makes the point that in many ways, social workers *are* researchers and already possess many of the skills that the practitioner researcher will come to rely on. But we underline the point that these are *transferable* skills. A social worker is no more automatically a researcher than a researcher is automatically a social worker. Practitioner researchers need to harness the considerable skills they have and apply them appropriately to a new, different task. Whilst we would not argue this is always easy, a social worker should find that the transition to researcher practitioner is not too difficult because of the transferability of the typical skill sets they possess – and therefore well within the reach of the everyday social worker. In this sense our prof-ession possesses strong foundations in developing its practitioner researchers. There is also a thorough examination of the ethics of social work research which considers the ethical principles we should adopt when going about our research. After all, social work research is likely to involve the vulnerable and disempowered. It is clearly not enough to simply have the skills to carry out research – especially in these complex areas. *How* we go about research in a way that affirms the values that under-pin our work is of fundamental importance.

The second section of the book takes the reader on a step by step, easy to read guide to doing social work research. It follows the typical path taken by most research projects looking at proposals, methods of doing research, analysis of data and writing up research reports. Thus, it looks at service user involvement in research, interviews, questionnaires, focus groups, observation and narratives. Each chapter draws on a range of research projects in social work areas to show how other people have man-aged the process and overcome the occasional obstacles that all research presents. They draw on a wide range of material from established research methods texts, through to contemporary journal articles, general social work texts and service user led projects.

Great emphasis is placed on developing the knowledge, skills and values that the practitioner researcher needs to generate knowledge in the workplace. We believe that this sort of activity is a part of the professional development of the social work and social care workforce. We believe that a critical, questioning approach to research informed practice – including researching one's own and others' practice – is funda-mental to the process of lifelong learning and keeping up to date. These are key components of good practice and, of course, are included in the National Occupational Standards and the Code of Practice.

The authors are both qualified social workers and have worked in various social work, social care, criminal justice and community settings before embarking on academic careers. They bring to this book all their practice experiences, but also the experience of teaching, supporting and enabling social work researchers for many years at many different levels. They have both been active researchers in the field of social work throughout their careers. Louise Hardwick is a Lecturer in The School of Sociology and Social Policy at the University of Liverpool and Aidan Worsley is Professor and Head of the School of Social Work at the University of Central Lancashire.

WHAT'S DISTINCTIVE ABOUT SOCIAL WORK RESEARCH?

OVERVIEW

This chapter will explore social work's knowledge base and the constellation of core values it draws on that predispose it towards enquiry that is both relationship-based and informed by a broader emancipatory mission. The questions 'What is research?' and whether there is a justification for practitioner research being seen as a valued perspective in its own right will be investigated. It is argued that, given the nature of social work practice, it is only to be expected that practitioners should seek research knowledge that both arises from, and reflects, the complexities of practice. It is also argued that practitioners themselves might contribute to this knowledge by engaging in research that can inform and influence practice and policy. To begin to understand the challenges facing practitioner research, we will look at the recent history of social work research's contribution to policy and the drive towards evidence-based knowledge and New Managerialism. We will suggest that practitioners who undertake research could provide both a situated understanding of the unique in each individual and circumstance and offer a challenge/critique of the practices, institutions and polices that militate against social justice. Doing research provides one route for practitioners to realise social work's emancipatory potential.

WHAT IS DISTINCTIVE ABOUT SOCIAL WORK PRACTICE?

The National Occupational Standards for Social Work draw on the international statement which identifies the social work profession as:

A profession which promotes social change, problem solving in human relationships and the empowerment and liberation of people to enhance well-being. Utilising theories of human behaviour and social systems, social work intervenes at the points where people interact with their environments. Principles of human rights and social justice are fundamental to social work. (International Association of Schools of Social Work and the International Federation of Social Workers, 2001)

This is a statement on the commitment of social work to humanitarian values and the promotion of social change. It provides the nucleus from which issue and permeate the six key roles of social work, and any social work endeavour.

National Occupational Standards for Social Work

Key Role 1: Prepare for, and work with individuals, families, carers, groups and communities to assess needs and circumstances.

Key Role 2: Plan, carry out, review and evaluate practice, with individuals, families, carers, groups, communities and other professionals.

Key Role 3: Support individuals to represent their needs, views and circumstances.

Key Role 4: Manage risk to individuals, families, groups, communities, self and colleagues.

Key Role 5: Manage and be accountable, with supervision and support, for your own social work practice within your organisation.

Key Role 6: Demonstrate competence in social work practice.

These key purposes combined with the humanitarian values in the International Federation's statement mean that for the social worker the service user is not just an individual in a social situation who is the subject of engagement, assessment and practice. The service user is also a unique individual in complex and uncertain circumstances that are influenced to a lesser or greater extent by collective socioeconomic forces. These forces demand acknowledgement and understanding if social justice and inequality are also to be addressed. Nonetheless, this collective emancipatory mission has been an area where the social work profession has struggled to move significantly beyond the rhetoric (Jordan, 2004) despite this fusion of regard for both unique and collective inequalities providing social work with its distinctive nature (Bisman, 2004; Webb, 2001). This is made even more challenging because social work is a highly complex and sometimes apparently contradictory pursuit. It is an adherence to this value base that helps navigate the practitioner through the quagmire that characterises practice. As Jordan argues:

… social work occupies an ambiguous role in society, negotiating with individuals in ways that try to validate their claims to autonomy, but from a position inside such institutions as public agencies, civil society organizations, churches or local groups, and one which involves a duty to criticize and challenge those very institutions, from the perspective of freedom, equality and justice. (2004: 12)

At an individual level of engagement the practitioner must always seek to facilitate a relationship which can enhance well-being and be characterised as 'relationship-based practice', an awareness of 'the uniqueness of each individual's circumstances and the diverse knowledge sources required to make sense of complex, unpredictable problems' (Ruch, 2005: 111). Social work also needs to move beyond the individual circumstance to understand and find ways to express concern for the societal inequalities and injustice that feed these individual circumstances. Practitioner research has the potential to express both these sets of values.

SOCIAL WORK KNOWLEDGE

Social work has always been multidisciplinary in its knowledge base and practice, drawing on, for instance, sociological thinking and research, psychology and social policy, and experiential knowledge (reflection). Through sociological thinking social work is offered an understanding of social differences and inequality such as class, disability, race, gender and age in the context of the laws and rules laid down by society. The sociologist gaze is bifocal – distinguishing between social presentation and social reality. Through psychology, social work is offered a knowledge of the processes that will influence and impact on individual behaviour and develop an understanding of personal attachments and relationships and how the nature of these can influence an individual's behaviour. Through social policy, social work is offered an understanding of the processes involved in the state distribution of resources amongst individuals and groups to meet welfare needs and how this is organised through a range of institutions from 'the family and the community networks in which the family exists, the market, the charitable and voluntary sectors, the social services and benefits provided by the state, and, increasingly, international organisations and agreements' (Baldock et al., 2003: xxi). Experiential learning is also important to social work knowledge because social work practice not only relies on technical expertise (theories and methods that can inform interventions and the legal and procedural requirements of the profession), but also on a tacit understanding that is a complicated combination of personal judgment, past experience and theoretical knowledge.

REFLECTION IN SOCIAL WORK

Experiential learning is explored in the work of Donald Schön who has analysed how professionals learn by focusing on what he calls 'the swampy lowlands' of professional practice (Schön, 1983). These relate to the inner resources professionals draw on when they find themselves having to make decisions in complex and/or controversial settings. For a social worker the obvious area for these kinds of decisions is regulatory practice, as for example the decision to take care proceedings under Section 38 of the Children Act (1989). However, less obvious situations – like the decision to follow up an intuition that may prove rooted or groundless – also requires complex decision making. Schön is fascinated by the inner resources and processes that influence how professionals can make these difficult complex and contingent decisions.

Schön has suggested that the professional develops a kind of 'artistry' which is different from their technical expertise. He has argued that this type of problem/situation cannot be dealt with by simply applying a technical competence. Instead, the professional has to build a 'repertoire' of past scenarios, precedents and case studies that can be drawn on to inform an understanding of the 'here-and-now' situation. These are accessed by applying knowledge from literature and research but additionally, and more significantly, by applying knowledge from the interpretation of experience. This process only becomes 'artistry' when the professional engages in a meaningful reflection on their past experience and practice. Reflection on practice involves:

- recapturing the situation;
- thinking about it;
- mulling it over (alone or with others);
- evaluating;
- acting on that evaluation. (Boud et al., 1985)

For Schön simple reflection is not sufficient as it ignores the social and situational nature of experience. Together with his colleague Argyris he argued that simple reflection will only produce 'single loop learning' (Argyris and Schön, 1974). With this kind of learning an individual will simply reinforce and defend old habits and behaviours because it fails to challenge their underlying assumptions, preconceptions and belief systems. You will doubtless be familiar with the attitude 'This is how I've always done it and no one has come to any harm'. For example, when reflecting on something like an altercation with a difficult colleague a practitioner may reflect that this colleague is always difficult and aggressive when asked for information when passing on the corridor. Single loop learning would be content to explore the problem as simply lying with the colleague. This approach lacks the critical reflection that challenges taken-for-granted understanding and problematises the process and motivation.

Alternatively, a competent professional will engage in 'double loop learning' which will challenge all previous understanding in a 'progressively more effective testing of assumptions and progressively greater learning about one's effectiveness' (Argyris and Schön, 1974: 86). This double loop learning may, for instance, question the appropriateness of asking for information on the corridor, why appropriate systems for information sharing are not being utilised, what the consequences of affixing the label 'difficult' on that colleague are likely to be. The process of critical reflection required for 'double loop' learning is inevitably difficult to achieve alone. The would-be learner can be the last person to recognise when their understanding is limited by long-held preconceptions that might go back to childhood because they are so enmeshed in the situation as to be incapable of objectivity. To avoid this Schön suggests what he calls a 'reflective practicum', where people come together to analyse an issue or problem and explore it from many different dimensions, including the individual's emotional response. Argyris and Schön developed their ideas on reflection from an educational discourse where they fundamentally questioned the value of professionals only using theoretical and technical knowledge for their practice. These ideas complement and cross-fertilise with reflexive knowledge, which is also important to the social work practitioner.

REFLEXIVITY IN SOCIAL WORK

Although reflexivity is a similar concept to reflection, it developed out of a social science discourse and has been used as an approach in social science research. It relates to researchers reflecting on the research process and locating themselves in this process (Fook, 2002). Reflexivity involves a more sophisticated exploration of the processes at play facilitating an emergent understanding of social situations that takes into account the social context, experience and values of the researcher (Powell, 2002). Sue White advocates using reflexivity in social work practice as well as research as a means 'of destabilisation, or problematization of taken-for-granted knowledge and day to day reasoning. Treated in this way, reflexivity becomes a process of looking inward and outward, to the social and cultural artefacts and forms of thought which saturate our practices' (2001: 102). This process of taking time to problematise all aspects of a situation avoids the rigidity which rides roughshod over the nuances of the particular. It also allows an opportunity for destabilisation and self-awareness rather than blindly acting on the basis of policies and procedures, research findings or strategies.

Since a reflexive approach takes account of values and questions taken-for-granted assumptions it is an approach which sits very comfortably with the situated and value-based requirements of the social worker practitioner. As Ruckdeschel and Shaw argue, ' ... all forms of social work practice can benefit from a reflective stance ... [but] reflective practice is of limited use unless the products of reflections are shared' (2008: 299). An effective method of ensuring that these reflections are rigorous and shared is available through the practitioner engaging in research.

WHAT IS RESEARCH?

Before we can focus in on practitioner research we need a brief examination of what we mean by research itself. All research involves the use of rigorous and systematic methods to explore questions, problems and topics with the aim of gathering data that will inform greater understanding. The discovered data and understanding may be very specific, or general, depending on the type of research being undertaken and the type of data sought. Research can range from basic/scientific to an applied social investigation. Generally speaking, with basic research the investigation will be driven by the researcher's interests and will be unrelated to immediate practical questions, problems or topics. In contrast, applied social research is more likely to be driven by social interests and be closely related to immediate practical questions, problems or topics (Stoecker, 2003).

Underpinning any research endeavour are key values associated with different research approaches and paradigms and these in turn will impact on the types of investigation undertaken. Positivism is an epistemological approach (theory of knowledge) which advocates the application of scientific methods to the discovery of social reality. This approach aims to reduce any possibility of contamination coming from the researcher themselves (researcher bias), the research equipment, the methods used, and the setting/laboratory or field setting, and is associated with the scientific methods found in the natural sciences. In contrast, the interpretivist approach requires researchers to investigate the subjective meaning of social reality. This approach is predicated on the belief that the social world is fundamentally different from the physical world and cannot be understood in all its complexity though the use of scientific methods.

There are two general approaches to gathering data – quantitative and qualitative – and these are not mutually exclusive. With the quantitative approach a researcher is more likely to remain objective and distant from the process and gather data which is often in the form of numbers. The data are analysed and interpreted using measurement and can be presented in the form of tables and charts. The types of methods associated with this approach are surveys, questionnaires and structured interviews. The qualitative approach is designed to allow for more complexity to emerge in the findings, thus allowing the intricacies of a situation to be acknowledged. Findings and data are often presented as prose. The interpretation of findings is more likely to be offered by the researcher and is therefore open to alternative interpretations, whereas with quantitative data the measurements and calculations will often speak for themselves. This approach lends itself to small-scale research that adopts methods of observation, unstructured interviews, focus groups and the use of narrative (Denscombe, 1998).

To summarise the differences between quantitative and qualitative:

The difference might be summarised by saying quantitative research is structured, logical, measured and wide. Qualitative research is more intuitive, subjective, and deep. This implies that some subjects are best investigated using quantitative whilst others, qualitative approaches will give better results. In some cases both methods can be used. (Bouma & Atkinson, 1995: 208)

In some research texts the two approaches will often be polarised. You will need to be cautious not to be too rigid in your understanding of these data gathering approaches.

TRIGGERS FOR SOCIAL WORK RESEARCH

There are numerous demands made upon social work research in what is a rapidly changing world. For example, in the UK people are generally living longer and healthier lives, but with increasing numbers of older people there is also an increase in the enduring health problems associated with ageing (see ONS/Social Trends 2009).[1] One example of this is the predicted impact on the cost of caring for an increasing number of older people with dementia (McCrove et al., 2008). This type of trend inevitably impacts on health and social care resources and makes demands on our understanding as social workers. Community Care Managers are likely to face numerous pressures, some of which will be in tension, when working with an elderly person with dementia. They must, for instance, consider self-reliance and autonomy whist at the same time ensuring there are sufficient resources in the community to support the elderly person to remain in their home environment. They must also balance the risks faced as a result of care in the community against the greater restriction that is part of a residential nursing home. They must consider whether the budget can meet the various costs and also, given the unique circumstances of the individual service user, which route would best respect their integrity and well-being. Answering these complex and potentially contradictory questions requires a recourse to the literature and research to discover what is already known about similar situations and discrete investigations to establish what is specific to a particular situation. It also requires an understanding of the sometimes unintended consequences of social policies that impact on people's lives. Through engaging in an exploration of research the practitioner is contributing to a comprehensive assessment of the situation. Through engaging in producing the research themselves there is the potential to develop an understanding that can be shared with others and influence both practice and policy.

Social work practice requires research on practice and policy initiatives that can impact on the social environment at a local and national level (Shaw, 2007). Historically, although social work might have wished to inform policy, the reality has been that social work has been at the receiving end of policy and subject to the prevailing political necessities of the day. This can be seen by tracking the recent history of social services research. With Seebohm (1968) and the setting up of social services departments, it was argued that it would prove 'wasteful and irresponsible' not to

---

[1]Social Trends is produced by the Office for National Statistics and can be accessed online at http://www.statistics.gov.uk. The ONS is an invaluable resource for the researcher.

monitor the effectiveness of social work. Research was to be concerned with two areas: 'First, the collection and analysis of basic data and, second, the clarification, evaluation and costing of the main options available in tackling the problem' (quoted in Payne, 1981). Building on this, in 1994 the Department of Health published a report called 'A Wider Strategy for Research & Development relating to Personal Social Services'. This looked at the links between research, policy and practice. It argued that research was being used to inform policy but that research findings were not being used more directly to inform practice. The report made a number of recommendations about the national, regional and local organisation, and dissemination, of social services-related research. Social services departments were to:

- have a known dissemination plan to keep their own staff and other service providers up to date with research findings;
- use in-house training to develop research findings;
- develop opportunities through secondments and fellowships to provide practitioners, researchers and trainers with experience of each other's work.

However, in reality most social services departments did little beyond employing small numbers of research and development staff whose remit was usually too wide to be able to implement these recommendations effectively. Eventually these recommendations and posts became re-shaped to meet quite different agendas. This point can be illustrated with reference to a Merseyside social services department.

Case study

Between 1995 and 1998 a Merseyside social services department became involved in a wide range of research which included:

- *projects undertaken internally*, such as evaluations of specific services – for example an evaluation of community care support to people with dementia (Hardwick, 2000);
- *projects commissioned from an external source*, for example a piece of work on local rehabilitation needs (McNally & Hardwick, 2000);
- *as participants in external projects*, for example in a study of community care assessment commissioned by the NHS from Lancaster University (Cornes & Clough, 2001).

Staff and service users were active participants in these projects, positively welcoming the opportunity to express a view on particular services or processes, receiving feedback on findings, and also being involved in discussions about the implications of those findings.

However, with the relentless raft of social care (and related health care) policy initiatives emanating from the Department of Health after New Labour came to office in 1997, interpreting policy for local implementation and following through that implementation with operational staff and managers became more of a priority. This resulted in the priority shifting again to performance management in the early 2000s with the introduction of performance indicators (Department of Health, 1998a). Work in social services departments became driven by the need to meet national performance targets. In this particular Merseyside social services department the shift was symbolised by the setting up in 2001 of a Policy and Performance unit, within which 'Research and Development Officers' became 'Policy and Performance Officers' with the inevitable move away from research and even policy towards performance management.

This change away from involvement (albeit very limited) in research is exemplified in this case study by the change of job title from 'Research and Development Officers' to 'Policy and Performance Officers'. However, at the same time the rhetoric coming out of government initiatives related to the 'modernising' agenda for social services recognised that practitioners should have greater recourse to research (Department of Health, 1998b). The White Paper states 'as in other professions, it is important that professionally qualified social workers base their practice on the best evidence of what works for clients and are responsive to new ideas from research' (Department of Health, 1998b, cited in Woodcock & Dixon, 2005: 955). This is not always as straightforward as this quote implies as has been acknowledged and strategically addressed in the Joint University Council Social Work Education Committee's (JUCSWEC) fourteen-year strategy, which states its aims are to:

- maximise the HEI contribution to social work and social care service improvement;
- develop a strong evidence base for social work and social care services;
- build a workforce capable of using evidence critically and effectively. (JUC/SWEC, 2008: 6)

WHAT IS AN EVIDENCE BASE FOR SOCIAL WORK?

In the arena of social work research there has been an increasing emphasis on evidence-based knowledge/research because of the pressure exerted by the moderising agenda with its 'ideological affiliations in favour of a pragmatic embracing of 'what matters is what works' (Davies & Nutley, 2002). As well as it being a vehicle to disseminate the 'what works' agenda to the social work workforce, a number of other reasons for this increasing emphasis on using evidence in policy and practice have been suggested. These include: the growth of a well-informed and educated public; an information explosion and corresponding improvements in information technology; a need for cost containment and increased productivity in service delivery; growth in the size and capabilities of the research community and an increasing emphasis on governmental scrutiny and accountability. Evidence-based knowledge also allows social work research to have credibility with more established scientifically-based academic disciplines and professions such as medicine. Take, for example, the drive towards interprofessional working – especially as this is backed by major research funding bodies like the National Institute for Health Research which includes social care/social work when considering issues related to the NHS (Cooksey, 2006). Social work research needs to be able to make a distinct contribution to this type of interprofessional research and not be swallowed up by the more resourced and larger health perspective.

When we talk of an evidence base for social work practice we are referring to a particular kind of knowledge that has been defined as 'the conscientious, explicit and judicious use of current best evidence in making decisions regarding the welfare of service-users and carers' (Sackett et al., 1996: 71). This is the idea that practitioners can intervene most effectively when they are drawing on a rigorous evidence base, the sources of which can be found in peer-reviewed journal articles, practice guidelines and systematic reviews (Corcoran & Vandiver, 2004). However, critics of an emphasis on evidence-based knowledge have argued that this approach to understanding indicates causal, linear thinking that is intrinsically flawed when dealing with human agency (King, 1997) and that using an evidence-based approach is built on the assumption that what has proved useful in one context is necessarily transferable to another, ignoring the significance of local information and interaction, and raising the question, 'Is a professional opinion inferior to a piece of research?'

Critics of the emphasis on evidence-based knowledge have also argued that research for it is often produced from a positivist perspective that believes standardised scientific methods will produce an objective truth about the social world and question how appropriate this view is for understanding the complexities of social work (Webb, 2001). In other words, that evidence-based researchers are too often academics who inhabit Schön's 'high hard ground' and who understand little of the 'swampy lowlands' of emergent, contingent and situated understanding.

These criticisms of evidence-based research may be legitimate if it is incorrectly applied and research becomes isolated from social work values. Use of evidence-based research requires the use of appropriate knowledge rooted in the values of social work practice. As Corcoran and Vandiver argue, ' … evidence-based practice requires that the practitioner structure the intervention into a workable treatment plan, which means that the session-by-session planning is unique and appropriate for the particular condition' (2004: 18). Munson further argues that 'relationship-based practice' and a recourse to evidence-based research is both compatible and necessary in practice as ' … evidence-based practice must be balanced with a relationship model. Practice cannot be grounded in only evidence, just as it cannot be formulated solely on relationship' (2004: 259)

In 2001 social work's evidence-based research bias was further strengthened with the establishment of the Social Care Institute for Excellence (SCIE) which set out to correlate a wide range of sources, and particularly research evidence, although they also acknowledged the need to listen to service user/carer views, to have a local evaluation of service deliveries and to hear about practitioners' experience of practice. SCIE was founded at a point when it was becoming increasingly recognised that the social work enterprise needed to be able to draw together the wide range of knowledge that informs practice and understanding.

Activity

- Log onto the SCIE website http://www.scie.org.uk/
- How many differing sources of knowledge can you discover from your search around the website?
- Write a term of interest such as 'dementia care' into the search box and identify from the results the range of issues that this throws up.
- Also identify the differing types of documents i.e. policy, article, etc. that come up.

DEVELOPING RESEARCH MINDEDNESS

A helpful way of thinking about social work research is to see it partly as a state of mind that can be acquired with rigour and professional discipline which opens up the possibility of exploring the interface between individuals and communities and the worlds they inhabit. This has been described as 'research mindedness' – a way of thinking and a habit of questioning that challenge our taken-for-granted assumptions so that we can *better understand* and reflect on the world that we, service users and communities encounter.

For example, as social workers this research mindedness could involve looking at an aspect of intervention or the context of a welfare provision including, perhaps, the agencies that provide services: for whom do they exist, and who is excluded? How are they funded? What are the culture, values and histories that impact on individuals and communities, and the particular policy initiatives that influence them? In fact, it could involve us opening our minds to any aspect of enquiry that can be related to the values, purposes and context of social work. (Developing ideas for research questions, problems and topics will be explored in detail in Chapter 2.)

Although all research is broadly about the advancement of scholarship and knowledge, if social work is to be beneficial to service users and carers this needs to be fine-tuned to the requirements of the profession and/or service users, in order to lead to a better understanding for practice and policy. If not, it will be indistinguishable from any other social science research and will also further marginalise the voices of service users, carers and professionals who live and work on the frontline of social injustices and need. Orme and Powell argue that ultimately social work research should be 'to improve professional practice for the benefit of service users and carers (2008: 2)

THE DRIVE TOWARDS PRACTITIONER RESEARCH

Social work practice takes place in the context of a global socio-political flux that is leading to accelerating changes in contemporary society. As Taylor-Gooby (2008) argues, governments throughout the world have been driven by these global pressures to develop new strategies for welfare reform. In the UK such welfare reform can be encapsulated by the New Managerialism that has taken hold of provision, which is predicated on the belief that to survive global pressures we need to increase cost-effectiveness and quantify outcomes to measure the effectiveness of welfare. Taylor Gooby also claims that running in parallel to these policy changes has been a subtle and implicit shift in the values legitimating welfare. The 'old' values coalesce around mutual trust, inclusion and a reciprocity between the state and the individual, endorsing the provision of a 'safety net' for the most vulnerable and ill informed in our society. However, Taylor-Gooby suggests that these 'old' values are being eroded by policy makers who are placing an increased emphasis on individual self-regard and the ability of individuals to make educated choices in the arena of welfare provision. The motivation behind this shift is the assumption that this will nourish competition, cost effectiveness and efficiency.

To encourage this individual appetite for informed choice amongst citizens the government has recognised the need to 'nurture and develop certain psychological characteristics – motivation, self-esteem, confidence, entrepreneurship and self-development' (Jordan, 2004: 10). These changes not only have implications for traditional welfare values but also the individual's ability to access services. Those individuals who are 'disabled and chronically sick people, those with heavy caring responsibilities, and those with fewest material resources and intellectual endowments' (ibid: 10) struggle in this welfare market environment. Who then does it fall to, to persuade and assist such individuals struggling to survive the requirements of this new welfare, but the social work profession? Social workers are expected to encourage service users to achieve this aspiration of self autonomy, while also to monitor, control and enforce a compliance with welfare reforms (Jordan, 2004). This produces an uncomfortable pressure on the practitioner to cajole service users into meeting the demands of the neoliberal state. This also places a heavy burden on the practitioner who is attempting to find forums to express core social work values and avoid buckling under the internal contradictions inherent in the contemporary social work role. By engaging in doing research that is emancipatory and grapples creatively with these tensions and contradictions the practitioner can make an emancipatory contribution beyond the individual therapeutic relationship.

EMANCIPATORY VALUES IN SOCIAL WORK RESEARCH

Social work research is usually driven by some issue or practical problem that someone wants to solve or understand i.e. it is purposeful in some way – seeking a particular end – and will make a difference to individuals, groups or organisations. Therefore social work research can be a vehicle for change, review, refocus and *empowerment* and can also make a real contribution to resolving the problem(s) we encounter. For social work research to be emancipatory practitioners will have to 'work together' with other parties associated with the social work enterprise to achieve change. These other parties might include employers, service users and carers, colleagues, other professionals and also academic researchers. Together they can ensure the research is properly disseminated to interested parties.

The general features expected if practitioner research is to be emancipatory are:

- an awareness of the situated nature of social work research, acknowledging the uniqueness of the individual;
- an awareness of the 'caring relationship' which has features of attentiveness, responsibility, competence and responsiveness;
- an awareness of seeking change in order to empower and search for social justice;
- an awareness of the need to work together with disempowered groups, individuals and communities – in other words, in a collaboration/partnership with the recipients of research.

CONCLUSION

When identifying what is distinctive about social work practice we have emphasised its humanitarian values, being relationship based and committed to the emancipatory principles of promoting social change and enhancing well-being to achieve social justice. These are intrinsically combined with the key roles/purposes of social work as identified by the National Occupational Standards, which involve drawing on a wide range of knowledge from other disciplines and practice expertise to work effectively with individuals, families, carers, groups and communities.

We have explained the concept of basic and applied social research and how the latter captures the applied nature of social work, where social work research emerges from, and reflects, the complexities of the context in which it is used. We have also drawn attention to how the social work community has become increasingly aware of the need to give legitimacy to the wide range of research enquiry that contributes to improving the lives of service users and carers. This includes evidence-based knowledge from a wide range of research sources as well as service user/carer views and practitioner expertise and research. A prerequisite to practitioner research is research mindedness, opening up the channels of enquiry that begin to further explore the interface between individuals and communities. Practitioner research is inevitably more likely to be concerned with a specific situation and context where practice takes place in an attempt to solve problem(s) encountered on a day-to-day basis. It has been argued that with this type of situational research the same professional values that apply to practice also apply to research.

Key points

- The situated nature of social work.
- The centrality of the 'caring relationship'.
- An engagement to seek change in order to empower.
- Working with others in partnership.

Further Reading

Bryman, A. (2008) *Social Research Methods*. Oxford: Oxford University Press.

Denscombe, M. (1998) *The Good Research Guide for Small-Scale Social Research Projects*. London: Open University Press.

Fook, F. (2002) 'Theorizing from practice: towards an inclusive approach for social work research', *Qualitative Social Work,* 1 (1): 79–95.

Jordan, B. (2001) 'Emancipatory social work: opportunity or oxymoron?' *British Journal of Social Work*, 34 (1): 5–19.

Marsh, P. & Fisher, M. (2005) 'Developing the evidence base for social work and social care practice', *Using Knowledge in Social Care Report No.10*. London: Social Care Institute for Excellence.

Robson, C. (2002) *Real World Research* (2nd edn). Oxford: Wiley/Blackwell.

Shaw, I. (2007) 'Is social work research distinctive?', *Social Work Education,* 26 (7): 659–669.

PRACTITIONER RESEARCH – ENGAGING WITH INDIVIDUALS, ORGANISATIONS AND COMMUNITIES

OVERVIEW

This chapter deals with the part practitioners can play in social work research and the imperative for practitioners to adopt research mindedness in order to begin to influence future welfare initiatives. This is not to minimise the part service users and carers can play in engaging in social work research but to point out that this will be addressed separately in Chapter 4. The purpose of this chapter is to help demystify research for practitioners in order to facilitate a research mindedness that not only relates to the ability to use research to inform practice but also the ability to identify critical issues for further enquiry. The practitioner research process will be explained with reference to a research continuum, where all practitioners will locate themselves at differing stages of this continuum and be 'research active'.

National Occupational Standards for Social Work

Key Role 1 of the National Occupational Standards for Social Work is: Prepare for, and work with individuals, families, carers, groups and communities to assess needs and circumstances. This chapter will explore how this can be achieved while meeting the requirement for research training outlined in Key Role 6: Research, analyse, evaluate, and use current knowledge of best social work practice. Contribute to the promotion of best social work practice.

WHO SHOULD UNDERTAKE SOCIAL WORK RESEARCH?

Developing a social work research capacity is not the exclusive responsibility of any one element of the social work community. Social work research is a complex system made up of diverse components which include academics, practitioners and service users (Orme & Powell, 2008; Walter et al., 2004). There is an agreement that any social work research undertaken is more likely to be put to good use if the various parts of the research community are encouraged to be 'research active' and if the various investigations are so aligned as to complement each other. For research to make a difference it should not be an isolated pursuit taken up by only one element of the social work community, but should instead reflect varied perspectives, thereby encompassing the multiple angles and standpoints that can shed light on subjects associated with service users' well-being:

> These include focusing on the relationship of individuals (practitioners and/or academics) with their employing organisation and the relationship between academia and practice. This means that specific opportunities have to be developed for social work academics (primary educators) and practitioners to engage in research ... In setting up an infrastructure for research training, it is also necessary to work in partnership with service users and carers to ensure that opportunities for research training involve them, either as recipients of training or as contributors to the training. (Orme & Powell, 2008: 11)

There is also an increasing awareness of and commitment to address the inadequate structural support offered to those multiple stakeholders who will be the beneficiaries of quality social work research (Orme & Powell, 2008). All parties in the process need to be included and encouraged to assume their role. Although this chapter relates specifically to the part that practitioners can play, it is predicated on the assumption that employers, funding bodies, academics and policy makers will recognise and support the potential of frontline practitioner research to contribute to the knowledge base for social work. All parties in the social work community require this recognition and infrastructure for each to take an active part – one that is intrinsically dependent on the other and the wider social work community – in order to work for the benefit of future service users and carers.

PRACTITIONER RESEARCH

Many social work practitioners see research as an activity that only experts engage in, and one that requires skills that are beyond the average practitioner. There is generally a lack of research opportunities combined with a lack of confidence to engage in the process. In addition there have traditionally been low academic expectations on qualifying social work courses, and social work is argued to have had a rather ambivalent relationship with academia (Orme & Powell, 2008).

A combination of these factors has contributed to the present invisibility of practitioner research and also resulted in the 'social work research pathway' being rarely trodden. This route should begin with the undergraduate student undertaking a qualifying course and then be followed by the social work practitioner engaging in post-qualifying activities, through to postgraduate research training both at a Master's and PhD level with the potential of funded opportunities via the Economic & Social Research Council (ESRC) or other major sponsors. Few practitioners become academic researchers in universities and even fewer actively engage in undertaking their own research. Since 2004 these low expectations have begun to be addressed with the three-year qualifying degree course, the Advanced Award in Social Work (although, astonishingly, even at this level it is not a requirement that the practitioner engages in research), and a slow-growing recognition of the need for research training at both degree and postgraduate level (Orme & Powell, 2008; Walter et al., 2004).

This book has been designed to contribute to this change and help encourage a demystification of research for practitioners. It seeks to encourage a research minded-ness which recognises that research is 'simply another word for enquiry' (Robson, 1993: x). This is not to say that practitioner research should not be rigorous and of quality. Practitioners need the skills, confidence and supporting infrastructure to advocate resonantly for both themselves and the services users and carers they serve. Social workers have tended to be passive recipients to changes in their role and the policies that influence their practice and, consequently and also indirectly, the well-being of service users. Practitioners need to begin to be committed to, and be structur-ally supported in, adopting research mindedness in relation to training, interventions and the settings and local communities where practice takes place. To focus briefly on social work training and the role, we would ask just how much voice have practitioners had in relation to these? As Jones and Novak have argued:

> Scarcely a year has passed without new legislation redefining the roles and responsi-bilities of social workers or introducing new structures, content and processes in the education system ... The structures and organisation of the institutions in which they [social workers] work have been endlessly reorganised, and professional training has been subjected to centralised control, stripped of its potential for critical questioning and subjected to the requirements of their managerial employers. (1999: 173)

Although this was written over a decade ago their observation remains applicable today. Perhaps if social work had, like other equivalent professions (nurses, teachers and health professionals), the infrastructure for effective research, and was not subject to constant re-organisations, practitioner research might be properly valued and be able to make a constructive contribution to future policies and practices.

THE SOCIAL WORK RESEARCH CONTINUUM

Any research investigation can only ever represent a partial understanding of the situ-ation and lived experience of individuals, yet it is important to recognise that social work practitioners can contribute to this understanding by joining academics, along-side service users and carers, in engaging in the research enterprise. This does not necessarily mean that each party will engage in the same sort of research but that each party's contribution would be recognised and valued. Critical thought involving reflection and reflexivity is a requirement for effective practice and this demands a questioning and problematising of our taken-for-granted assumptions – a process of looking inward and outward that not only informs our understanding but also makes us more aware of what it is we do not know. We can begin with the 'here and now', with the specific situation, investigating what we think we already know (tacit knowl-edge) and making it explicit. This is further informed by our recourse to literature and research evidence to deepen and challenge this understanding. This type of enquiry is an early stage along the research continuum.

Therefore when we observe and know something of the practice situation we have already embarked on the first stage of the research continuum. We can then draw on research and literature in order to deepen that understanding or to question/challenge what we already know. Walter et al. (2004) identify a number of barriers that practitioners will experience at this point, such as a lack of research skills, limited access to literature and research, and a lack of time given the competing priorities of professional practice. However, if these barriers are overcome a number of routes can emerge. For instance, enquiry may endorse and give legitimacy to what is already known, or it may challenge aspects of understanding leading to a re-evaluation or further investigation. Moreover, it may identify areas where there is little existing literature or research evidence, or where that evidence is contradictory or inadequate thus leaving unanswered questions. This process exposes subjects which should elicit a more rigorous investigation.

Research enquiry can entail a variety of roles for the practitioner. A baseline for all practitioners should be that they are research minded and informed in their everyday practice. This will lead to the possibility of identifying subjects and/or research questions. These frontline issues can then be passed along to employers or academic researchers as subjects worthy of further enquiry. Alternatively, the practitioner can take an active role in the enquiry by becoming a research participant or collaborator/partner with interested parties such as employers or academics. If properly supported, practitioners can even take on the role of principal investigator in an enquiry. Every practitioner should be located somewhere on this research continuum and be 'research active' (Orme & Powell, 2008) as this situated knowledge and understanding is an integral part of good practice.

Elements of the social work research continuum for the practitioner researcher include:

- an identification of what we know in the 'here-and-now';
- a recourse to research and literature to endorse/challenge/inform what we already know;
- an identification of subjects for further enquiry;
- an engagement with research enquiry.

As practitioners in the field we are often at the 'coal face' of practice and therefore well situated to identify issues and potential research questions arising from what we see and experience since 'practitioners are frequently aware of important practice-related questions long before scholars and academics. Such questions may arise out of difficult clinical situations, policy changes that affect delivery of service, or demographic changes that affect the characteristics of those who seek service … ' (Vonk, Tripodi & Epstein, 2007: 234). This can be a rather frustrating situation to be in if we have no means of articulating or feeding back our queries/observations or no possibility of instigating our own research questions. Anecdotally, from our own years in practice and our observation of the career-paths of qualified students, we have seen many who decided to move on to other careers. This is sometimes due to frustration when on a day-to-day basis, they observe problems in policy and in their practice and/or organisational context, but have no forum for voicing or no channel for communicating these observations. They therefore grow frustrated at being denied the means to contribute to a systemic review and change. This can in turn lead to feelings of disillusionment and disempowerment. By engaging in research, practitioners can potentially provide rigorous evidenced knowledge of the contemporary practice context and its related problems.

The strength that practitioners and service users can bring to bear in the complex arrangement that can be called 'social work research' is inductive knowledge: 'bottom-up' knowledge that is specific to the situation and context from which it emerges (Fook, 2002). This can be contrasted with deductive knowledge that is 'top-down' and builds on theories and research that are not necessarily specific to the situation. Practitioners are more likely, because of their situation, to undertake the inductive types of enquiry and as such their enquiries are more likely to be small scale and to be evaluations that directly relate to service delivery and local communities (Shaw, 2007). Shaw, in his review of practitioner research, concluded that at present the wider infrastructure supporting social work research marginalises practitioner research into 'a "street market" version of mainstream research' (2005: 1231). This has meant that there has been little opportunity for practitioner research to contribute to and generate social work theory. To address this, Fook (2002) has called for the adoption of an action research approach for the practitioner which would give legitimacy to their perspective:

> Action research recognises that theories are generated in context, influencing, and being influenced by a context of interactions as they are in the process of being developed. (2002: 83).

An action research approach is predicated on a 'bottom-up' strategy. This type of approach is ingrained in a commitment to research as an empowering activity for all concerned (Punch, 2005). In this way practitioner research is similar to an action research approach. Another comparable characteristic between the two approaches is the ambition to seek out partnerships and collaborations with relevant parties (such as services users, other professionals, managers and academics) and the adoption of a reflective and reflexive questioning of the process. This involves the research process engaging in a cycle that combines action and reflection which in turn will allow the researcher to be flexible and responsive to the changing circumstances of a practice context. Equally, both practitioner research and action research set out to solve practical problems specific to local situations.

The characteristics of an action research approach include:

- a participatory/collaborative process;
- action and reflection in a cyclical process;
- seeking to solve practical problems;
- being concerned with change that empowers individuals and communities.

The major challenge for practitioner researchers is to begin to not only identify subjects that emerge from their specific situation, but also to begin to problematise those subjects thus allowing research questions to be generated. As we have explored earlier, a fundamental part of engaging on the research continuum is consulting research and literature to deepen an understanding of, and to question/challenge, what is already known. As Walter et al. (2004) state:

> Using research can mean many different things: raising awareness of research findings; challenging attitudes and perceptions; or changes in policy or practice or in outcomes for service users. (Walter et al., 2004: 9)

If all practitioners are to be engaged with research they have to have knowledge of how to access sources of research, and they must be supported in using research to effect a change for the better. Below are a few indicators of where to go to find literature relating to research and although this is by no means comprehensive, some of these sites could act as a springboard to further enquiry.

Activity

Access each of these useful sites for social work research:

- www.evidencenetwork.org
  This is a joint initiative between Barnardo's, City University and York University and part of the UK-wide 'Evidence Network' and provides summaries and findings on particular interventions.
- http://www.scie-socialcareonline.org.uk/
  This provides a free database of social care information which includes everything from research briefings, to reports, government documents, journal articles and websites.

Useful journals include:

- *Community Care*
  http://www.communitycare.co.uk
  This is a very practice orientated journal exploring issues in all aspects of practice, as well as policy and legislation and discussion boards.
- *British Journal of Social Work*
  http://bjsw.oxfordjournal.org
  This peer-reviewed journal covers a wide range of social work activity, with topical discussions on practice and theories.

Activity

- Think about how often you investigate social work research to inform your understanding of day-to-day practice and its context.
- Do you know where to readily access this research?
- Can you think of a particular social work situation that would benefit from you accessing related research? Why?

PRACTITIONER RESEARCH ON SOCIAL WORK INTERVENTIONS

To assist you in the process of engaging in developing research mindedness and identifying subjects for further enquiry we are going to use the fictional case study of Melissa, a social worker in Liverpool. Melissa's story will be told by looking at her practice, the organisations where she has worked, and her local community and its welfare history. Using this situated understanding will demonstrate how ideas for further enquiry can be generated from 'coal face' experiences. There will also be activities for you as a practitioner to engage in, so you also can begin this process of identifying areas for enquiry within your own practice and welfare context.

Practice interventions: Melissa's story

Melissa is presently in a part-time post in a voluntary sector organisation called Draycott Family Support (DFS)*. DFS offers advice, advocacy, and support to parents and families who are involved with the social services due to child protection concerns.

DFS was established in 1992 by a parent in response to her personal experience of a child protection investigation. The parent identified a massive gap in advice and support services available to families in similar situations. The service was designed to complement both the services offered by the child and family division and legal services during a child protection inquiry. This parent became the full-time manager and eventually secured funding to recruit a part-time social worker (Melissa) and a legal adviser to ensure service users understood child protection procedures while being adequately supported and prepared for case conferences, reviews and court hearings. DFS also recruited a number of volunteers to supplement the core service offered by the paid employees.

*Draycott Family Support (DFS) is a pseudonym

In the UK, unlike the USA, there has not been a tradition of practitioners engaging in research to evaluate and test out particular practice interventions (Shaw, 2005). This partly relates to the many obstacles facing practitioners in engaging in social work research identified earlier in this chapter, such as a lack of confidence and limited research skills combined with the inhospitable research infrastructure to support and nurture this process. However, it also relates to an awareness of the ethical considerations that apply when a practitioner investigates an intervention where the respondents might also be service users with whom the practitioner may have a professional relationship. Padgett argues that the practitioner's legal duties may be in conflict with 'standards of confidentiality, informed consent and withdrawal from research/treatment' (1998: 376). As with other professional groups who engage directly with practitioner research, especially the range of health professionals, these ethical considerations need to be paramount but should not necessarily be insurmountable. Another potential problem with practice research on practice interventions is the potential for research becoming self-serving. For example, a practitioner who has a vested interest in kinship fostering is more likely to design an investigation that endorses this view rather than an impartial approach. This is another serious ethical issue, but again one which can be overcome with due ethical scrutiny. (Ethical considerations will be discussed in greater depth in Chapter 3.)

The British Association of Social Workers actively contributes to a recognition of frontline practice issues and the encouragement of practitioner research through their peer reviewed journal *Practice: Social Work in Action*.[1] This journal publishes articles written by practitioner researchers as well as welcoming contributors from other elements of the social work community.

---

[1]This journal can be accessed online via http://www.basw.co.uk/Default.aspx?tabid=98

Here are two examples:

- Shaw, C. & Palattiyil, G. (2008) 'Issues of alcohol misuse among older people: attitudes and experiences of social work practitioners', *Practice: Social Work in Action,* 20 (3): 181–193.
  At the time of writing this article, Catherine Shaw was a practitioner with an Older People's Team and George Palattiyil was a social work academic. Together they undertook a small-scale qualitative study that focused on the experiences of social workers *vis-à-vis* older people and people who misuse alcohol. Their study identified the need for an 'age-specific' approach to alcohol misuse to target the needs of older people more effectively.
- Preece, D. (2009) 'Effective short breaks services for families with children with autism spectrum disorders: how one local authority in the United Kingdom is working to meet the challenge', *Practice: Social Work in Action*, 21 (3): 159–174.
  At the time of writing this article, David Preece was a manager with Northamptonshire's Social Care Services for children with autism spectrum disorders. This article drew together the findings of two previous investigations undertaken by Preece which explored the views of parents with children with ASD. His findings highlighted the importance of respite care for families with ASD and the range of obstacles they encountered when seeking support in Northamptonshire.

Both these studies emerged out of the direct experience of practitioners working with specific user groups.

Practice interventions: areas for further enquiry emerging from Melissa's story

- Literature and research on the experience of parents in child protection cases.
- The legislative and practice guidelines that relate to supporting parents who are involved in child protection concerns.
- The service users' and stakeholders' perspectives on DFS's information and advice, together with the advocacy and legal support offered.
- Service users' and stakeholders' perspectives on family courts.
- The needs of carers/parents involved in child protection investigations.
- The ethical considerations that relate to the above areas given Melissa's professional role within the organisation and her engaging in any research enquiry.

Activity

- Think of the range of interventions you engage in through your practice and the potential impact of these on service users. What literature/research exists that relates to these and what are the gaps in knowledge?
- Begin to identify any ethical considerations that relate to engaging in a piece of research connected to any of these interventions.

PRACTITIONER RESEARCH WITH AND FOR ORGANISATIONS

Working in organisations: Melissa's story

Since qualifying in 2001 with a Master's from the University of Liverpool, Melissa has worked in a range of social work settings. Initially she joined Family Service Unit (FSU), a voluntary sector organisation that pioneered casework for vulnerable families with the aim of keeping them together. After a few years she decided that she wanted to broaden her experience to statutory child care. She hoped to secure a position with Liverpool's Child and Family Division. However, she was surprised at how few permanent jobs were advertised and therefore joined a social care job agency who quickly offered her agency work with a team in the division. In a relatively short period of time she had a heavy caseload that included Section 47 Child Protection Inquiries and applications for Section 31 Care Orders. What she found most difficult about the work was that her team manager was on long-term sick leave and that there were unfilled vacancies in the team. This had a knock-on effect on the rest of the team. One member had to 'act-up' as manager. The remaining members (who, like Melissa, were agency workers) covered only high priority cases.

By 2004 the pressures of the unmanageable workload and concern over the lack of recruitment across the whole Children & Families Division resulted in a local social work strike. It was at this point Melissa decided to return to the voluntary sector and applied for her present post in DFS.

The organisational context of our working lives is influenced by the key trends in welfare policy. These trends inevitably impact on our practice and on the experiences of service users and carers. Understanding and investigating the influence of these forces should include the settings where social work takes place. Social work activity is located in welfare organisations that may be statutory, voluntary or private, which are situated in specific local communities where these settings will have a crucial impact on the practice experience and the type of service offered. Wilson et al. argue 'Social Work students and practitioners need to understand how positive and productive relationships can be fostered within the context of the social and organisational problems and constraints that confront them' (2008: 67). This assumes that some of the responsibility of overcoming constraining organisational issues lies with the practitioner. Investigating these can not only lead to offering a more effective service but also could potentially lead to a greater awareness of those areas requiring further enquiry. To assist the practitioner in identifying constraining organisational issues, we will refer to the work of Watson (2006) on organisations. His conceptualisation of organisational processes through 'process-relational framing' allows practitioners to develop a reflexive understanding of the multi-layered processes and communications taking place in any work setting.

Watson understands 'process-relational framing' to mean that organisations are made up of sets of relationships and ways of understanding that are contingent on the dynamics, relationships and culture of the body of people who work in them. This challenges the pervading assumption that organisations are somehow self-determining in their own right and able to make decisions and decide roles and procedures as if they are entities that are independent of their membership.

'Process-relational framing' acknowledges that organisational boundaries are always permeable, even if at first they appear to be rigidly defined. The organisation is composed of sets of relationships that exist both within it and beyond it (Watson, 2006). A 'process-relational framework' draws attention to the continuous flow of 'exchange, negotiation, conflict and compromise' (2006: 30) that is central to the performance of any organisation. Watson argues that these processes include and encompass the emotions of individuals, managers and all associates of the organisation. For social work organisations this also applies to service users/carers and students, all of whom will contribute in various ways to the character of that organisation. Watson urges the enquiring observer to look beyond the overt and rational manifestations of what is happening, including both inward to internal processes and outward to the socioeconomic and cultural/political circumstances that will impact on the particular setting and situation.

Activity

Map out your own practice history including pre-course experience, practice placements and agencies that you've worked in.

Activity: Working in organisations: areas for further enquiry emerging from Melissa's story

- Consider the impact of under resourcing in social work settings on both practitioners' interventions and their well-being, and the well-being of children where there are child protection concerns.
- Looking inward at both the Child and Family Division and DFS raises questions about the roles within each setting. What are the differences and the similarities between the two settings and the implications of these for Melissa?

Activity: Working in organisations: areas for further enquiry emerging from your practice

- What are the sets of relationships and roles that make up your organisation/placement setting?
- What are the stated organisational tasks? Are there any always achievable and if not what obstacles are faced?
- How does information get exchanged in your organisation? What are the practices and procedures that you follow? What are the positive and negative outcomes from these practices and procedures for managers, social workers, other professionals, service users and students?
- Identify the current socioeconomic and political/cultural forces that might impact on your organisation.

For practitioner research to be of benefit to anyone it has to happen in organisations that are receptive to change and research and not totally preoccupied with meeting government targets and managerial goals (Orme & Powell, 2008). An organisation that can move beyond immediate concerns is termed a 'learning organisation', where the emphasis is not solely the individual learning but also includes the organisation adapting and changing through continual enquiry.

LEARNING ORGANISATIONS

Senge's (1990) work *The Fifth Discipline* developed the concept of learning organisations. He identified five disciplines required for a learning organisation:

- *Systems thinking* – an approach which involves a recognition by individuals in the organisation that they are part of a whole system where each role is interconnected and dependent on others and part of the bigger picture (1990: 8).
- *Personal mastery* – an approach that acknowledges the organisation can only learn if the individuals within it also learn.
- *Mental models* – an approach which refers to the tacit knowledge or 'professional repertoire' that individuals develop within a working context.
- *Shared vision* – an approach that is dependent on good leadership within the organisation and their ability to influence the workers.
- *Team learning* – this is the combination of a collective shared vision and individual learning leading to people acting together for change.

According to Senge learning organisations are:

... organizations where people continually expand their capacity to create the results they truly desire, where new and expansive patterns of thinking are nurtured, where collective aspiration is set free, and where people are continually learning to see the whole together. (1990: 3)

Engaging in practitioner research relates closely to the requirements of Senge's personal mastery. When this personal mastery approach is espoused practitioners are supported to develop research mindedness and actively engage in learning from reflection while working in collaboration with service users, colleagues and managers to achieve beneficial changes for all concerned. This type of research cannot happen in isolation, but, at the very least, requires the support of a practitioner's organisation and their managers. Argyris and Schön (1978) applied their understanding of individual reflection to the way organisations learn (as discussed in Chapter 1). In relation to an organisation, with single-loop learning that organisation can fail to question underlying assumptions and habits. In this case the learning is likely to reinforce existing policies and objectives. When an organisation engages in double-loop learning it will challenge these taken-for-granted understandings and is more likely to modify its policies and objectives. Realistically, many social work organisations will have difficulty in combining all the qualities required to be an effective learning organisation, given the internal and external pressures to ensure sustainability and cost effectiveness and to meet performance targets. This, however, does not mean that organisations should not strive to support the working conditions that facilitate learning at both an individual and organisational level.

Activity

- Think about whether your work organisation has any of the characteristics of a learning organisation.
- Identify some of the forces that militate against your organisation having these characteristics.

PRACTITIONER RESEARCH FOR UNDERSTANDING LOCAL COMMUNITIES AND THEIR WELFARE HISTORIES

Understanding local communities and their welfare history: Melissa's story

Melissa was born and still lives in an inner city area of Liverpool with one of the oldest Black communities in the UK. Understanding the welfare history of Liverpool takes us back to the eighteenth and nineteenth centuries when Liverpool was one of the richest cities in Europe, with its central trading role across the Atlantic sustained by the slave and cotton trades. However, with this wealth came previously unseen depths of poverty and a growing imperative to tackle this poverty through the development of various forms of welfare provision (Simey & Bingham, 2005). In this way Liverpool became a forerunner and pioneer of many welfare services as well as being a recipient of centralised welfare responses from the state (Simey & Bingham, 2005).

In early Victorian times Liverpool established a significant number of homes and orphanages for destitute children, for example the Female Orphan Asylum (1840) and Boy Orphan Asylum (1858) which were to amalgamate into the Liverpool Society for the Prevention of Cruelty. This was later to give rise to a national organisation (the NSPCC). This organisation played a pioneering role in highlighting the need for legislation to protect vulnerable children both locally and nationally (Starkey, 2000). This was a period when there was a clear division of responsibility between the state and voluntary sector, with the Poor Law (1843) providing the central response of the state to the problems associated with urbanisation. Locally, a Poor Law workhouse was established. Such were the appalling conditions of this establishment and others like it that a provision from charities was sought above this kind of harsh state response, resulting in the emergence of numerous charitable enterprises supported by many outstanding local individuals and groups (Simey & Bingham, 2005).

The University of Liverpool established the Liverpool School of Social Science (1905) and later the first social work training course. This saw a partnership between the school and the local branch of the Settlement Movement (originally set up in London by Canon Barnett to establish partnerships between universities and settlements in deprived urban areas, in order to facilitate social reform). The aim was to 'integrate higher education and students into the local community through partnerships with organisations' (Gilchrist & Jeffs, 2001: 238). One of the first such partnerships was between the Liverpool Domestic Mission Society and the University of Liverpool.

Later in the century there was a national reversal of this trend of charitable assist towards state provision resulting from the establishment of the Welfare State (The Beveridge Report 1942). This pushed the voluntary sector into the role of supplementing these state services. This is exemplified with the passing of the 1948 Children Act which placed the burden of responsibility for the welfare of children predominantly with local authorities (Starkey, 2000). In wartime Liverpool a few voluntary organisations managed to survive this trend. One example is the Family Service Unit (FSU) where Melissa was eventually to have her first post-qualifying post. This service eventually led to other FSUs being set up in similarly deprived inner city areas across England (Starkey, 2000).

By the 1970s, and with a national economic recession, there was a marked shift to multiple sector providers and the re-emergence of voluntary provision as a significant provider. One aspect of this reversal back towards the third sector was the fragmentation of practice between sectors, with statutory provision becoming increasingly dominated by targets for performance, tight budgets and increased bureaucracy. Moreover, third sector provision was now being seen as more flexible and responsive to welfare needs and particularly responsive to local needs (Deakin, 1998; Kendall & Knapp, 1996).

By 2006 many of the services originally provided by the local authority social service departments had been contracted out to third sector organisations, resulting in larger charities on Merseyside delivering increasing levels of public welfare services (Charity Commission, 2007). In this climate of fragmentation of welfare provision, the University of Liverpool withdrew its MA in Social Work in 2005, thereby ending the historical partnership between social work training at Liverpool and local welfare agencies.

Nationally, this was a period of rapid shifts in social policy causing a number of threats to third sector organisations. As expectations arose regarding their ability to become major deliverers of welfare services this in turn had significant implications for the sustainability of some voluntary sector organisations, particularly smaller organisations that might struggle to retain their independence and experience increased financial insecurity and a 'squeezing out' of welfare provision (Charity Commission, 2007; Kendall, 2003; Scott et al., 2000). FSU was no exception and went into liquidation in 2005, leaving DFS's future then in doubt with no secured funding beyond April 2010.

In the same way as organisations need to be understood both in relation to internal as well as external processes, so too do the communities where practice takes place. To fully understand the needs of users of welfare organisations and the context of social work service delivery and policy, there also has to be an awareness of the specific community where practice takes place, with its welfare history and the political ideologies that have influenced and navigated developments in the past and which influence the present and future (Defilippis et al., 2006).

Social work education and practice in the UK does not have a tradition of conceptualising social work as community-based in the same way as happens in social work education across Europe (Lorenz, 2006; Lyons & Lawrence, 2006). In Germany for example there is a tradition of social pedagogy and community work in social work education. One implication of this is that social work education does not confine itself to focusing on social problems but takes a broader view, acknowledging that all individuals and communities experience and are subject to social adjustment (Lyons & Lawrence, 2006). This holistic outlook acknowledges the complexity of human experience and facilitates an approach that encourages the practitioner to look both inward to individuals and outward to communities.

In the UK, like in Germany, the practitioner is also at the interface between service users, communities and the policy makers and broader social and economic forces that impact on lives. Practitioners are therefore well situated to identify the subjects that relate to communities, and particularly the socially excluded. Just as Watson (2006) adopted a 'process-relational framing' of organisations to avoid a one-dimensional understanding of these, it is possible to do the same when understanding community issues. However, despite this central position of social work it has not been a primary player in New Labour's attempts to tackle social problems. Nor has social work been used to help identify the underlying causes of social exclusion. Rather, social work has been expected to pick up the fractured pieces of service users lives and attempt to enhance their autonomy and self-development regardless of these underlying socioeconomic causes that militate against restoration (Jordan, 2004). Regeneration policies and capacity building initiatives have tended to focus on enhancing social inclusion in local communities through 'the ability of individuals, groups and communities to participate in the opportunities provided by wider regeneration processes and outcomes' (Burchardt et al., 2002: 41). Implicit in many of these policies has been the assumption that social inclusion can be addressed through micro activities of social engagement such as those identified by Putman in his (1995) discussion of 'social capital'. These include activities like voting, community and volunteering work, and undertaking informal social activities like visiting friends. As Defilippis et al. (2006) argue, these activities in themselves are not without worth for communities but they can mask the macro political and economic forces that underlie the experience of social exclusion for individuals and in communities.

UK welfare history demonstrates the negative changes that have taken place between social work, social work organisations and the communities served. As Jordan argues:

> The profession of social work increasingly finds itself working in an extensive set of individualised, commercialised and fragmented services, within a mixed economy of care and a set of often small and under funded community initiatives. (2001: 533)

This would certainly tally with some of Melissa's story where she found local authority social work under-resourced and smaller charity organisations 'squeezed out' of welfare provision (Charity Commission, 2007). Since before New Labour came into power, both the third sector and statutory sectors of social work have been forced to participate in centralised agendas which are determined by the requirements of the market economy and actively undermine professional values. Most social workers are interested in working in organisations where the service contributes to service user well-being and addresses the wider social issues of social justice in the local community. Their primary interest tends not to be on whether the service is competitive and cost-effective and can be quantified into measurable outcomes (Gilchrist, 2003).

Social work practice is often on the frontline of observing some of the unintended consequences of social policy on individuals, organisations and communities. An awareness of these unintended consequences and their impact can be credited to the founding father of social policy as an academic discipline, Richard Titmuss, who by researching policy interventions was able to evidence how the outcomes of many of these initiatives were not what had necessarily been intended (Baldock et al., 2003).

Activity: Understanding welfare histories and communities: areas for further enquiry emerging from Melissa's story

- What issues emerge from the enquiry into Melissa's personal history and connection to the local community?
- What issues emerge from the welfare history of Liverpool?
- How has this welfare history influenced innovations in welfare?
- What has been the impact of national strategies and intervention on welfare provision in Liverpool?
- Identify any potentially unintended consequences of policy initiatives which you have noted in Melissa's story.

Activity

- What can you discover about your local welfare history?
- Where does social work take place locally?
- What are the present day demographic issues impacting on your local community? (You may want to begin by searching on Neighbourhood Statistics on http://neighbourhood.statistics.gov.uk/dissemination/)
- Where are welfare needs being predominantly met, or not met, locally?
- Can you think of any unintended consequences of welfare policy initiatives in local communities?

Key areas for future research enquiry are:

- your interventions with service users and carers and other professionals;
- identifying organisational constraints and issues;
- understanding your local community and its welfare history and how this relates to the lived experience of service users and carers;
- understanding past welfare policies and their unintended consequences on individuals, organisations and local communities.

CONCLUSION

Social work practitioners are situated in organisations at the interface between individuals and communities and therefore can and should engage in social work research which develops a rigorous analysis of these circumstances. This will help influence and contribute to the future development of welfare initiatives that will be of benefit to service users and carers.

For practitioners to be 'research active' they need to develop an approach that is research minded and engage with the research continuum, where practitioners can draw on research evidence to deepen and challenge their understanding of interventions, organisational settings and communities, leading to the identification of subjects that can form the basis for further enquiry. A major challenge for many practitioners is becoming informed about where to find social work research evidence and other sources of knowledge to help their understanding, and how they might identify appropriate subjects that can form the starting point for a research enquiry. This chapter has guided the reader to key areas for reflection, questioning and problematising from a practice perspective. It has advocated that practitioners should look both inward to individual circumstances and the internal organisation processes and outward to the local community with its specific history as well as the broader socioeconomic and cultural/political circumstances that impact on the particular practice setting. This multi-layered focus will open up a wealth of areas for further enquiry that may be of benefit to service users and carers.

Key points

- The various parts of the research community should be encouraged to be 'research active' so that these investigations can actively complement each other.
- Employers, funding bodies, academics and policy makers should recognise and support the potential of frontline practitioner research to contribute to the knowledge base for social work.
- The research continuum for practitioners begins with an identification of what they know in the 'here-and-now' followed by a recourse to research and literature to endorse/challenge/inform what they already know. This can lead to an identification of subjects for potential research and to an active engagement with a research investigation.
- The strength that practitioners and service users bring to bear in the complex system that can be called 'social work research' is inductive knowledge: 'bottom-up' knowledge that is specific to the situation and context from which it emerges.

Further Reading

Beresford, P., Croft, S. & Adshead, L. (2008) '"We don't see her as a social worker": a service user care study of the importance of the social worker's relationship and humanity', *British Journal of Social Work,* 38 (7): 1388–1407.

Fook, F. (2002) 'Theorizing from practice: towards an inclusive approach for social work research', *Qualitative Social Work,* 1 (1): 79–95.

McLaughlin, H. (2007) *Understanding Social Work Research.* London: SAGE.

Shaw, I. (2005) 'Practitioner research: evidence or critique?', *British Journal of Social Work,* 35 (8): 1231–1248.

Warren, J. (2007) *Service User and Carer Participation in Social Work.* Exeter: Learning Matters.

THE ETHICS OF SOCIAL WORK RESEARCH

OVERVIEW

For the practitioner, research (like practice) is not just about individuals in social situations who are in need of professional engagement, there is also an awareness and acknowledgement that service users are unique individuals living within complex and uncertain circumstances. As we engage in social work research, we are not simply extracting information from particular respondents within certain groups. We are engaging with people to make a difference. The practitioner researcher needs to fore-ground an approach that is 'relationship-based' and aims to achieve changes for the better for individuals, groups and communities. When this research directly involves gathering data from people (human subjects) an ongoing ethical scrutiny of all aspects of the research process is necessary. It could be argued that social work research, by its very nature, is more likely to deal with vulnerable people, the disadvantaged, those with learning disabilities or mental health problems, the young, the old and so forth. It is central to our professional Code of Practice, as well as to the good practice of research, that in carrying out research with service users and carers (and, indeed, staff), we do so while being *ever mindful* of the way in which we conduct ourselves and the effects of our actions. In this sense research ethics provide us with *norms of conduct* that define what is acceptable and unacceptable in how we go about research. These norms form a sort of moral code for the researcher practitioner, establishing what is 'right and wrong' and enshrining appropriate values. So central is this issue to research that it is not generally considered acceptable for the researchers themselves to decide what is and is not ethical. Research ethics are therefore usually subject to externally agreed guidelines that act as a reference point for researchers to reason out the most appropriate way of thinking and behaving both as individuals and members of a profession.

This chapter will explore the issues surrounding ethical social work research and how the social work practitioner researcher can go about obtaining ethical approval for their research. We will examine key ethical issues and how you might address these in your research. We will also provide an historical context to research governance for health and social work/social care dating back to the Declaration of Helsinki (World Medical Association, 1964) through to the introduction of the current framework for ethical review of research in the form of the *Research Governance Framework for Health and Social Care* (DoH, 2005).

In exploring how to approach the ethics and governance of social work research the authors draw on a notion of situational ethics which advocates a willingness to be 'open' and to 'listen' to the situation under investigation by engaging in a reflexive interrogation of all aspects of the study, rather than by holding an unquestioning and inflexible reliance on ethical guidelines and policies as 'givens' that do not necessitate reflection. As Bryman argues:

> While the codes and guidelines of professional associations provide some guidance, their potency is ambiguous and they often leave the door open for some autonomy with regard to ethical issues. (2004: 520)

That said, the balance needs to be drawn conservatively for the beginning researcher, between the clear merits of looking at the individual situation and the broader generic norms of ethical research conduct.

National Occupational Standards for Social Work

The ethics of social work are, of course, central to both the National Occupational Standards and the GSCC Code of Practice. Element 19.3 insists that practitioners work within the principles and values underpinning social work. Element 19.1 is about the exercise and justification of professional judgements. Element 19.2 notes the need to exert professional assertiveness in the justification of decisions related to practice, values and ethics. Unit 20 is specifically concerned with the management of complex ethical issues and Element 20.2 is targeted on the need to devise strategies to deal with ethical issues, dilemmas and conflicts.

BEGINNING CONCEPTS

To begin this discussion of ethics it is helpful to borrow the four key principles that, for many years, have formed the cornerstone of ethical guidance for the health professions. Whilst originally outlined as general behavioural and 'bioethical' guidelines for medical staff, they apply equally to social work researchers who, until very recently, had no similar code. We shall consider a social work-specific code later in this chapter, but these principles help to establish a platform for later discussions and should ensure that the reader is clear about what we mean by an 'ethical approach'.

- *A respect for autonomy* – the research must respect the notion that people are free to make their own autonomous decisions about involvement without any controlling influence, fully understanding what the research entails. Informed consent is a central element of the principle of autonomy.
- *Nonmaleficence* – the research must not do any harm. As we engage in our research projects we must be sensitive to the potential for causing harm or distress in any way, especially where it may not be seen as reasonable in the context of the particular research project.

- *Beneficence* – the research must be of benefit to those engaged in the research. This should apply both to the individual respondent as well as to society as a whole.
- *Justice* – the research should be fair and just, for and to, the wider community.

With these principles in mind we can begin to unpack the core elements of an ethical approach. Two points must be made: first that it is clear that ethics are inextricably linked with morals. Concepts such as justice and fairness are irrevocably interconnected with our own individual moral compass and our perceptions of such concepts will inevitably differ. This leads us to our second point – that ethical issues can often tend to lead into areas that can best be described as the grey between the black and white. If, for example, research should never distress any respondent, does this mean we can never ask interview questions that involve difficult issues? What if our research will offer little benefit to the individual, but may possibly lead to an increase in resources for the community? The next sections of this chapter will tackle some of these dilemmas and hopefully help steer a sensible course through these difficult waters.

HARM VERSUS RISK

The harm versus risk dichotomy is about avoiding exposing participants to physical or mental distress or danger. For the practitioner researcher this is most likely to relate to the potential of causing psychological distress rather than physical harm. One of the most obvious ways this may occur is when an investigation creates upset, contributes to the stigmatisation of participants and/or draws attention to potentially deviant, risky or illegal behaviour. Less obvious ways might be when participants are left with feelings of exposure – perhaps they have revealed more of their private affairs than they would have wished to. Alternatively, they may feel under-valued, that it is only the data they reveal which is of worth and they are not recognised as individuals.

To militate against harm researchers have to take responsibility to ensure that the benefits of their investigation strongly outweigh any potential negative impact and/or psychological distress, a process which is a continual balancing act that requires reflection and the problematization of specific circumstances.

Case study

A practitioner wanted to investigate the benefits of a youth club for young people who were staying with their mothers in the local women's refuge. In order to evaluate the service, the practitioner wanted to gather qualitative data from the young people about how they felt about the youth club.

To build a rapport with the young people, the researcher asked the mothers for their consent to attend sessions at the youth club and speak directly to the young people about their

(Continued)

(Continued)

experiences. She also explained the study to the young people, and asked for their consent to conduct semi-structured interviews with them. She found them compliant with this, but unenthused by the prospect. Added to this, having spent time with the young people, the practitioner became aware of how relaxed and carefree they were during these sessions and she realised that her intrusive questions might fracture the calm of the youth club sessions, possibly the only current opportunity for the young people to put their family problems to one side.

In the process of balancing the potential psychological harm against any benefits the researcher revised her methods for gathering data. Instead of directly interviewing the young people, as an alternative she recorded her observations of the sessions and conducted semi-structured interviews with the mothers.

PROTECTING VULNERABLE GROUPS

The example above not only highlights the harm versus benefits dichotomy, but also the sensitivities of investigating 'vulnerable' individuals, groups and communities. Before going any further with this debate we should acknowledge that the word 'vulnerable' itself is problematic. Who decides who is vulnerable, and is this label always beneficial to the recipient or is there potential for it to be damaging and cause psychological distress or disadvantage in itself? This tension reveals the implicit power differentials at play in any research investigation as it is almost unheard of for the researched to be powerful or for the researcher to be disempowered (Lee, 1999; Oliver, 1992). Despite the contested nature of this word it can be used effectively if seen as a statement to encapsulate the notion that participants may be powerless, at risk and/or lacking defence. Participants in this position are likely to have a weak voice and a weak representation in society. Given this, researchers have a responsibility to act to protect their interests and where possible to address any power differential. This may sometimes mean that, as in the example above, a researcher may have to decide (despite the informed consent from participants) not to invade their privacy and interview them as after consideration the balance may weigh more towards harm than benefit. In the example given, the researcher after some reflection asked herself how free were the young people from the youth club to withhold their consent in their specific situation. Did the importance of the data justify the insecurities that might arise from a 1:1 interview?

On the other hand, it is possible that this researcher may have decided that it would indeed be in the interests of the young people. There appears to be a real dearth of research about young people, perhaps in part because of ethical concerns and issues surrounding parental consent. In ethical considerations there are no clear-cut right and wrong approaches and we would not want these and other vulnerable groups to be 'erased' from research in this way. Children and other vulnerable groups have a right to have their lived experience heard and understood and there should not be an assumption that such 'protection' equates to their non-participation. However, the reflexive researcher should ask themselves whether they have the expertise to sensitively use research methods that will directly engage with vulnerable groups. This requires skill and experience and should only be taken on if the researcher is confident of their own abilities. These considerations are of necessity complex, contingent and uncertain – and they also require considerable reflection and a problematization of the specific situation by the principal investigator if they are to reflect this.

INFORMED CONSENT

The Social Research Association defines informed consent as:

> ... a procedure for ensuring that research participants understand what is being done to them, the limits to their participation and awareness of any potential risks they incur. (2003: 28)

Informed consent involves ensuring that all potential research participants are fully informed about every aspect of the investigation and any issues that might influence their decision to participate. You might think this straightforward, but the SRA's definition presents an interesting example of how easy it can be to make assumptions that everyone approaches ethical issues in the same way. Does the social work practitioner researcher do research 'to' – or 'with' – service users and carers? Consent is normally seen as having three elements which must be in place for the consent to be valid. First, the person must be capable of making the consent decision, i.e. they are competent. Second, the person must be acting voluntarily and must not, for example, be placed under duress or an obligation to give their consent. Finally, the person must be provided with enough information to enable them to make an informed decision – hence 'informed consent'.

A comprehensive profile of the investigation should be explained in clearly spoken and/or written language with no hidden agenda and no area of the study considered outside the brief and/or understanding of any of the participants. This means all aspects of the process, from the beginning to the end, should be totally transparent to everyone concerned. Informed consent is often facilitated by the production of a Participant Information Sheet (PIS) which explains everything the participant needs to know. Respondents should normally sign a consent form confirming this for the researcher – which is generally seen as good practice unless there is a contrary rationale. Participant Information Sheets will obviously differ from project to project but will tend to have similar headings and cover similar areas. The headings (see below, Table 3.1) are taken from a recent sheet produced by one of the authors.

Table 3.1 Typical headings for a Participant Information Sheet

1 Who is doing the research?	2 What is the purpose of the study?	3 Why have I been chosen?	4 Do I have to take part?	5 What will happen to me if I take part?	6 What are the possible disadvantages and risks of taking part?
7 What are the benefits of taking part?	8 What if something goes wrong?	9 Will my taking part in the study be kept confidential?	10 What will happen to the results of the research study?	11 Who is organising and funding the research?	12 Who can I contact for further information?

Of course, the whole issue of informed consent is problematic in regard to the many different social groups that social work practitioner researchers may be dealing with and we will now look at two examples in particular.

CHILDREN, YOUNG PEOPLE AND THE ISSUE OF CONSENT

In the UK the term 'child' will generally apply to anyone who is under the age of 18 (Masson, 2004), although there are significant legal differences between England, Scotland and Wales – researchers need to ensure they are fully cognisant of these differences. Gatekeepers often surround children and, quite rightly, will seek to ensure that they come to no harm in a research process. This can mean we must deal not only with parents and teachers but also with local authorities who, of course, have parental responsibility for those in their care. In England, the matter is broadly within common law following on from the Gillick competence case (Wheeler, 2006), the essence here being that where a child or young person is deemed capable of giving consent then they are free to do so. Legally speaking it's a matter of both the maturity of the child and the seriousness of the matters being researched (Masson, 2004). Having said this, one would normally apply a general principle that practitioner researchers ought to seek parental consent for the purposes of interviewing any children and young people. For those young people aged 16 and above, one might reasonably assume they are capable of giving their consent independently if the research model has good cause to do so and, of course, where ethical approval has been granted.

Activity

Imagine you are doing a small-scale research project on what children between the ages of 14 and 16 think about the social work services they receive in a particular school. What are the ethical issues you may face in gaining informed consent? Decide on how you will go about gaining such consent and draft out a participant information sheet for both children and parents.

PEOPLE WITH LEARNING DISABILITIES AND INFORMED CONSENT

As with children and, indeed, any vulnerable group, there is a danger that the particular challenges of managing the ethical issues surrounding research with people with learning disabilities will deter people from engaging in such activity (McCarthy, 1999). In this way research can further marginalise and disempower an already disadvantaged group, leaving them anonymous, voiceless and unheard. Essentially our starting point as researchers is that it is right to assume that adults, with or without learning disabilities, are capable of making their own decisions. Where any doubt exists then an assessment of capacity needs to be made that draws on specialist knowledge within this area (DoH, 2001). For people to have this capacity to make a decision as to whether to engage with research, they need to be able to comprehend and retain the information given – and to understand any implication of their being and not being involved. Then, of course, they need to be able to weigh up that information for its pros and cons. People with learning disabilities might demonstrate this through the use of paraphrasing, the comparing of alternatives and applying this information to their own situation. Family members, carers and other advocates can also assist. Some also advocate the use of 'stop' cards. Whatever the eventual methods used, the authors can only express their concern that practitioner researchers take great care in working with people with learning disabilities: the challenges that can be presented are perhaps the most complex ethical issues in all of social work research and, as such, there are no simple answers. Our main advice is to gain assistance and advice from an expert and to engage in these areas as (or with) an experienced researcher rather than as a beginner. It is also extremely important to educate yourself proactively as a researcher about the ethical issues you may encounter with this group as with any other. The work of Wiles et al. (2007) is a good place to start in this particular instance.

Activity

Think through the ethical issues and respond to the prompts of working with these two groups:

- *Older people:* How do we define older people? Are age and biological age the same? How might cultural difference impact? How do we avoid assuming that physical frailty is the same as mental incapacity? Do we need to consider consent as an ongoing issue, rather than fixed at an early point? How can we involve older people as advisors on our research? How do we deal ethically with the gatekeepers that surround older people?
- *LGBT (Lesbian, Gay, Bisexual and Transgendered) people:* Why is there so little demographic information about this group of people? How might we avoid assuming this group is a homogeneous community? How do we avoid the dangers of replicating cultural stereotypes? Do we deal with the issue of privacy differently in this case? Are there different levels of being out? How may this affect our research process?

THE RIGHT TO PRIVACY

Securing privacy for participants involves ensuring that they are given an opportunity to control if, when, and under what circumstances they reveal or grant access to personal information on their behaviour, values and/or beliefs. This right encompasses almost all of the data that are likely to be collected which relate to participants. There are three established ways of protecting participants' privacy:

- Confidentiality – ensuring that information or the data collected from participants in the investigation is not revealed in a form that can be linked or traced back to individuals.
- Anonymisation – ensuring real names are replaced by pseudonyms, thus protecting the participant's identity. Anonymity (where researchers do not know the identity of the respondent) can obviously be a tool for ensuring privacy.
- Editing – allowing participants to see data that relate to them and decide whether they wish these to be revealed or edited out.

ETHICAL ISSUES INVOLVING AND ARISING FROM VESTED INTERESTS

Sometimes ethical considerations will arise from either the sponsor of the research or a partner in the study having a vested interest in the data revealing certain outcomes or being presented in a specific way. This can usually be forestalled if sponsors and collaborative parties have drawn up some kind of contract where issues around intellectual copyright and dissemination are mutually agreed. Pressure to modify or withhold data will challenge the integrity of a study and researchers and will also undermine the validity of the findings – this should be strongly resisted.

Activity

What are the considerations that relate to these situations?

- A sponsor (who is also your employer) expressing unhappiness with an aspect of the findings.
- Someone asking you to revise an aspect of the research report to present a more favourable picture.

DATA PROTECTION

Inevitably, practitioner research is concerned with dealing with personal or confidential information about individuals, groups, communities or members of an organisation. As with social work practice, it is essential that practitioners respect the confidentiality of the information and do not disclose it to unauthorised persons and that they follow the Data Protection Act (1998) which requires, amongst other things, that personal and confidential information is kept in a secure, locked location or on PCs that are firewalled and password protected.

Key Principles of the Data Protection Act 1998

Personal information must comply with the following principles which require that it is:

- fairly and lawfully processed;
- processed for limited purposes;
- adequate, relevant and not excessive;
- accurate and up to date;
- not kept for longer than is necessary;
- processed in line with such rights;
- secure.

Thus, data should only be used for the purposes they were collected for and not disclosed to others without consent and individuals should have the right to access the information that is kept about them.

(The Information Commissioner's Office can be found at www.ico.gov.uk)

RECRUITMENT, RELATIONSHIP AND REIMBURSEMENT

There are particular ethical issues that will accrue when we begin to consider recruitment for research projects as researcher practitioners. In more traditional forms of research we can observe recruitment as a relatively straightforward process, based on a variety of factors. Are we looking at whole populations – as with the census – or students at a particular university? Or perhaps a sample of a population, driven by certain characteristics such as age, programme of study, professional role, etc.? Researchers can simply send out letters, adverts, or e-mails to a mailing list asking for volunteers. With all these suggestions, there is the underlying notion of anonymity, where the researcher doesn't know the potential respondents and they are thus strangers. But, even so, we do have to be mindful of the impact of our approach and its suitability for what we wish to achieve. Complications will exist when we require access from gatekeepers to certain groups. How, for example, do we recruit offenders? And what would the Youth Offending Team's view be?

For the researcher practitioner, what will cause more concern is the notion of recruiting and researching those we know through the course of work, either as service users, carers or colleagues. Traditional research practice would simply advise that it is best not to interview those we know already and our advice would be that the beginning researcher practitioner should follow that path until they gain experience. The argument quite rightly follows that if, as a social worker, we are interviewing one of our clients, as a researcher, then we are less likely to get an honest response as the roles can conflict and people might be less willing to open up to us. Fundamentally, such an approach may interfere with the autonomy of informed consent. A service user may feel obliged to be part of their social worker's research. However, if, through our situational ethics approach we are trying to locate our research within a caring relationship, then, of course, there is an opportunity to involve those we know in our research. If that is the path we choose, then we must give careful consideration to the challenges this method brings and be prepared to argue this rational approach before ethics committees. We also need to take into account the issues of consent and so forth and to develop strategies for their management. We would argue that the basic premise of social work research is concerned with care and social change and that offers a form of potential override in certain circumstances:

> What is more important – an academic commitment to a particular way of knowing and researching the world, or the alleged abuse, extreme boredom and poor quality care that some service users say they experience? (Glasby & Beresford, 2006: 280)

As with all ethical issues, these are not straightforward problems and they do not arrive with straightforward solutions. Our awareness of the potential impacts of the paths we choose and our ability to manage the problems that we can foresee and those that arise as we engage in research are key to being good researcher practitioners.

Finally, in this section we should also mention the issue of reimbursement. Again, for very good reasons a traditional research approach would instruct researchers not to pay or reward respondents for taking part in research on the grounds that it interferes with consent, forms an obligation and is likely to distort responses. Clearly, if we are working with service users and carers we need to be mindful of the expenses they will incur such as travel costs and it is perfectly legitimate to fund such items. Some authors would also argue that whilst we must always strive to reduce bias, the dangers of making payments can be outweighed by the advantages. There is evidence that some forms of payment can increase levels of participation, construct an appropriate acknowledgement of respondents' time engaged with the research and go some way to evening out the power imbalance between researcher and researched (Thompson, 1996). As we noted in the introduction to this chapter, ethics deals with shades of grey and there are very rarely black and white answers to ethical dilemmas. However, there are certainly general approaches and expectations that the process of research governance rightly requires.

RESEARCH GOVERNANCE AND ETHICAL REVIEW

It is a broadly accepted principle that all research involving human participants is subject to a proper, formal ethical review (Wiles et al., 2007). Beginning practitioner researchers should be aware that ethical approval does not normally apply to the collection of 'secondary' data – i.e. where the research exclusively uses existing data gathered by someone else (government statistics, journal articles, policy documents and so forth). Rather, where the researcher themselves is gathering 'primary' data from individuals then ethical approval will be required. Where you are in any doubt, make the appropriate enquiries. Thus, it is both likely and desirable that as a practitioner researcher you will be required to submit your research proposal to ethical scrutiny before an ethics committee. Remember that it is most important that ethical approval is obtained before any contact with respondents.

There are three main avenues for consent that need to be considered for the typical social work practitioner researcher:

- local authority (or social care employer) ethics committee;
- health ethics committee;
- university ethics committee.

A fourth avenue, the newly established Social Care Research Ethics Committee (SCREC), is being designed as a subset of the Health Ethics Committee structure. It is essentially managed by the Social Care Institute for Excellence (SCIE) and operates only at a national level. SCREC will look at adult social care research funded by the Department of Health, research involving those lacking capacity and service user led research. Further details can be found at its website: (http://www.screc.org.uk/). As SCREC complements rather than replaces the three main avenues our advice is to look to local processes in the first instance.

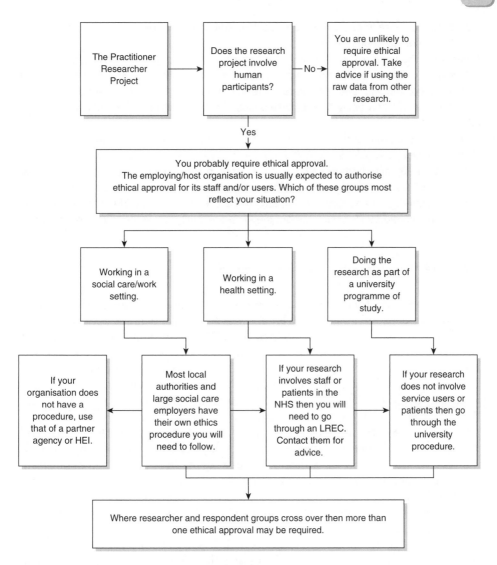

Figure 3.1   A flowchart for ethics approval

WHERE DO I GO?

The question facing all researchers is 'Where do I go for ethical approval?' The flow-chart in Figure 3.1 offers fledgling guidance to help start the practitioner research off on the right foot.

Here are some scenarios requiring ethics approval.

- *Example 1*   You are doing a Master's in social work and for your dissertation are conducting a small-scale piece of research on student attitudes towards the personalisation agenda. As you are planning to interview students you will need ethics approval from the university. Most health and social care faculties will have their own ethics committee and you should contact them for advice.

- *Example 2*   You are a social worker in a large local authority in a looked after children setting and wish to do a piece of research involving asking service users their views about their initial contact with social workers. Here you will need ethics approval from the local authority which will probably have its own ethics committee which you should approach for advice.

- *Example 3*   You are a social worker in a community mental health team and wish to interview your colleagues (CPNs and AMHPs) about joined-up working. You will almost certainly need ethical approval from the NHS Local Research Ethics Committee and should seek advice. LRECs will sometimes advise that some forms of research are 'evaluation' rather than research per se and these may therefore be exempt from requiring ethical approval. You may also need ethics approval from the local authority and will need to take advice.

GOVERNANCE OF HEALTH RESEARCH

Frankly, the process of gaining ethical approval from health committees is complicated and time consuming. Health-related research usually requires approval by the Local Health Research Ethics Committee (or LREC – pronounced 'L' Reck) if it involves primary data, although there are a number of exceptions and parameters that you will need to consider. The NHS is moving towards a centralised online process via the National Research Ethics Service ('N' Rez) and its website can be found at http:// www.nres.npsa.nhs.uk . This process uses the Integrated Research Application System ('I' Raz) which is a daunting procedure and one not to be undertaken either lightly or without consultation from someone who has dealt with this before. This process will apply to workers or students wishing to conduct any research involving any NHS- or health-based staff, students or patients. If your proposed research involves health in any way then our advice is to seek advice from your local LREC as to your next steps. It ought to be noted that this process can take quite a long time to see through and you may need to factor several months into a research process if approval from your LREC is required.

In Europe the ethical review of health research has been strongly influenced by the Declaration of Helsinki, in which Article 5 states that in 'medical research on human subjects, considerations related to the wellbeing of the human subject should take precedence over the interests of science and society' (Cave & Holm, 2002: 320 citing the World Medical Association, 1964). It is interesting to note that the Declaration drew largely from the Nuremburg Code of 1947, produced directly after the Second World War following concerns about human experimentation.[1] In the UK, the Declaration of

---

[1]Sadly, there are numerous examples of the failures of research to follow what one might expect to be reasonable moral and ethical standards in modern times, a commonly quoted example being the now infamous 'Tuskegee syphilis experiment' where 399 poor, Black sharecroppers were denied antibiotic medical treatment for syphilis to see how the disease naturally progressed. The research project was run by the US Public Health Service and was only stopped, after 40 years, in 1972. A more recent, but less dramatic, example of research ignoring the issue of race was analysed by Ranganathan and Bhopal (2006).

Helsinki initially led to the establishment of independent ethical review committees funded by health authorities and then also to the creation of 'multicentre research ethics committees' with the aim of addressing possible inconsistencies between local committees and providing a structure to support multi-site applications (Cave & Holm, 2002).

For the public, confidence regarding the governance offered by these health authority review committees was undermined by two high profile cases. The first was the Bristol heart scandal followed by the Alder Hey organs scandal in Liverpool (*Guardian Unlimited*, 2001). Both these cases raised concerns regarding informed consent as bereaved parents discovered that across the two sites nearly 1,000 dead children's vital organs had been removed without parental knowledge. At the same time, within the health service itself, there was a growing awareness of the need for a framework for health research that would be compatible with the European Directive 2001/20/EC on clinical drug trials (Cave & Holm, 2002).

In light of these considerations a framework for a review of research was established in the form of the *Research Governance Framework for Health and Social Care* (RGF) (DoH, 2005). This was an attempt to address issues of accountability and responsibility and to draw attention both to the law and good practice relating to ethical considerations. Given the history surrounding Bristol and Alder Hey it was inevitably focused on avoiding future distressing medical malpractices that had nothing to do with social work research.

GOVERNANCE OF SOCIAL WORK RESEARCH

Under the RGF, social care services must have:

- systems to deal with applications from people wanting to carry out research;
- checks to ensure that all agreed research has a sponsor;
- systems to record study details, adverse occurrences, complaints, etc.
- procedures for providing information to service users, carers and staff regarding completed research;
- made staff aware of their responsibilities under the RGF;
- systems for the safe handling and storage of data;
- a person or group to assess the plans for research studies;
- systems to ensure there is a documented research plan;
- systems to ensure that research has been subject to a scientific and ethical review.

It is our experience, however, that different local authorities are at different stages of development in these areas and therefore the situation faced by the researcher practitioner will inevitably be localised. All we can say is that it is necessary to approach the relevant authority to gain guidance and approval in line with what they will require. Sadly, the situation is even less clear when we come to consider the broad range of agencies across the private, voluntary and independent sectors that populate so much of our social care provision. This is an emerging issue that is far from being resolved. Researchers in such situations should consider using existing ethics committee in partner organisations and local universities in such circumstances.

Activity

Think about your research project and what ethical issues will arise. Using these typical headings, work through what responses you would provide to an ethics committee – what would you say about:

- avoiding harm and distress?
- potential benefits for participants?
- health and safety issues for researchers?
- participant recruitment, criteria, reimbursement and relationship?
- informed consent and confidentiality?
- management of data?
- vulnerable groups?

Historically, unlike health, the governance of social work research has been predominantly unregulated unless it has fallen under the auspices of an NHS research review, existing academic ethical review bodies, or other review systems. This lack of regulation has begun to be addressed in the code of research guidelines and ethical considerations mapped out in the RGF and the Code of Ethics for Social Work and Social Care Research (JUCSWEC[2], 2008).

Code of Ethics for Social Work and Social Care Research (JUCSWEC, 2008)

1 At all stages of the research process, from inception, resourcing, design, investigation and dissemination, social work and social care researchers have a duty to maintain an active, personal and disciplinary ethical awareness and to take practical and moral responsibility for their work.

2 Both the process of social work/care research, including choice of methodology, and the use to which any findings might be put, should be congruent with the aims and values of social work practice and, where possible, seek to empower service users, promote their welfare and improve their access to economic and social capital on equal terms with other citizens.

3 Social work and social care researchers should seek to promote emancipatory research and work together with disempowered groups, individuals and communities to devise, articulate and to achieve research agendas that respect fundamental human rights and which aim towards social justice.

4 In the case of all those who are the subjects of research, but particularly those made vulnerable by age, health, disability or social disadvantage, social work and social

---

[2]The Joint University Council Social Work Education Committee is a body which represents the majority of Higher Education providers of social work education. Their Code of Ethics can be found on their website at http://www.juc.ac.uk/swec-res-code.aspx

care researchers must retain a primary concern for subjects' welfare and should actively protect participants from physical and mental harm, discomfort, danger and unreasonable disruption in their daily lives or unwarranted intrusions into their privacy.

5 Social work and social care researchers must not tolerate any form of discrimination based on age, gender, class, ethnicity, national origin, religion, sexual orientation, disability, health, marital, domestic or parental status and must seek to ensure that their work excludes any unacknowledged bias. Where appropriate, social work/care researchers should seek to predicate their work on the perspective and lived experiences of the research subject.

6 In establishing the aims and objectives of their research, social work and social care researchers are to consider the ascertainable consequences of their actions for the users of social work/care services, both in particular and in general, in order to ensure that the legitimate interests of service users are not unwarrantably compromised or prejudiced by the proposed investigation.

7 In their chosen methodology and in every other aspect of their research design, social work researchers are to ensure that they are technically competent to carry out the particular investigation to the highest standards of social science as currently understood, recognising the limitations of their own expertise. In relation to research carried out primarily for educational or instructional purposes, this responsibility is shared by the student's supervisor.

8 In relation to every participant to the research process, including service users, colleagues, funders and employers, social work and social care researchers have a duty to deal openly and fairly. In particular, there is a duty to inform every participant of all features of the research that might be expected to influence willingness to participate, especially but not exclusively when access to services may be, or may be perceived to be, dependent on participation.

9 Only in cases where no alternative strategy is feasible, where no harm to the research subject can be foreseen and where the greater good is self-evidently served, are procedures involving deception or concealment permissible for social work and social care researchers.

10 The social work and social care researcher will at all times respect the individual participant's absolute right to decline to participate in or to withdraw from the research programme, especially when the researcher is, by any means, in a position of authority over the participant.

11 Participation in any social work/care research activity is to be predicated on the freely given, informed and acknowledged consent of the research subject. Particular care must be taken in obtaining the consent of those who have impairments that might limit understanding and/or communication. Third party consent in the case of those who are incapable of giving consent directly may only be obtained from a legally authorized or other appropriate person.

12 Consent must be secured through the use of language that is readily comprehensible to the research subject and which accurately and adequately explains the purpose of the research and the procedures to be followed.

13 Any data or other information produced in the course of social work/care research is confidential except as agreed in advance with the research participants (including research subjects) and prescribed by law.

14 Social work/care research findings must be reported accurately, completely and without distortion and note any significant variables and conditions that may have

(Continued)

(Continued)

affected the outcomes or the interpretation of the data. This includes a duty to report results which reflect unfavourably on agencies of the central or local state, vested interests (including the researchers' own and those of sponsors) as well as prevailing wisdom and orthodox opinion. In addition, social work and social care researchers have a responsibility to make every reasonable effort to ensure that public communications of their work reported through the mass media do not contain unfavourable stereotypes or other derogatory or damaging representations of service users. Social work/care researchers should also seek to ensure that their findings are not otherwise misused, especially where this is to the detriment of service users or of any partner to the research process.

15 The publication of social work research findings should properly, and in proportion to their contribution, acknowledge the part played by all participants to the research process.

The JUCSWEC code directly addresses social work research and has been rightly and warmly welcomed by the social work research community. Drawing these key considerations together had been considered a vital task as it was feared that otherwise social work might be crowded out by adjacent professions, especially health. For example, the RGF was principally based on a medical-style code of ethics, orientated towards positivist research approaches that were appropriate for medical drug trials (Butler, 2003) but were also potentially unfit for reviewing social work research. As has been discussed in earlier chapters, practitioner research is more likely to use interpretative methods appropriate to small-scale investigations that might be considered less rigorous or valid when reviewed through a positivist orientation (Butler, 2003; Parton, 2003; Shaw & Gould, 2001).

To take account of these different orientations in the RDF, a public consultation process was set up to develop guidelines relating to social work and social care research (Pahl, 2004). These state that the composition of a system of ethical review must include a range of disciplines that reflect social work's knowledge base, as well as service users and their relatives. There are also very clear and helpful guidelines on the process for ethical review (2004: 30–33) and working in tandem with the JUCSWEC code SCEI's newly set-up National Social Care Research Ethics Committee (NSCREC); these demonstrate a concerted effort by the social work community to develop appropriate ethical awareness and governance for social work in a multi-disciplinary climate. However, the researcher practitioner needs to retain awareness that when they engage with the 'health'-focused ethical approval processes they may well feel disadvantaged because of their social care background – simply because these particular committees can lack an understanding and knowledge of social care and its research. Glasby and Beresford (2007) recently found LRECS to be almost entirely staffed by medical and health professionals, with a strange preponderance of 'lay' members who are either Christian chaplains or the retired. You must understand what this might mean for your research, gather the support you need and be prepared to explain why you want to do things in the way you do to someone who, simply, may think differently about the research task.

USING SOCIAL WORK RESEARCH ETHICS

Having looked at some of the more straightforward (!) aspects of research ethics, we now need to consider some of the deeper issues that can affect how we may choose to understand our use of social work ethics. As we have established in the previous chapters, caring is a fundamental concept implicit in social work values. In relation to social work ethics, our understanding of this can be deepened with reference to the feminist discourse on the 'ethics of care' (Parton, 2003). Drawing on the work of Tronto (1993) and Sevenhuijsen (1998), it is argued that for the feminist caring is not an abstract concept but an active engagement in a relationship with another in order to develop an 'ethical relationship of care' (Noddings, 1984). This begins with a particular individual in their specific situation before broadening out to encompass wider, more abstract concerns related to their situation (Engster, 2004). This attention to the individual in a specific situation can be related to situation ethics (Hardwick & Hardwick, 2007). The situation ethics approach is concerned with the specific and takes into account all aspects of the situation, all the permutations relating to the investigation, by adopting an attitude that is 'open' and willing to 'listen'. This is in contrast to the deontological approach which is concerned with more universalistic ethical principles. The word 'deontological' is derived from the Greek for 'necessary' or 'imperative'. Deontological ethics presents principles as 'givens'. For the deontological ethicist, the approach is to follow the guidelines and diktats laid out for ethical approval. The problem with this is that it does not necessitate a reflexive interrogation although it does not exclude the possibility. It is orientated towards accepting the procedural requirements as something 'given'.

The situation ethicist would accept, like the deontologist, that ethical maxims are significant, pertinent and demand respect. However, unlike the deontologist, in a given situation, and having read the pertinent ethical maxims relevant to the situation and the implications, the researcher may be prepared to set aside the relevant principles if, after critical reflection, the benefits of doing so outweigh any possible harm caused.

> Situation ethics is willing to make full and respectful use of principles, to be treated as maxims but not as laws ... We might call it 'principled relativism' ... Principles ... or general rules are *illuminators*. But they are not *directors*. (Fletcher, 1966: 31 quoted in Hardwick & Hardwick, 2007)

For situation ethicists, principles are guides rather than laws that must be obeyed because they see each situation as unique – in the sense that it is in some way both unprecedented and unrepeatable. Each situation will provide the clue as to the most appropriate strategy. For example, a situation ethicist might argue that although one should begin from the premise that seeking informed consent is a 'given', having listened and being open, there may be a one-off situation when this should be set aside.

Example of a Possible Scenario for Setting Aside 'Informed Consent'

An investigation is undertaken using covert participant observation to gather data on child care workers in a residential setting with the objective of gaining further understanding of the practices and procedures that facilitate institutional abuse. The use of covert methods and the inevitable setting aside of informed consent from participants might be justified on the grounds that any awareness of the investigation would influence the behaviour of the child care workers and lead to a contamination of sensitive data. Given the history of institutional abuse in UK residential homes (Corby et al., 1998; Stanley et al., 1999) it might, in certain specific circumstances, be argued that a greater good is served by covert methods, because it will increase understanding that will help reduce institutional abuse, even though that knowledge has been gained through the infringement of the principles of consent and privacy for participants.

Is it right to say that all ethical principles such as informed consent are absolute and unbreachable, which therefore takes care of all situations? Or can we say that these principles while enlightened can sometimes be set aside if, after reflection, a greater good is being served? Situations that give rise to the setting aside of well-established principles should be extremely rare and also demand rigorous and ongoing review from both the principal investigator and ethical review processes.

A very persuasive argument for a situation ethics approach is that it requires a systematic interrogation by the researchers of their own reasoning and behaviour. It places this at the forefront of any ethical consideration, clearly locating responsibility with the researchers to ensure they are 'open' and 'listen' to what is the most appropriate course of action. This can only be achieved through the researcher adopting a reflexive approach to ethical review. Reflexivity is:

> ... a term used in research methodology to refer to a reflectiveness among social researchers about the implications for knowledge of the social world they generate, of their methods, values, biases, decisions, and mere presence in the very situations they investigate. (Bryman, 2004: 543)

This is particularly pertinent to the practitioner researcher as taking time for critical reflection and the use of reflexivity is argued to be a prerequisite for allowing the complexity of social situations to emerge in all types of social work research (Powell, 2002). This type of understanding relates to 'process knowledge'. Process knowledge is a knowledge that is not fixed but rather emergent and contingent, where all the facts may never be fully known or understood. This contrasts with 'product knowledge' that is static and factual (Sheppard & Ryan, 2003) and relates more to the deontological position. Thus, because the social work researcher practitioner deals with such complex, fluid practice/research situations, they need to be ever mindful of the ethical issues and dilemmas that may emerge in this non-static situation. Things change. Nothing stays the same.

Part of the process of a reflexive, situated ethical review is thinking through the implications and permutations of all aspects of the research and weighing these in the benefits/harm balance. There can be no absolute answers, but there can be evidenced and sensitive deliberation. It is not unknown for research proposals seeking ethical approval to casually state that written consent will be sought, and questions will be sensitively phrased to meet the needs of the participants. What does this mean? Where is the evidence of reflexive deliberation? If care and time are not taken, this is simply paying lip-service to the reflexive process. A systematic review of the implications of decisions made and methods used allows researchers to take personal responsibility for the research process and avoids a reliance on unthinkingly following ethical guidelines. This gives the opportunity for immersion in the ethical review rather than taking the facts for granted.

Critics of situation ethics have argued that this focus is too personal, constrictive and time consuming (McCabe, 1968). Inevitably there is a tension in situation ethics between becoming indulgently micro and remaining mindful of the overall context and macro issues that are also relevant in a meaningful, ethical review. It is not a matter of 'either/or' but 'both/and'. The micro and the macro situation interplay and complement each other with the researcher engaging in a process of looking both inward and outward. This is a time-consuming pursuit, but then so are all aspects of doing research and given that the time taken is to promote emancipatory research, sensitive to the implications of methods used, then it is time well spent.

ETHICAL CONSIDERATIONS WHEN DOING PRACTITIONER RESEARCH

In order to begin to identify the reflexive process needed for ethical scrutiny we will analyse a scenario and consider the range of ethical issues which it reveals. Situation ethics acknowledges the infinite possibilities that might emerge in each unique situation and therefore this scenario should only be used as a guide for exploring possibilities and not as a precedent for use in a similar situation. Each principal investigator ultimately has to take personal responsibility for ensuring a comprehensive review of the implications of their specific research.

Proposal for an Ethical Review

Title: An investigation into the involvement in crime of young people in a neighbourhood in a Yorkshire town.

The practitioner researcher: A youth justice worker in the district Youth Offending Team.

Research aim: To ascertain the involvement in crime of young people aged 16–18, both in education and outside of it, in a neighbourhood with a high Asian heritage community.

Methods: To gather data from professionals working in the neighbourhood through in-depth interviews and from young people through a series of focus groups. These will consist of six young people with separate groups for males and females, and those in or out of education.

Sampling: A purposive sample of young people from the neighbourhood will be achieved though liaising with local sixth forms and information held by Connexions and neighbourhood youth clubs.

(Continued)

(Continued)

Ethical Considerations

1 The study does not involve participants who are vulnerable or unable to give informed consent.
2 No covert methods will be used at any time.
3 There won't be any discussion of sensitive topics that may cause distress or embarrassment to the participants or potential risk of disclosure to the researcher of criminal activity or child protection issues.
4 There is no potential for the study to induce psychological stress or anxiety or cause harm or negative consequences beyond the risks encountered in normal life.
5 Written consent will be obtained and participants informed that their participation is voluntary and that they can withdraw at any time.
6 Participants will be informed of any aspect of the study that might influence their continued participation.
7 Benefit to participants will be achieved through a half-day conference held in the neighbourhood to share findings and promote discussion.

DISCUSSION OF ETHICAL CONSIDERATIONS

Before a situated, reflexive interrogation can take place this study needs to be situated within a local and national policy context related to the criminal activities of young people. Also required is socioeconomic information about the neighbourhood which should include information specific to all ethnic groups and their educational attainment, employment rate and criminal activity. Is there any current research exploring related subjects?

Without this contextual analysis it is not possible to understand the specific situation and ethical considerations ensuing from this. Therefore in the light of the contextual background:

• Is it true to say that the study will not involve participants who are vulnerable? These participants are young people aged 16–18 of mixed ethnic origin, some with disadvantaged circumstances. It may be appropriate to consider how issues related to specific vulnerability may be handled, i.e. power and race differentials between the young people themselves and between the young people and researcher, how issues of literacy and intellectual capability could be partially equalised, and also to consider the possible community issues such as group or gang alliances.
• The commitment given – that there will be no covert methods used – can only be guaranteed if the research is meticulously planned and managed.
• Is it possible to know whether there is going to be any discussion of sensitive topics? Given the key theme for discussion is participation in crime, a highly sensitive topic in its own right, how are participants to be protected from potential criminal disclosure? What if someone says that they were involved in a robbery or carried a knife for their own protection? Also, will the young people be briefed about the limits of confidentiality in relation to child protection issues and have contingency plans been made for a disclosure of abuse? How will issues of race and potential Islamophobia be handled should they arise if they have 'ethnically mixed' focus groups?

- Given the above, is it helpful to say that there will be no psychological stress, anxiety, harm or negative consequences beyond the risks encountered in normal life? More helpful would be an awareness of how to steer the discussion away from topics that might cause psychological stress and an awareness of how the unexpected might be handled. Also, will there be no debriefing at the end or after the focus groups with youth workers or counsellors available? These focus groups will require someone experienced in working in groups with young people. If the youth justice worker is experienced they are likely to have the required skills, but this is not discussed. If they are to conduct the focus groups, why is there no consideration of the impact of this on the young people? Will the researcher be known – and if so, in what capacity by some of the young people, and how might this impact on the data gathered?
- How is written consent to be obtained? Will parental consent be sought and how do notions of consent differ between ethnic groups?
- How will participants be kept informed of any aspect of the study that might influence their continued participation? Is there to be ongoing briefing sessions, or will the researcher decide what constitutes significant information?
- How will the opportunity to attend a community conference/feedback session to debrief and discuss the research make the study of benefit to the participants? Is there any potential for change ensuing from the study, and how will such change be initiated?

Activity

Imagine you are writing a research proposal investigating the involvement in crime of young people aged 16–18, both in education and outside of it, in your working neighbourhood.

- Explore the local and national policy context related to activities of young people in crime. Also, gather socioeconomic information specific to your work neighbourhood and any current research exploring related issues.

Address each of the following questions which may be raised in response to your imaginary proposal:

- Does the study involve participants who are vulnerable or unable to give informed consent?
- Will any covert methods be used at any time?
- Will there be any discussion of sensitive topics that may cause distress or embarrassment to the participant or a potential risk of disclosure to the researcher of criminal activity or child protection issues?
- Does the study have the potential to induce psychological stress or anxiety or cause harm or negative consequences beyond the risks encountered in normal life?
- Will written consent be obtained and participants be informed that their participation is voluntary and that they can withdraw at any time? If so, how will this be done?
- Will participants be informed of any aspect of the study that might influence their continued participation in the study? If so, how?
- Will this study be of potential benefit to participants, and if so how?

CONCLUSION

According to Butler, good social work research is research that has a comprehensive underpinning of social work values and calls for, 'a sophisticated form of ethical awareness that goes beyond questions of governance' (2003: 26). However, it remains an absolute that ethical approval for research must be honestly and properly obtained through the correct channels that we have outlined. We have argued that the social work practitioner researcher ought to go beyond an unquestioning approach to ethics and be ever mindful of the dynamic scenarios that can unfold before them in the course of their research – and which may prompt new and emerging ethical dilemmas.

This chapter has argued that a sophisticated ethical awareness embedded in social work values can be achieved through the development of an 'ethical relationship of care' that begins with the particular individual in their specific situation, before broadening out to encompass wider concerns related to this. Attention to the individual in a specific situation can draw upon situation ethics, which is a helpful discourse for understanding the process required for a social work-focused ethical review.

There are a number of implications to adopting this orientation. A challenging one is that in rare circumstances ethical principles can sometimes be set aside if, after reflexive interrogation, a greater good is seen to be served by doing so. This requires an even greater than usual systematic interrogation and review from both the principal researcher and the ethical review process. Yet again we must emphasise caution here, especially for the beginning practitioner researcher as they develop their skills of reflexivity and become more familiar with the relationships that research can engender. Situation ethics is particularly appropriate to an 'ethical relationship of care' because it fully legitimates and affords the exercise of the faculty of moral discernment and conscience (reflexive interrogation) in any ethical review. This allows for the possibility of the space, time and intellectual rigour to focus on both the uniqueness of the situation and the capacity to reveal social injustice or social discord in its specific manifestations. The situation ethics approach can be taken alongside the existence of preordained ethical procedures and implicitly acknowledges that knowledge is temporal, transient and located in the specific.

Key points

- Obtain ethical approval when required.
- Take full account of ethical principles but do not use them as 'givens'.
- Have awareness of the uniqueness of each situation.
- Foreground a 'relationship-based' approach.
- Seek a change for the better for individuals, groups and communities.
- Be willing to be 'open' and to 'listen', allowing for a reflexive interrogation of all possible permutations.
- Foreground moral discernment and the taking of personal responsibility.

Further Reading

Department of Health (2005) *Governance Arrangements for the NHS Research Ethics Committees*. London: DoH.

Fraser, S. et al. (eds) (2004) *Doing Research with Children and Young People*. London: SAGE.

Glasby, J. & Beresford, P. (2007) 'In whose interests? Local research ethics committees and service user research', *Ethics and Social Welfare*, 1 (3): 282–292.

Lee, R.L. (1999) *Doing Research on Sensitive Topics*. London: SAGE.

Wiles, R., Crow, G., Charles, V. & Heath, S. (2006) 'Informed consent and the research process: following rules or striking balances', *Sociological Research Online* 12 (2). Available at http://www.socresonline.org.uk/12/2/wiles.html and last accessed 5 November 2009.

SERVICE USERS, CARERS AND SOCIAL WORK RESEARCH

OVERVIEW

There's a rather old joke that asks how many social workers it takes to change a light bulb. An answer we prefer amongst the many on offer is that it's the system that needs to change, not the light bulb. We can transfer this idea to the involvement of service users and carers in social work research. Anyone who is broadly familiar with the general canon of research in social work can't but fail to query why it is that service users are so little involved in social work research, with their usual role being that of passive respondents. They are seldom genuine partners in the very research that concerns them most and there are literally only a small handful of examples in the UK where service users have actually led research projects. The system – albeit an evolving one – does need to change to meet the demands on it that an empowering form of social work research would expect. This chapter aims to explore this situation, looking at methods and techniques of involving service users and carers in research projects in meaningful ways, and also looking at some examples of service user- and carer-led research.

It's helpful to reflect for a moment on what we actually mean by service users and carers in this context. 'Users' of services in the broadest sense can include a vast range of people – those in government, those who work in organisations, users of research, researchers themselves and so on. We would do well to think, as researchers, which users we need to relate to most. However, for the purposes of this chapter we will look at a specific area: people who use services, be they social services, health services and so forth within the social care world. This includes those who care for others and in this chapter we shall use the term 'service users' in this inclusive sense. At the same time an understanding of this group should not stop there, we mustn't take for granted the elements of this rather simplistic definition. There are positive and negative factors which go beyond the notion of an entitlement to benefits and support, not least of which is the tacit understanding that service users and carers tend to be in unequal relationships with the society in which they live. There is also an underpinning notion of service users as the passive recipients of support, which in some senses restricts their identity – we must be careful not to equate the notion of 'service user' as the whole person – reducing the complexity of their life to, for example, a disability, a health problem or a care need.

Beyond all this there is also an understanding that the experiences of service users can connect in a meaningful and powerful way. As stories are shared in supportive environments people can become less isolated and more aware that others share their situations and feelings (Branfield & Beresford, 2006; Shaping our Lives & University of Leeds Centre for Disability Studies, 2007). If we are to consider how, as researchers, we can involve service users in research we need to understand and reflect on these profound issues and the differences in our experiences. Some authors have used an alternative nomenclature in an attempt to capture different aspects of this issue, notably, 'experts by experience' (Preston-Shoot, 2007) and indeed the term 'survivor research' (Halliday & Sherwood, 2003).

National Occupational Standards for Social Work

These relate directly to the notion of service user involvement in research – as in practice. Element 1.2 talks of promoting the wishes of service users. Element 1.5 asks social workers to advance equal opportunities for service users. Element 3.4 raises the notion of paying attention to resource or operational difficulties that may impact on care delivery. In terms of process, practitioner researchers should note Element 3.8 concerning the responsible use of power as a social worker and Element 5.2 which ensures that no one is exploited, be they service users, carers or colleagues.

WHY IS SERVICE USER INVOLVEMENT IN RESEARCH IMPORTANT?

As social workers who are engaged in research, it is clearly important that service users are involved: we feel this on an instinctive level. It is critical that social workers stay in touch with the grassroots experience of service users and equally it is essential that the research they engage in is meaningful and relevant to those lives and experiences. At its heart (and we use that phrase advisedly) social work research should be about change – the kinds of changes desired by service users (Turner & Beresford, 2005). Such research can also be an empowering personal experience which supports service users in having a voice, a say in their lives and, in working alongside others, this can develop solidarity. One survivor researcher talks of how research played such a role amongst psychiatric system survivors and helped raise the expectations of those who had been 'educated' to live with an unacceptable quality of life (Faulkner, 2006). At a more day-to-day level, evidence suggests that other benefits of involvement include the development of the capacity to be useful and the identification and pursuit of new issues (Beresford, 2007b). As social workers engaged in research we are probably drawn to these examples of why service user involvement is so important – because it affords us all a place to meet and to share. Preston-Shoot (2007) recounts a service user telling how a social worker visited them one day, but only softly knocked on the door before walking hurriedly down the garden path and then, a few days later, sending a letter indicating they were sorry the person wasn't in. The service user, who was indeed at home, told of how they assumed the social worker was frightened of coming to discuss a difficult subject. The service user reflected on whether the social worker understood that they too were frightened: 'What I most regret is that we never had the opportunity, the social worker and I, to talk about what it meant to be frightened' (2007: 350).

Activity

Using the Social Care Institute of Excellence website (www.scie.org.uk) select an area of practice that interests you and track down three journal articles or research reports on that theme. Read these pieces and pay particular attention to the involvement of service users and carers. Was this done? How was this done? How might you have done this differently?

BACKGROUND

Before we look at some of the practical examples of service user involvement in research it helps to begin to understand some of the context in which research takes place. Within our introduction, we noted how little research in social work is led by service users or executed jointly with them. The question we must ask is, why? There are several elements to any reasonable answer, the first of which is probably that social work research generally tends not to be done by social workers and therefore such researchers are not as steeped in the values of the profession and are less likely to place an equal merit on service user involvement in research. A second element of an answer must be that there is simply much less of social work research compared to many other forms of research, particularly that which looks at perhaps our closest neighbour – health. Figures show that health spends 5.3 per cent of its entire budget on research and development compared to a meagre 0.31 per cent of a social services' budget. Similarly, the overall research and development spending per member of staff is 135 times greater in health than it is in social services, roughly equating to £25.00 for each social services' employee and £3,400 for each health employee (Marsh & Fisher, 2005). It is also very important to note that even in health settings, user involvement in research is in its infancy. Evans and Jones (2004) report that only 17 per cent of NHS research projects in 2004 had user involvement at any stage at all. Fundamentally, research is probably not a common component of the average social work office.

Beyond this, there are numerous concerns stemming from the generally academic base of social work research and a growing body of evidence that service users find it difficult to 'fit in' to academic structures and settings (Branfield, 2007). Research has found that academics tend not to value service user inputs highly enough, and are also rigid, lack a conduciveness to change and their institutions present problems of access. Indeed, evidence suggests that academics might put up barriers to service user involvement, fearing their knowledge and approaches to practice issues will be exposed as out of date (Branfield et al., 2007). This is all presented both as an understanding of why service users are so little involved and also as a guide to what some of the issues are for social work practitioners to act as researchers. The whole approach of this book is offered as one way forward in these developments – an attempt to shift the location, direction and purpose of social work research. Of course, we wouldn't want to paint a picture showing that all academic-based researchers are bad and, indeed, that all service user-led research is good. But there is a sense in which it seems an insufficient emphasis has been placed within existing research communities on the involvement of service users, carers and practitioners. It has to be up to them to open the doors: it is academia that has to change. We would firmly encourage the development of partnerships between these groups, where each other's strengths are valued amongst equals. For the practitioner researcher the process of user engagement must emerge as their very first thought …

Activity

Imagine inviting a group of service users to your workplace to discuss research. Compose a letter inviting the group to a meeting. How do you think the letter would be received and what would be their first impressions of your workplace? What sort of issues might this present to you? What sort of challenges might stem from the organisation, the buildings you inhabit and your working patterns? How would you go about addressing these challenges?

WHO GETS RESEARCHED?

When we ask the question, '*Who gets researched?*', we should take a moment to consider the research we are familiar with across a broad spectrum, before we can perhaps come up with the observation that the answer tends to be, '*The less powerful*'.

> … people who are poor, unemployed, mentally ill, women, black people, disabled people and children are all frequently studied. In comparison research has uncovered little about the lives and activities of psychiatrists, bank managers, policemen, politicians, policy makers, political terrorists, captains of industry or even researchers themselves. (Oliver, 1992: 110)

Perhaps the challenge for us here is to understand the use of power as it applies to social workers who can be seen as powerful, professional experts. We can also add that researchers are likewise seen as influential, knowledgeable people. As Oliver (1992) continues to argue, the powerful are rarely studied because they have the resources to protect themselves from scrutiny. How can social workers deal with this dilemma of wanting to conduct research that benefits service users without further disempowering them? The answer here is perhaps more straightforward than might be first thought – and is all to do with the approach and involvement. Collaboration, as was once said, can sometimes be what service users are told they are doing when they become involved in research projects designed or conceived by academic researchers (Faulkner, 2006). The point of principle is to ensure that such collaboration and involvement has meaning for all those involved by thinking about the issue as part of

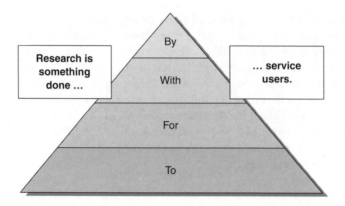

Figure 4.1   Service user involvement in research (Evans & Jones, 2004)

the practitioner researcher's approach. It is helpful to conceive of a continuum of service user involvement in research.

Looking at Figure 4.1, on the lowest level we can see that research can be something that is done 'to' service users, leaving them as passive and fragmented symptoms. As we progress the involvement in research we can see it move to research done 'for' service users, 'with' them, and finally done 'by' them. Levels of choice, control, participation and partnership over the process then increase as we reach the apex. In this way, we can begin to see the shifts required as we move from consultation, through collaboration, to control.

The peculiar dynamic that authors in this field seldom deal with is the relative distance of practitioners from research, academics from practice, and service users from having much say in either. Traditional academic research in social work tends to exclude both service users and practitioners. The task for practitioner researchers reading this book who wish to develop a research project can therefore be doubly hard. However, practitioners are arguably far closer to the realities of service users' lived experiences than academic researchers – and this experience can be used as its own 'expertise'. Indeed, as we have discussed elsewhere, social work skills are readily transferable to research skills. Nowhere is this more evident than with service user involvement. One might say that it is a natural orientation for a social worker's moral compass towards participative and empowering practice, as it therefore ought to be to research as well.

RESEARCH APPROACHES

Different research approaches are associated with service user involvement in research and we shall briefly consider three of the main approaches in the literature as we try to understand what underpins this idea and what its antecedents are. The approaches discussed will all benefit from further reading. Practitioner researchers considering a critique of traditional research practices can see how they have not only excluded service users and carers but also other marginalised groups in society. There is an increasingly dissatisfied group of authors writing about research who are identifying serious flaws in research approaches that don't demonstrate an understanding of power.

Feminist research methodology

There are, of course, so many approaches to research from a feminist perspective that one cannot readily reduce these to a few simple statements (Harvey, 1990). However, writers in this area tend to be critical of traditional research practices which they see as having been largely done by men, focusing on men, yet often drawing conclusions that are attributed to entire populations: 'malestream' research producing a masculine view of the world (McLaughlin, 2007). Their response to this problem is to reject these (often positivist) approaches and place much greater emphasis on the individual, arguing that the 'personal is political'. In so doing they highlight the politics of research and pay far greater attention to the individual, the researcher's relationship to them, and the power relationships they will engage in. In placing such an emphasis on the daily lives of people, their thoughts and their feelings, the links between feminist methodology and service user involvement in social work research are apparent.

Participatory Action Research (PAR)

In a similar vein, PAR refers to a variety of research practices that take people's lived experiences as their starting point with the idea of creating positive social change as a central driving force. PAR has been defined as:

> ... collective, self reflective enquiry undertaken by participants in social situations in order to improve the rationality and justice of their own social ... practices. (Kemmis & McTaggart, 1988: 5)

There are a number of key principles that make PAR distinctive, which also chime closely with what we are seeking from service users' involvement in research. First and foremost is the notion that research is undertaken by those that are personally involved. Typically, PAR also includes an emphasis on changing social practice, authentic participation and collaboration. The dynamic processes of PAR are also revealed in its general development of self-critical communities committed not only to learning about themselves and the world around them but also to emancipating themselves from the power constraints that affect them. However, an important corollary of this rather grand and taxing notion is that PAR *starts small*. It begins by working on issues of change that are manageable, within small cycles of research and small groups of people. This is a particularly useful point for service users' involvement in research.

Emancipatory, disability and service user-controlled research

Developments under these headings owe a lot to colleagues in the health professions and include, for example, disabled people's research movements and psychiatric systems survivor research. Oliver (1992) has been a key author in the movement which sought to develop a more emancipatory form of research around issues of disability, noting the medicalisation and clinical bias of research that brought with it a positivist approach which, as with feminist approaches, has been severely critiqued. For Oliver, the problem with this kind of research was that it inherently reinforced an individual model of disability where the problems people faced were being caused by their individual impairments. He neatly revealed this in an interrogation of questions taken from the Office of Population Census and Surveys National Disability Survey in 1986. Here are three of the questions that were used in the survey and Oliver's (1992) re-framing of them from his emancipatory perspective. He gave us a salutary lesson of how many ideological assumptions about power relationships could be infused into seemingly straightforward questions:

- Are your difficulties in understanding people mainly due to a hearing problem?
- *Are your difficulties in understanding people mainly due to their inabilities to communicate with you?*
- Did you move here because of your health problem or disability?
- *What inadequacies in your housing caused you to move here?*
- Does your health problem/disability affect your work in any way at present?
- *Do you have problems at work because of the physical environment or the attitude of others?*

In contrast, survivor research is a phrase used to capture, in this context, both the experiences of those surviving the experience of mental health problems as well as their treatment and engagement with mental health services. Supporters of these particular approaches argue that the inherently subjective nature of mental health problems means that survivors should lead and define research about themselves. Such an approach, they say, will provide a greater insight into their needs and more accurately identify their views and experiences of services, support and treatment. This approach also argues that control of these research agendas is an empowering component for the survivors themselves and affords a generally more holistic view of mental health than that normally taken by academic and clinical researchers.

AN ETHICAL BASIS FOR SERVICE USER INVOLVEMENT IN RESEARCH

Having considered some of the methodological and theoretical backgrounds of participatory research we can see the context for the emergence of service user involvement in social work research. Core themes have been developed around meaningful involvement, social justice, empowerment and language and are clearly evidenced in this area of work. In turn these themes are clearly located in the Joint University

Council Social Work Education Committee's (JUCSWEC) Code of Ethics for Social Work and Social Care Research. The Code forms an excellent starting point for connecting the values of the professional social worker, research and service users. (Its origins were discussed in the previous chapter.)

Activity

Look at the first five statements below from the Social Work Research Code of Ethics (JUCSWEC, 2008). Try to make connections with some of the ideas of service user and carer involvement that have been considered in this chapter. What might these statements mean for your research project?

1 At all stages of the research process, from inception, resourcing and design, to investigation and dissemination, social work and social care researchers have a duty to maintain an active, personal and disciplinary ethical awareness and to take practical and moral responsibility for their work.
2 Both the process of social work/care research, including choice of methodology, and the use to which any findings might be put, should be congruent with the aims and values of social work practice and, where possible, seek to empower service users, promote their welfare and improve their access to economic and social capital on equal terms with other citizens.
3 Social work and social care researchers should seek to promote emancipatory research and work together with disempowered groups, individuals and communities to devise, articulate and to achieve research agendas that respect fundamental human rights and which aim towards social justice.
4 In the case of all those who are the subjects of research, but particularly those made vulnerable by age, health, disability or social disadvantage, social work and social care researchers must retain a primary concern for subjects' welfare and should actively protect participants from physical and mental harm, discomfort, danger and unreasonable disruption in their daily lives or unwarranted intrusions into their privacy.
5 Social work and social care researchers must not tolerate any form of discrimination based on age, gender, class, ethnicity, national origin, religion, sexual orientation, disability, health, marital, domestic or parental status and must seek to ensure that their work excludes any unacknowledged bias. Where appropriate, social work/care researchers should seek to predicate their work on the perspective and lived experiences of the research subject.

The Code encourages social work researchers to see themselves as moral agents – as persons who are cognisant of what is good and bad and who have a responsibility to act within a sense of what is right and wrong. The research we engage in should therefore be open to scrutiny and criticism should it not appropriately respond to the ethical and moral demands placed upon it. There is also a clear sense that the values of social work research are congruent with the values of social work. This is an unusual position for many researchers across the broad spectrum of research who don't posses such an external reference point. But, more fundamentally, social work research is seen as 'empowering' for service users – it should work towards change, achieve social justice. This, it ought to be acknowledged, clashes in some ways with notions of research 'objectivity' and knowledge generation being free from prejudice and intent. If these notions are promoted then social change becomes something of an irrelevance, as the researcher is merely reporting factual observations and not lobbying. Becker, writing in the 1960s, coined the famous phrase 'Whose side are we on'?, meaning that the researcher needs to understand and be aware of the 'team' for which they are playing (Becker, 1967). We would argue that social work research is very much on the side of the service user: it's about improving their lives, it's about social change.

Activity

Consider the issue of morality and service user and carer involvement as you examine these three famous examples of research. Find out what you can about each in turn. These are challenging topics about very sensitive areas.

- The Tuskegee experiment.
- The Bristol Royal Infirmary inquiry.
- The Alder Hey organs scandal.

SERVICE USER-LED RESEARCH

As was noted before there is an understanding in the approaches we have considered and the Code of Ethics reproduced above that all is not well with 'traditional' research. Indeed, it is arguably the failings of such social work research in not embracing service users in research activity and being unwilling or unable to understand or work with the complexities of people's lives that give rise to the need for service user-led research. 'Traditional' research tends to focus on the individual – asking each person questions, getting them to fill in a questionnaire, observing them and so on. However, just as Oliver (1992) argued, this process focuses on one aspect of the person, be it their disability, their offending pattern, or even their choice of daily newspaper. In this sense people become fragments, reduced to the status of research subjects and restricted, by the process of research, to a small range of behaviours, namely what they can and can't talk about. The researchers themselves are only interested in a small portion of their complex lives and, in effect, use people – treating them *as* their illness, their disability, etc.

Some writers argue this process is alienating as it treats issues such as disability as the subjects' fault, leaving them essentially alone (Rowan, 1981). Furthermore, an inherently individualised approach means that the whole notion of someone's place in the world becomes invisible, which in turn tends to ignore the causes of those situations that are to do with social forces, structural factors and institutional constraints (Lukes, 1972). How can the practitioner researcher afford to lose sight of such issues as poverty, unemployment, housing, stigma and dependency? Surely we must seek to understand people in their social situations, their friendships, their communities?

EXAMPLES OF SERVICE USER-LED RESEARCH

As we have noted above, while there are not many examples of service user-led research, it is also the case that more and more are emerging, especially in the area of health and social care. We shall examine two examples before looking in a little more detail at one the authors have been involved in.

Children and young people as partners in the designing and commissioning of research (Morrison et al., 2008)

This project, commissioned by Scottish Women's Aid, explored the views, experiences and needs of children and young people who have had to move home following abuse. Children and young people were involved in the commissioning, design and dissemination of the research. The project challenged assumptions (and indeed the fears) that many researchers have about not only the involvement of children in research (as participants as well as collaborators) but also about emotionally complex situations such as the topic of the project. They note that most of the literature around domestic abuse stems from adult accounts produced by professional researchers and mothers:

> In keeping with this understanding of children and our commitment to a child's right to influence matters that affect them, we actively sought to involve children and young people in the design and the development of the research project. This meant having children and young people participate in a meaningful way that went beyond participating in the study as respondents. We anticipated that involving children and young people in this way would result in the research being more informed and more reflective of their experiences. (Morrison et al., 2008: 5)

Children and young people helped set the research agenda through focus group discussions about the important issues that arose for them in moving house. An advisory group consisting of five adults and two young people led the process through 'workshop'-style gatherings as opposed to more traditional, formal meetings. They met together on Saturday mornings or after school. The group was later to acknowledge that intensive support was required for everyone to contribute and also that issues of time and commitment proved to be very important. They identified three key factors that helped the group work:

- *Shared values* – in terms of commitment both to the project and to the idea of participatory research. Time was taken to build relationships within the group.
- *Finding ways for everyone to contribute* – time was taken to develop research skills amongst the group and to value the skills and knowledge brought by everyone there. A 'young person's facilitator' helped move this process along.
- *Valuing members' contributions* – it was important that all group members' contributions were heard and valued equally.

The research project discovered many things that could be of use in the development of practice and the lessons learned from such projects often tend to be very direct and practical. It is interesting to note that projects such as these aren't truly user led until the users – in this case young people – are in control: accessing the research budgets or directing what it is they wish to research. That said, the collaborative ideas and flexibility shown in this project provided a model template for such an activity, whilst also reminding us that such an involvement is costly in terms of time and resources. These are not easy options but, arguably, are likely to provide greater accuracy in findings:

> The children and young people talked a lot about the kind of things that had helped them. A lot of young people thought that staying in touch with their friends had helped. Unfortunately, many of the children and young people were unable to keep in touch with their friends. Those who managed to stay in touch felt as though their friendships were still affected. The majority of the children and young people thought it was helpful to have someone to talk to about their problems. (Morrison et al., 2008: 15)

Activity

Involving children and young people in studies is a difficult ethical area for research. Reflect on the particular challenges you would meet and how you might address them in the following:

- A focus group of young male offenders looking at car crime.
- Several one-to-one interviews with mixed gender young people on the subject of teenage pregnancy.
- Engaging with a large group of young people who all attend the same youth club in order to try and construct a research project that would be led by them.

We are not stupid (Taylor et al. 2008)

Like many of the service user-led research reports that one reads, *We are Not Stupid* begins with a familiar sense of disillusion with the traditional forms of research and professional support that have apparently overlooked this particular group of people with learning disabilities:

> Jennifer has explained why we are doing this research: ... People like psychiatrists and doctors and teachers and stuff are writing stuff about us saying that we are stupid and can't do stuff, but we are not stupid. We've got our own minds. We know what's good for us and we know what we want in our lives, not them telling us what we want in our lives. They're the ones who are wrong. (Taylor et al., 2008: 28)

The project was led by People First Lambeth, with support from the Shaping our Lives Network, Brunel University and Trust for London, and its first thought was to start from the perspective of the service users leading the project. Fundamental questions asked at the outset of any research project will shape its future in often unalterable ways. It is interesting to see how this project reported on the issues that it wanted to investigate, especially if we reflect on a list that might not look like the kinds we see within 'traditional' research reports. The researchers wanted to write about the things they cared about most and what was happening in the lives of people with learning difficulties, which included:

- People going to day centres and not getting properly paid jobs.
- People being nasty to people with learning difficulties and making us feel stupid.
- People with learning difficulties being controlled or bossed around by people without learning difficulties.
- The names people with learning difficulties get called.
- People with learning difficulties trying to get what they/we want but not always getting somewhere. For example people wanting to move and Social Services saying they will do something for months on end without any changes happening. (Taylor et al., 2008: 19)

One of interesting issues this raises is that of language: presenting text in this straightforward, everyday, language seems at odds with the formal academic styles in which research is usually presented. Equally, we might, as social workers, compare our tendency to write in a professionally centred language that might not always be as accessible to the range of people who use services as it ought to be. The report goes on to consider the various issues which it set out to examine. Its directness and candour are revealing and create a significant emotional impact on the reader by allowing them to connect with the authors' experiences, stories and lives. For example, one of the researchers, Roseanne,[1] speaks of how she interviewed Mihesh who told her about his work at a day centre for which he used to be paid £2.75, but that now he receives nothing (Taylor et al., 2008: 84). Elsewhere, the report talks about Marlene's experiences during the period of the research she was raped by a resident but chose to share this experience for the report. This is part of what she said:

It didn't go to court because there wasn't enough evidence. He didn't get away with it anyway because I reported him. The court people said I would make a good witness. I'm helping out all the other women who have been raped. I'm telling everybody to look out for yourselves, so that it doesn't happen to the other women besides myself. On the 17th February 2003 I spoke to the inspectors [of Heath Road].[2] We had an inspection and I told them that the doors in the bedrooms can't lock so could we have the lock changed and he said yes. [Before then] I asked the Deputy Manager if we could have, if I could have another lock on my door and he said 'no' because of safety reasons in case there is a fire and you couldn't get out. It's wrong not having a lock inside the bedroom because people can just walk in and it's your room. Staff say 'you are not to go in other people's rooms' but Patricia goes in and I say 'get out'. We need a lock so that people can't just barge in when they feel like it.

Six months after Marlene was raped at Heath Road she said she heard one member of staff tell another staff member what was in the minutes of the staff meeting. This included information about the rape. The staff were talking in the lounge in front of other residents. Marlene said: They were looking back in the staff meeting. Marlene was very upset by this because as she put it: I thought it was confidential. I thought it was not supposed to be said about what happened to me upstairs. I didn't want all the staff to know about it not everybody. Now they all know, even the agency staff and even the handyman and that's not fair. (Taylor et al., 2008: 49)

---

[1] All names were changed in the report.
[2] All place names were changed in the report.

This is without doubt a very powerful and concerning statement that anyone coming across will remember for a long time. Furthermore we hope – indeed believe – that this is the sort of research that will affect change and improve lives and that can only be a good thing. It is not our argument that such personal testimony is some form of requirement and that service user-led research provokes some kind of need to bear witness to the hardships and injustices of people's lives. Rather, we would argue that service user-led research leaves the fundamental choices of what is to be researched and what experiences are to be shared up to the people who are living those lives. We, as readers, social workers, academic researchers, must acknowledge the strength of such evidence and work together to affect the change that this research points us towards – to improve people's lives.

Activity

So little research is conducted from service users' or, indeed, social workers' perspectives that the practitioner researcher should reflect on what they think would happen if they asked a group of a) service users, b) carers, and c) workers linked to their particular area of practice what they would like to research because they cared about it most.

- Sketch out the three lists.
- How far do the three lists overlap?
- Reflect on how the different groups' actual responses might differ.
- Ask at least five colleagues what they would like to research.
- Compare their answers with each other and your original list.

What have you learned from this activity?

Walk this way! (FOCUS and the University of Chester, 2008)

FOCUS (Forum of Carers and Users of Services) worked with staff at the University of Chester in a service user-led research project into post-qualifying (PQ) training for mental health workers. The project was funded by Skills for Care and the university. The first phase of the research involved training a small group of service users and carers in research methods. From this base point the group made choices about how they would evaluate the PQ training provided locally, paying particular attention to the involvement of service users and carers. The group gathered data on module evaluations and constructed an interview schedule arranged into key thematic areas. The group then interviewed the social workers on the programme. They analysed the data they had gathered and led the construction of the final research report. The group was assisted throughout this process by a research assistant and also staff at the university. In general, the findings were extremely positive regarding the beneficial impacts on practice coming from the service user and carer inputs. It might be helpful to dwell a little here on the issue of training in research methods. If we are serious about service user-led research then those involved in it need to be empowered to be fully involved and must receive training to ensure that their research is rigorous, conducted appropriately, of merit, and valid in its own right.

FOCUS selected a group of several researchers who had had a variety of experiences as users and carers (some linked to mental health) which was soon reduced down to a core group of four people who led the project until the end. The group undertook some bespoke training on the various aspects of the research process. These included sessions on literature searching, making effective notes, gathering information and report writing and general research methods. Whilst these sessions were designed to be comprehensive, they had varying levels of success with the group. As the background and experience of those service users and carers involved in the research differed, problems were apparent with a 'one-approach-fits-all' style of training. The key learning appears to be around the need to teach in line with notions of adult learning, in addition to high levels of personal engagement with the learning and the project – promoting a 'learning by doing' approach rather than a more didactic method. Valuing previous experiences and transferable skills that the service users and carers possessed appeared to lead to an increase in confidence and an enthused willingness to take part in all aspects of the project. Approaching the training was initially problematic due to the mystique surrounding the research process. The more successful sessions capitalised on the service users' and carers' previous experiences of transferable elements of research, such as calculating household bills (data analysis) and paraphrasing stories from the newspaper (a form of note-making). Whilst it was not a primary aim of the project, many people involved in the team changed their perception of research. The service users and carers began to think of research as something approachable and at which they could succeed. The training was later condensed into a publication entitled 'Service Users' Guide to Research' (FOCUS & University of Chester, 2008).

GOOD PRACTICE

This chapter has tried to afford an overview of service involvement in research by looking at the continuum of research done 'to' service users right through to concrete examples of research done 'by' service users. To conclude, we shall now pull together some good practice guidelines for service user involvement in research. FOCUS made some useful general observations generated from their experience as a group of service users and carers leading a research project and these are reproduced here:

- Tailor the project to account for the individual needs so that the researchers can stay committed. This may require flexibility from the group.
- Control the group size – make sure there are enough members to give ideas but not so many nothing can be agreed upon.
- Always consider the role of the Carer in the research.
- Ensure that the ownership of the project is clear from the start and that everyone knows what is expected of them and others.
- Expect problems and be prepared to deal with them.
- Be aware that the Service Users and Carers involved may be dealing with their own problems alongside the research.

- Involve Service Users and Carers from the beginning of the project.
- Realise that everything may take longer than you expect and, as such, may also cost more than you expect – keep a close eye on your budget!!
- Make sure everyone feels comfortable in the setting – give an induction to give information about facilities (e.g. drinks/photocopying/toilets).
- And CONGRATULATE yourself! Research is a challenging, but very rewarding experience!
  (FOCUS & University of Chester, 2008)

Drawing on Turner and Beresford's excellent (2005) review of the literature combined with discussions with service users and the INVOLVE project which considered what it called 'effective deliberative public engagement' (INVOLVE, 2008), these principles afford a useful summary of the factors practitioners must take account of when engaged in service user-led research as well as other levels of collaborative working. They suggest the following:

- Clarity and transparency in the aims, objectives and processes of the research, which are explained carefully and clearly to all participants in the research.
- Confidentiality – this must be assured for all.
- Information – when information is given by service users it should be experienced positively and this may involve a two-way sharing of information with the researcher.
- Equal access – in terms of communication, physical and cultural access to enable the positive involvement of everyone. Researchers' projects must pay attention to ensuring the right numbers of the right kind of people are engaged with the project.
- Payment – this should be made to all those involved and it should be done promptly.
- Feedback – this should be assured for all participants at all stages and a priority should be placed on their discussions.
- Democracy and integrity – in the way the project is constituted and operated.
- Change – improving the lives of service users is a key component. Make research make a difference. Projects should be reviewed and evaluated to ensure they improve practice.

CONCLUSION

In adhering to what evidence suggests is good practice, we must be vigilant that users' involvement in research meets the values of the professional, moral and ethical demands placed upon it. There are no ready-made answers to exactly 'how' this might work best: 'there is as yet no consensus about the role service users can play in knowledge formation (Beresford, 2007b: 330). Underpinning this chapter has been the tension of uncertainty as to how best the social work practitioner should develop a relationship with service users in the construction, pursuance and execution of research. Some would argue that we simply need to adopt a variety of roles in any given situation:

> The role here, however, is to be an ally, an advisor, an enabler and maybe a partner to users undertaking research. (Evans & Jones, 2004: 9)

Surely this remains good advice? Social workers can also be deeply attuned to the issue of the colonisation of user-controlled research by non-users, whether they be academic or, indeed, practitioners. For the time being it may well be that practitioner researchers can work with both academic researchers and service users in a three-way relationship that focuses on building the capacity for research in this emerging area. Most importantly such an alliance can perhaps provide the impetus to make sure that the research focus emanates from the wishes and interests of service users and is focused on achieving change and social justice.

Key points

- Be aware of the different levels of involvement that service users can have with research.
- Involve service users from the very beginning to the very end.
- Think of how best to facilitate service user involvement at all stages.
- Maintain the emphasis on change, even if this is in small steps.
- Think creatively about involving groups that are marginalised.
- You may need to 'let go' of your research project to enhance other people's control.

Further Reading

Beresford, P. (2007) 'The role of service user research in generating knowledge-based health and social care: from conflict to contribution', *Evidence and Policy*, 3(3): 329–341.

Holland, S. (2009) 'Listening to children in care: a review of methodological and theoretical approaches to understanding looked after children's perspectives', *Children and Society*, 23(3): 226–235.

Marsh, P. (2007) *Developing an Enquiring Social Work Practice: Practitioners, Researchers and Users as Scientific Partners*. Houten: Bohn Stafleu van Loghum.

Preston-Shoot, M. (2007) 'Whose lives and whose learning? Whose narratives and whose writing? Taking the next research and literature steps with experts by experience', *Evidence and Policy*, 3(3): 343–359.

Taylor, J. et al. (2008) *We Are Not Stupid*. London: People First Lambeth and Shaping Our Lives. Available at: http://www.shapingourlives.org.uk/documents/wansweb.pdf

Turner, M. & Beresford, P. (2005) *User Controlled Research: Its Meaning and Potential*. Brunel University: Shaping Our Lives.

INTERVIEWS AND QUESTIONNAIRES

OVERVIEW

There is no task more fundamental to social work than asking questions, no more universal process for social workers than interviewing. For those looking to construct an argument that social workers, by transferring their very professional skills, would make excellent researchers, they may well begin with a discussion about interviews. Indeed, Kadushin and Kadushin argue that 'interviewing skills are the central skills on which all components of the social work process depend' (1997: 3). As Allen and Langford (2008) proceed to contend, because social work deals with the social needs of individuals, an ability to understand those needs and respond to them is vital and that can only be done 'by talking'. Of course, social workers have very different kinds of conversations with a wide range of people – some more serious and structured than others. Social workers asking questions of a colleague, service user or carer might do so in a relatively loose and unstructured way (as in an interview), or at the other end of a continuum may follow pre-prepared questions often in the shape of a form (as in a questionnaire). As researchers, social workers might, in the same sense, construct questionnaires that they will administer or ask others to complete. That said, we need to be clear that there are very different power dynamics between the roles of social worker and researcher. When interviewing service users as social workers we carry the power located in the professional role, such as gatekeeper to resources. This will, inevitably, affect the interview. Likewise, as researchers we will have different, perhaps less pronounced, power differentials between the role of respondent and researcher. In both scenarios, we need to be very conscious of the impact of these differences. The advantage for the practitioner researcher is that they possess high quality transferable skills in such situations.

National Occupational Standards for Social Work

There are numerous examples showing where research skills around interviewing link into the Occupational Standards. Element 2.2 talks of working with others to gather, analyse and understand information. Element 2.3 considers how we work with others to clarify and express strengths and expectations. Element 3.1 is about the assessment and review of the preferred options of individuals, families, carers and communities. More generally, Element 6.4 looks at reviewing the effectiveness of plans with those involved.

This chapter will look at both interviews and questionnaires – seeing them, as Robson (2002) and Bryman (2008) do, as points along the same continuum. The parallels with social work skills are clear as interviews and questionnaires are probably the most used methods of qualitative research and draw on probably the most used social work skills. We would stress that researchers need to understand that there are fundamental differences to the interviewing of, say, service users for professional purposes rather than for research purposes. It would be fundamentally dishonest and perhaps an abuse of power to confuse the two. Social workers can be researchers but it is usually best to keep the roles separate for those who know about you in a professional capacity.

When used in the research context, we can think of interviewing as a form of exchange through dialogue which can involve speaking, either one to one with an individual respondent or with a group (the latter being covered in the chapter on focus groups). Interviews can often posses a style that is informal, face to face, and present as more of a discussion than, for example, a questionnaire. Here lies the fundamental reason that interviews are such a popular method of social research – they have an unrivalled capacity for allowing opportunities for the researched respondents' voices to be heard. They are a flexible, adaptable approach that can accommodate the unexpected and respond to the different directions that human conversation can take. What comes with these aspects are problems of validity and reliability as consistency between interviews is difficult to maintain.

Depending on one's ontological perspective (how we see our ability as social scientists to get at the 'facts'), there is a sense within research interviews that the dialogue we engage in is not necessarily a pure reporting of fact as both parties can create and share meanings and understandings in an interactive and dynamic way. People may lie, people may choose to present themselves in particular ways. Because of this we might better appraise interviewing as the construction or reconstruction of knowledge rather than the excavation of it (Mason, 2002). We should therefore approach interviews and questionnaires with a certain reflexive attitude, being careful to consider the limits of their validity. We must always strive for rigour in our approach. Some would argue that questionnaires, because their questions tend to be less complicated and shorter, are more impervious to challenges to validity. Although perhaps this seems a little unfair – a respondent can choose to say or write what they wish in either circumstance. But in engaging with an interview or questionnaire we are aware both as researchers and respondents that there is a rationale, an objective, a reason for so doing. This is not an aimless, chaotic, chance encounter. There is a sense of purpose to this activity – it is headed in a particular direction and has its own research purpose – to which researchers and respondents are usually committed. In this final sense, it is useful to note Robson's observation that, the (research) interview is, 'a kind of conversation; a conversation with a purpose' (1993: 228). This directly links to Kadushin and Kadushin's description of a social work interview as, 'a conversation with a deliberate purpose that the participants accept' (1997: 4). Therefore social work skills in the purposeful interpretation of communication, assessment of information and judgement are readily transferable to the process of interviewing for research purposes.

QUESTIONNAIRES

At their simplest questionnaires are a series of written questions requiring a written response (Hek & Moule, 2006). They are often delivered in the research process as something to be 'self completed', although this needn't be the case – researchers can complete them under the direction of a respondent. Another common component of delivery is that they will arrive by post or through e-mail. As Bryman (2008) notes, the main difference between an interview and a questionnaire is usually that the interviewer is not present with the latter. The implication must be that there is a greater burden of clarity with the questionnaire which must be easy to follow and asking questions that are straightforward to answer. Postal questionnaires are useful in that they can be targeted at particular addresses or workplaces for which you have the details. Of course, they are also reliant on people not treating them as 'junk-mail' and often postal questionnaires suffer from especially low response rates as a result. Having said that, the postal approach gives people time to think and arguably they might be more honest if completing it on their own.

Conversely, you have no guarantee that the person filling in the questionnaire is the one you sent it to! In a similar way, questionnaires sent by e-mail whilst usually arriving at their target can often be treated as 'spam', but obviously these save on postage and seem to benefit from higher response rates. Practitioner researchers should be aware that response rates vary enormously and can be as low as 20 to 30 per cent, which can have a severe impact on the actual numbers of replies which you can use for analysis. Online surveys are something to consider in this area. A typical example is www.surveymonkey.com – a free online survey creation tool that can be used for simple tasks in this area of data collection. It must be noted that online surveys, as with other questionnaire approaches, can not only struggle with response rates but also with self selection. People who respond to certain surveys may do so simply because they have something particular to say and have selected themselves as respondents to convey their message. Thus if we are using an online survey method to ask social workers in a certain office what they think about their working conditions, the danger is that those who have a particular concern about an issue (such as a lack of facilities) may be the only ones who respond. However, their views wouldn't necessarily be representative of the whole group.

We need to understand this issue when choosing to deploy these kinds of methods: they each have their opportunities and advantages but are rarely sufficient in and of themselves to gain an accurate picture of an issue. We suggest using the concept of triangulation which means employing more than two different methods (e.g. survey, interview and focus group) and triangulating the results from each. If all three are saying the same thing, then this affords a good measure of validity. Conversely, if two say one thing and your online survey says another, then it might be that self selection has played a role and you will need to evaluate what to do next. It is also worth noting that a form of triangulation can take place with existing secondary data. In this scenario we may have done some interviews and a focus group and our findings are correlating to what existing, pre-published research has found.

Activity

Using surveymonkey.com create a basic online survey, asking different types of questions for a particular audience. How might you use this survey with other methods to increase its validity?

ASKING QUESTIONS

Whilst we have already argued that social work skills are directly transferable to research interviewing, it is important to reflect on the particular qualities that inhabit the terrain of social work research. Social research, in its broadest sense, deals with the general public. Whilst it is certainly also true that those who are researched tend to be less powerful than those doing the researching, this is especially the case with social work. It is a particular facet of the professional role that we deal with relationships which are often with the vulnerable or with those who in any number of ways might be different to ourselves – by age, race, class, culture and so forth. These are difficult and challenging areas of interviewing for research purposes. Here we can reflect on the role of social workers and the complex ethical issues that are generated by, for example, interviewing those with learning disabilities, those who are under the age of 18, those who have dementia and those whose first language might not be English. These kinds of challenges must all be addressed in preparation for the complex areas of research in which social workers might engage, simply because they reflect the working role and moral impetus of social care practitioner researchers. (We explore some of these issues in the chapter on Ethics.)

Robson (2002) notes that, at heart, we are trying to find out what people know, what they do, and what they think or feel. He helpfully reduces this down to the questions we ask in interviews being concerned with facts (insofar as we can attribute them such an objective presumption), with behaviour, and with beliefs or attitudes. That said, we might well cover all these areas within the space of a few questions but it helps to begin conceptualising our questions in advance of the interview in the form of an *interview schedule*, which is basically a list of the questions that we are going to ask with directions about the conduct and process of the interview.

Case study

A particularly interesting example for social work of an interview schedule comes from the Shaping Our Lives service user-led collective. In their research report entitled *We are Not Stupid*, service users with learning difficulties described their research process and their findings on the experiences of people with learning difficulties:

(Continued)

(Continued)

We found out a lot from talking to each other and other people with learning difficulties in People First. We also talked with different people with learning difficulties who are not People First members and interviewed them. At the interviews we decided to ask people these questions:

- What do you like in your life?
- What don't you like in your life?
- What do you do in the daytime?
- What do you do at night?
- What do you do at the weekend?
- How do staff treat you?
- Does anyone boss you around or stop you from doing anything?
- If you are being bullied can you say what happens?
- Are you allowed to have a boyfriend or girlfriend? Can you tell us about this?
- How do you want your life to change? What do you want in the future?

We wanted to find out about their experiences and how they live, what their life is like now. It took us two days to talk through the questions with people.

(Taylor, J. et al. (2008) *We Are Not Stupid*. London: People First Lambeth and Shaping Our Lives. Available at: http://www.shapingourlives.org.uk/documents/wansweb.pdf)

Questions need to be written in a way that meets the needs of the research whilst also meeting the needs of respondents. The level of structure an interviewer brings to the process is another major source of delineation. If, for example, we think of a structured interview, we envisage a rather more formal process characterised by a close adherence to a structured interview schedule. Semi-structured interviews, whilst not without a level of organisation and purpose, allow for a 'free-er' flow of exchange. Within the relatively rarely used format of unstructured interviews, respondents basically lead the way and talk about whatever they want. This can sometimes be an aspect of life story work, but for obvious reasons it sits uneasily with given tasks and deadlines.

Case study

Virkki (2008) reports a interesting study on Finnish social workers' and nurses' attitudes regarding client perpetrated violence. As with the overwhelming majority of journal articles, we do not get to see the interview schedule. However, the author goes into considerable detail on the process of interviewing 20 social workers and 15 nurses who were each given thematic, one to two hour interviews on violence originating from both clients and the professional community. All interviews were transcribed. Virkki notes:

The interviewed social workers are employed in city or municipal social welfare agencies in central Finland, working in various branches of the social sector. Their ages range from 25 to 60 years and all but three of them are women. The interviewed nurses work either in various departments of the central hospitals or at municipal health centre wards in central Finland. The interviewed nurses, all of them women, were aged 24 to 61 during the time of the interviews. I sought for interviewees through various methods; by personally emailing nurses and social workers, by sending information about my research on selected intranet mailing lists and workplace newsletters, as well as by sending handouts of the study to be delivered at workplaces. I aimed at acquiring voluntary informants rather than ones handpicked by their superiors. (2008: 250)

Through these interviews and some written accounts the author found evidence that suggested social workers and nurses consistently underestimated the risk of the violence they were exposed to – despite being the most affected professional group in Finland. It is argued that this is because these particular professions place undue emphasis on trust in client relationships and this can obscure the risks of violence to which they are exposed.

(Virkki, T. (2008) 'Habitual trust in encountering violence at work: attitudes towards client violence among Finnish social workers and nurses', *Journal of Social Work*, 8(3): 247–267.)

Broadly speaking, questions can be closed, open or scale. Closed questions, as their name implies, have a narrow focus, resulting in limited options for response. The typical 'closed' question is one that requires a simple yes or no answer. Other closed questions might offer a limited range of responses; typically these might refer to basic demographic data (age, gender, race and so forth) or simply options to choose from. A variation on this theme is the 'scale' question, which might ask you to rate something out of ten, or a variant such as the Likert (1932) scale, which we are all familiar with, which will often ask whether we strongly agree, agree, neither agree nor disagree, disagree or strongly disagree. Of course there are many permutations of these scales and we shall consider some of them as they apply to the social work research setting shortly. This leaves the final type: the open question. As its name suggests this question opens the door to a wide variety of responses, depending on respondents' particular views, experiences and so forth. A very open example might be, 'Tell me about your life' or 'How would you describe your personality?' Rather less open questions (but still not closed) might include, 'What is your opinion of this service?', 'How might you respond to this situation?' Whether writing questions for interviews or for questionnaires, what is vital is that they work towards the research ends in a proper way by being clear and straightforward. Robson (2002) summarises the typical things to watch out for when constructing questions:

- *Offering cues* – for example, 'Are you against sin?'. The cues are both in the concept of sin (which arguably predefines a particular world view) and in the manner of the question. These lead the respondent down a particular path which may not coincide with their actual views.
- *Long questions* – respondents will lose track of a question the longer it becomes. A general rule of thumb is to split a long question into two (or more) separate ones.

- *Double-barrelled questions* – this is where we ask two or more questions within one e.g. 'How do you feel about racism compared to five years ago?' This is asking the respondent to think about a) how they felt about racism five years ago; b) how they feel about racism now; and c) what are the differences between the two. All this makes it a very difficult question to answer.
- *Jargon* – social workers, as with many professionals, will use the shorthand of jargon so frequently that it can become too easily forgotten how those outside the profession might not understand its meaning.
- *Leading questions* – for example, 'How much do you like this social service department?' is a question that leads the respondent down a path of admitting how much they like something rather than whether or not they like it to begin with.

These are all helpful points when constructing a list of questions. Basically, these comments simply bring out what a period of reflection would reveal and it is important as a practitioner researcher to save some time in the process to think through how you would go about creating the right ambience for the interview process. The nature of the questions you ask must meet this agenda as well as that which concerns the quality of the communication. It is always a good idea to 'pilot' (or test out) your questions before using them directly for research, maybe with friends, colleagues or someone with the same characteristics as the group you intend to interview – do they think your questions are clear and straightforward?

Activity

What changes might you make to the following questionnaire?

This questionnaire is part of my research study about poor people and access to private child care. Please tick all relevant boxes, unless otherwise stated. Your responses are anonymous.

1 *Which one of these do you receive?*

☐ Income support ☐ Housing benefit ☐ Mobility allowance
☐ Child benefit ☐ Disability allowance

2 *How old are you?*
3 *Do you agree or disagree with the following:*

I find it easy to access childminders
I am entirely satisfied in accessing childminders
I have used childminders many times
I have never complained
I prefer to get my family to provide child care
The requirements for becoming an registered childminder should be changed

4 *Have you ever felt discriminated against*   No   Yes

Thank you for your time and co-operation. Please return the completed survey to me as soon as you can.

(Stapleton et al., 2008)

Practitioner researchers should avoid ambiguous questions and remember that those which require respondent recall might get answered less accurately. Similarly, hypothetical questions ('If you were to deal with this situation, what might you do?') are hard to answer, especially when they reach the hinterlands of a respondent's experience. Obviously, one should avoid offensive questions or those that aim squarely at personal problems. For example, an attempt to find out whether or to what extent someone is selfish is highly likely to falter if the question asked is, 'How selfish are you?' or 'How selfish would you rate your self on a scale of one to ten?' These types of issues, including attitudes like racism, homophobia, ageism, sexism and the like, are very difficult to reach directly through interviews – far better to avoid these areas if you are a beginning researcher or, perhaps, use scenario-type material to allow an opportunity for them to emerge. Simply put, very few of us are likely to seek to portray ourselves in a poor light.

Activity

- You are doing research on the drinking habits of students. Write down one or more questions that aim to find out how much alcohol they are consuming.
- You are doing some research on criminal behaviour in young people. Write down one or more questions that aim to find out if a respondent has done anything criminal for which they have never been caught.
- What are the issues you have thought through in constructing these questions?
- What are the issues that you believe might affect the veracity of responses?

One of the basic truths of interviews is that they are a relatively easy way of finding things out. They are certainly less problematic than observation and watching behaviour. When we are interviewing in a face-to-face environment it can also be easier to follow up interesting things that your respondent says, whilst also allowing the researcher an opportunity to observe body language in a way that might both illuminate particular responses and allow us to see whether the respondent is comfortable in the process. However, interviews are clearly time consuming: compare, for example, the time involved in interviewing (and arranging to interview) four social workers with sending out four questionnaires. Interviews also require a considerable amount of preparation if one is going to achieve a level of co-operation that suits the research process. Of course, by their very nature interviews bring with them problems of reliability and bias. The idea that just by asking open questions we can put power back with the respondent who is free to answer as they choose is not only misleading but also perhaps dangerous. The more structured the interview, the more likely it is that it will create or replicate hierarchical relationships (Silverman, 2006). However, as Silverman continues, the idea that data are problematic just because they include misinterpretation problems between the interview and interviewee is possibly false. Might this simply be a normal facet of human interaction that gets reproduced within an interview setting and should, therefore, be studied in its own right?

CONSTRUCTING QUESTIONS

When we begin to ask questions of respondents we are entering a complicated and dynamic relationship. Situations can be open to manipulation on both sides and it behoves the practitioner researcher to approach the interview with a critical awareness of ethical issues relevant to the situation. One could argue that the social work researcher should have a level of reflexivity that allows for a fundamental critique of structural concepts, as well as an understanding of 'who' they are and 'why' they are doing this research. Writers in the feminist research tradition stress the importance of an awareness of one's own position and the need to acknowledge that we – as practitioner researchers – will impose ourselves at all stages of the research (Dana, 1999).

Basic questions

Let's start to look at how we might construct some basic questions and begin to think about some of the issues involved. How do we ask about age, race, gender and class?

- *Age* – Typically this gets asked about in a closed fashion, usually by a range statement (such as ☐ 18–25 ☐ 26–35 and so on). People may have mixed feelings about revealing their age and, in essence, the 'age' question should only be asked if you intend to use the data for a solid purpose: do you really need to know the age of these respondents? People may be more inclined to give a range rather than a specific response. Of course, the ranges selected need to be thought through. With younger people, for example, a five year range isn't helpful: people at 10, 15 and 20 are very different. Alternatively, a date of birth can be asked for where it is felt to be appropriate – this is a common method in larger demographic studies such as the 2001 Census.
- *Race* – Again, this is a question to ask only if you have a clear rationale for gathering this type of data. There are two basic ways to go about this: self definition and some form of closed categorisation. Whilst self declaration can appear attractive initially, one needs to bear in mind that to make sense of the self categorisation one still requires categories. Furthermore, as with many of these types of issues, they are open to people's own perceptions of themselves and even their whims. Thus, for example, one may choose to define oneself racially as 'Welsh'. The use of an 'other' category can also be a way for some to side-step the issue. Subversion is an interesting facet of interviews and questionnaires particularly, a recent example of this being the 2001 Census campaign to have 'Jedi Knight' listed as an 'official' religion in the UK.[1]
- *Gender* – This is superficially perhaps a less complex area for the interviewer as the traditional 'male or female' approach is still prevalent. The 2001 Census asked simply whether your 'sex' was male or female. However, gender identity is a complex area and, depending on your research, consideration might need to be given to those who might choose to define themselves as transsexual, transgendered, male to female, female to male, or unsure.
- *Class* – A concept that appears less frequently than it once did, but is still interesting nevertheless as an issue which the researcher can struggle to define. Typically this will be asked about through income and occupation. The most common expression of these

[1]Following an internet campaign in advance of the 2001 UK Census, 390,000 people declared their religion as 'Jedi Knight' (http://news.bbc.co.uk/1/hi/uk/2757067.stm).

classifications is the National Statistics Socio-Economic Classifications or NS-SEC (formerly known as the Registrar General's social scale) which runs down various occupational categories from 1 at the top to 8 at the bottom (the long-term unemployed). Thus, category 1.1 includes Higher Managerial and Professional occupations through to 1.2 Higher Professions (including doctors, lawyers, teachers and social workers) who are apparently a step above 2. Lower Managerial and Professional (nurses, midwives, prison officers) and so on (see http://www.statistics.gov.uk/methods_quality/ns_sec/).

What all these difficult aspects of interviewing have in common is the fact they are at once structural issues for society and also completely personal aspects of our own individual world, perceptions, judgements, prejudices and, most fundamentally, our identity. These types of questions, often swiftly driven past as 'basic socio-demographic data', actually encapsulate society's shorthand for defining us – and whilst as individuals we might agree or disagree with the notion, we are all aware of its truth. How we choose to present ourselves in interviews or when answering a questionnaire is beyond researchers' control, whether today we wish to declare ourselves as Jedi Knights or exercise a choice not to share our transgendered status.

What perhaps exacerbates this problem of self presentation is the fact that we are, as practitioner researchers, most likely engaged in 'volatile' and 'fleeting' relationships with those we are researching. Researchers could be characterised as sweeping into peoples lives to investigate something that interests them rather than those they research and, of course, this project is far more likely to be in the researcher's interests than those of the researched. What is in it for respondents after all? They may simply choose to construct fabrications about themselves for their own amusement, or indeed because they are just not committed to your research endeavour (Denzin, 1970).

STRUCTURING THE INTERVIEW AND QUESTIONNAIRE

Having considered some of the many matters that researchers need to reflect on when constructing questions, we shall now turn to cover some broader overarching topics, namely the general structure of an interview schedule or questionnaire and larger matters of our connection with respondents. When constructing a schedule we need to remember that another facet of our usually transitory relationship with the researched is that we need to ensure the pace and progression of the questions fit with those relationship qualities. It would be imprudent to begin an interview with the more intimate of our questions – we need to build up to these and develop a confidence in the process as we work through a logical sequence that makes sense to the respondent. We would advise, as a general rule of thumb for the beginning practitioner researcher, that it might be best to avoid particularly personal questions. What follows is a fairly standard main structure for an interview schedule:

- *Introduction* – Introduce yourself and be courteous, explain the purpose of the research, the use of confidentiality. Double check the informed consent and (if appropriate) the permission to record that you will have previously established. Most researchers will be using a participant information sheet which covers these items.
- *Warm up* – Use non-threatening questions to settle both interviewer and interviewee. This can start with broad socio-demographic data, but also needs to include the first few full

questions. It might be helpful to think of warm-up questions as relatively 'bland' and impersonal, yet related to the main topics. For example, a question asking for experiences of professional training might afford an easy way into many areas of professional practice.

- *Main body of interview* – Present the main purpose of the research and instil a logical progression to the questions. 'Risky' questions should come later in the sequence. It might be helpful to think of a small number of sections with questions linked by a theme.
- *Cool off* – Use straightforward questions to defuse any tensions as it is important not to end with any provocative questions. The questions in this section must move away from the personal and may, for example, ask 'How do you see this issue developing over the next five years?'
- *Conclusion* – Express your thanks for the respondent's time and involvement. Interviewees need to be clear about how they can contact someone in the future about the research. Make sure there is time for respondents to talk with you, perhaps when the tape has been turned off when it is not uncommon for respondents to say, 'Just one more thing ... '[2]

However, all this only takes us so far. The structure of an interview schedule or questionnaire also needs to include an understanding that certain questions you wish to ask will come in 'clusters': these can be grouped together because they are asking about different aspects of a similar theme. Thus, for example, if we are constructing a questionnaire for service users about day centre provision we might have sections related to staff, resources, food, transport and so forth. These themes need to be thought of before constructing the questionnaire and can be very helpful when breaking down the later analysis and writing up your findings as they can become chapter or section headings.

Activity

You have been asked to prepare some interview schedules for a small piece of research on a local Youth Inclusion Team which wants to gather evidence of the services it provides. There are two key areas that they wish to look at:

- One to one interviews with young people who have used the service. These are generally 'disaffected' youths, mostly male, and often offenders who receive a volunteer support service – mentoring support. The aim is to simply assist in making beneficial changes in the lives of young people.
- The network of agencies that refer to and link up with the YIT team. It is anticipated that this will be done primarily by telephone – feedback from the people who refer to the programme.

Prepare an interview schedule for the task and structure the schedule into (at least) four key areas. Then prepare a number of questions in each area and reflect on the use of language, sequencing, introduction, endings, confidentiality and ethical issues.

---

[2]Researchers need to anticipate issues such as these and how they will choose to deal with the information. A general rule of thumb is to ensure you have agreed beforehand with the respondent any uses for anything they may say after the tape has been turned off.

INTERVIEWING DIFFERENT GROUPS

It is rather surprising that most of the general texts on social research methodologies, such as Robson (2002) and Bryman (2008), dwell almost exclusively on the practicalities of interviewing rather than on the complex issues emanating from the process of interviewing the types of vulnerable and/or disadvantaged groups that social workers deal with as a matter of course. Having said that, some authors such as Kvale would argue that 'ethics becomes as important as methodology on interview research', due to the complex dynamics of power (2006: 497). We would agree that ethical issues are just as important as the structures of the research we create and require an equal, if not greater, amount of attention. (If you haven't already read the chapter on ethics, we suggest you do so before engaging with the following section.)

Children

To begin with, we might consider the role of children in research. In many ways, this is depressingly new territory for researchers because children have so often in the past been overlooked as people in their own right with their own opinions and attitudes. But another reason is also the complex issues of consent that arise when seeking to interview children which was previously covered in our chapter on ethics. Children and young people can (wrongly) be assumed to somehow be less expert in their own lives, less competent or rigorous in their response to questions. There is a highly succinct example here of a researcher asking a 10 year old girl a question in pursuit of information on children's consent to surgery, 'So, you're having your legs made longer?', to which the girl replied 'I suffer from achondroplasia and I am having my femurs lengthened' (Alderson, 2000, cited in Kellet & Ding, 2004: 165).

Whilst taking this message on board, we still need to think about engaging children and young people – being especially sensitive to the impact of age, language and process – as *how* we go about interviewing children is of vital importance. This may involve adapting traditional interview techniques to include word showers ('What words do you link with this … ?'); ranking exercises ('Place these in order of importance to you … '); visual prompts such as pictorial faces and expressions ('Which face represents best what you think about this … ?'); pictorial vignettes 'What do you think is going on in this picture … ?' and sentence completion such as 'I am happiest when … ' (Kellett & Ding, 2004). Backett and Alexander (1991) reported on an interesting study of child health using discussions about drawings done by children prior to interview. Other authors have suggested taking the lead from the child as to what they might find interesting to talk about and also taking the time to learn and use the child's language. In a similar vein, Tammivaara and Enright (1986) suggest data collection is combined with another activity that is already known to the child, such as 'show and tell' or familiar game routines (Darlington & Scott, 2002).

Different cultures

Different types of sensitivities will accrue when researchers begin to think about researching peoples from different cultures to themselves and indeed researching those who have a different first language to that of the practitioner researcher. It is interesting to note that problems in power relationships can be more pronounced when researchers 'join' a community rather than entering as experts (Crigger et al., 2001). There is a growing body of research that suggests participatory methods of research work best in these circumstances. But many of the same ethical considerations will apply, albeit in a more 'intense' format (Marshall & Batten, 2004). Informed consent must be sought and questions should be asked in a safe environment, should be straightforward rather than complex, and should be translated where appropriate and so forth. It is the practitioner researcher's responsibility to ensure they are sufficiently aware of different cultural mores (e.g. around eye contact and disagreement) to allow the process to be experienced in a positive way (Darou et al., 1993). Different issues will accrue with the use of interpreters and there is an interesting body of literature emerging that critically examines this subject. It seems essential to ensure that interpreters are familiar with a research project and also that they work with researchers in the challenges to validity that might occur (Kapborg & Bertero, 2002).

People with learning difficulties

Earlier in the book we drew an example of an interview schedule from *We Are Not Stupid* (Taylor et al., 2008), a research report about people with learning difficulties *by* people with learning difficulties. This is, of course, a valuable example of a rarely seen approach from a group of people who are seldom researched – and who even less appear as researchers (Friar, 1998). Darlington and Scott (2002) provide a useful statement of the requirements of research interviews in this area: that we value the experiences of those who are verbally challenged; that we accept their experiences are valid in and of themselves and 'not inferior or a threat to our own way of being in the world'; and finally, that we find a way for their voices to be heard.

Certain suggestions do tend to be offered such as the use of observation and gaining a familiarity with the care records of respondents to enhance a researcher's understanding of the respondents as individuals while avoiding false assumptions. Of course, this would have to be done with the appropriate consent clearly established. Familiar environments are seen as a boon for interviews and consideration might be given to the involvement of a person known to the respondent to assist with language difficulties. More specifically, research suggests it might be wise to avoid comparison questions and the broader open questions (Biklen & Mosley, 1988; Booth & Booth, 1994a, 1994b). Visual cues, pictures and photographs can also help with information gathering and answering open-ended questions (Darlington & Scott, 2002).

There is a whole range of research on offer to inform these types of interviews and social work researchers need to become familiar with best practice in these areas before beginning.

SAMPLING

As we come to the end of this chapter, it seems appropriate to reflect on what might seem a rather tangential matter to the subject of interviews and questionnaires. A frequently perplexing question for the practitioner researcher is 'Who shall I ask?'. As we have just considered this can be in reference to particular qualities of the respondent, but it can also refer to how many respondents should be interviewed. A significant amount of social work research in the workplace is small scale and, if funded at all, operates on a very low budget. It is unlikely therefore that practitioners engaged in research will be dealing with large samples. Researchers call the selection of participants 'sampling'. The purpose of sampling is usually to try and get a sample that is in some way 'indicative' of the larger population. Broadly speaking, the less indicative your sample is, the less valid your data are likely to be. However, provided researchers are explicit about their approach and don't make inappropriate claims for their data, then small samples can be an effective way of illustrating research. There are a number of different types of sampling.

Random sampling is where you choose people at random, perhaps by drawing names from a hat. This equals the chances of each person being chosen. Rather more complicated is the issue of *stratified sampling* whereby the sample you choose directly reflects a particular aspect of the whole group. This is a very useful concept to understand so let's explain it further. Imagine 100 social workers work for Newtown Social Services and, following general national patterns, 20 of them are male and 80 are female. A stratified sample of 10 per cent would mean that you selected two men and eight women. In this way the sample comes to be representative of the whole group. One might add in *systematic sampling* where the researcher simply selects every nth individual in a population. Other forms of sampling that social workers are likely to come across can include *cluster sampling*, which involves the selection of a particular group or clusters such as the members of a single parent group or the residents of a street; *opportunity sampling*, which involves selection merely by the occasion of, for example, passing the interviewer in the local shopping centre; and *snowball sampling*, which is an interesting process whereby word of mouth is used to connect initial respondents with subsequent ones. A good example here might be researching drug users, where the first person interviewed is able to put the researcher in contact with his friends/acquaintances who also take drugs.

Yet for all these forms of sampling researchers must be very careful about the claims they make for their data, especially about their findings' applicability to the population. It will simply not be possible to interview small numbers of service users or social workers and make generalisations from your data that will allow you to infer certain characteristics on all service users or social workers. Small-scale researchers have to be modest in their claims. (This subject is pursued in a later chapter on data analysis.)

CODING

One more thing to bear in mind when constructing interviews and especially questionnaires is coding. This is the systematic labelling of all text which refers to the same issue in a similar way. For example, if you were analysing attitudes to higher education amongst teenagers in foster care, you might want to know what proportion of teenagers would actually consider going to university. To do this, you might code all the positive statements about entering university '1' and all the negative statements '2'. Then you could count up all of the positive statements and calculate the percentage of your sample likely to go on to further study. Statistical software packages (such as SPSS) require you to construct numerical codes for all data so that you can cross reference, for example, the responses from students in a certain age group, gender or race. We looked above at the possibility of asking respondents to describe their ethnic origin. If they did so, the analysis of the data will, in effect, have to code the responses into certain categories.

This process can also be used to manage the analysis of the general data you gather from interviews or questionnaires. It is a way of breaking down what respondents tell you into more manageable chunks of data using variables that you can (relatively) easily compare and contrast. It is probably easier to see this in Table 5.1 below where the variables are given a code. This example covers a social worker staff evaluation of a cafeteria.

Of course, research projects will use different methods – questionnaires, interviews and focus groups – and then compare the data they find in these various ways with what is available in a national and/or published format. This process of 'triangulation' is an important concept that can assist in strengthening the validity of small-scale samples. The reason we have briefly considered coding here (and will continue to do

Table 5.1   An example of coding

Assigned code	Variable name	Example quote/s
01	Too crowded	'Every time I go in there, there's like nowhere to sit so I just take the food outside.' *Tony, 32* 'It would be better if you could just sit down.' *Julie, 48*
02	Too expensive	'It's like 50p for a pack of crisps! I can get them from the vending machine for 35.' *Mike, 31* 'It's cheaper to go the local newsagent.' *Kath, 22*
03	Poor range	'I'm on a diet and there is just nothing there I can eat.' *Ruth, 27* 'They don't stock my favorite crisps.' *Lawrence, 71*
04	Staff pleasant	'I go in there a lot and the staff are always friendly.' *Geoff, 50*
05	Uncomfortable	'Even the chairs in the staff room are comfier than the ones in there!' *Carl, 31*
06	Good food	'I particularly like the scones.' *Phil, 61*

(Adapted from Stapleton et al., 2008)

in the chapter on data analysis), is simply that we need to have in mind the issue of coding when we are constructing our interviews and questionnaires.

CONCLUSION

Kvale (1996) has contrasted two metaphors – one of the researcher as a miner and one as a traveller – and both are particularly illuminating when reflecting on research interviews. Each relates to different ontological and theoretical perspectives and it is helpful to consider how the social worker might approach the task of asking questions of others. With the miner metaphor, knowledge and data are seen as valuable nuggets of precious metal, waiting to be unearthed by the researcher. This knowledge is extracted (by asking questions), purified (by being transcribed) and then compared in the full light of day to an objective, real world. In contrast the traveller metaphor sees the interviewer as someone 'on a journey that leads to a tale to be told upon returning home' (1996: 4). What the traveller hears is constructed as a story, interpreted by them and described qualitatively, and it may have its own effect on the traveller themselves. Interviews can have that transformative effect.

We have spoken earlier of social work's awareness of the uniqueness of the individual's complex life and the need for diverse sources of knowledge to make sense of this complexity. Ruch (2005) describes this as 'relationship based practice'. Perhaps we can begin to move forward from our metaphors to consider whether, as social workers, we are engaged in relationship based research? We are not simply travellers seeking material for our stories; rather we should see ourselves engaged in asking questions through interviews and questionnaires as partners with those with whom we converse. Perhaps we are less concerned with unearthing nuggets and more concerned with achieving change? Undoubtedly, whichever approach we favour, the skills required to get the most out of these forms of enquiry are possessed in abundance by social workers who are sensitive to issues of phrasing, situation, language, ethics and process. Furthermore, our approach to the process of interviewing and asking questions can only benefit by being informed by and assessed against the values of social work. Underpinning all these ideas and notions is the view that as social workers engaged in research we will have a particular professional, ethical and moral framework that will inevitably help shape our research and 'whether we want to admit to it or not, we cannot completely divorce ourselves from who we are or what we are' (Strauss & Corbin, 1989: 47).

Key points

- Interviews and questionnaires can allow direct access to individual viewpoints.
- Construct questions carefully using the language of respondents.
- Respect the difference that each respondent brings.
- Only ask those questions that need to be asked.
- Pay attention to coding and themes.

Further Reading

Barbara, A., Chaim, G. & Doctor, F. (2007) *Asking the Right Questions 2.* Canada: Centre for Addiction and Mental Health.

Darlington, Y. & Scott, D. (2002) *Qualitative Research in Practice: Stories from the Field.* Maidenhead: Open University Press.

Gillham, B. (2005) *Research Interviewing: The Range of Techniques: A Practical Guide.* Maidenhead: Open University Press.

Kvale, S. (1996) *Interviews: An Introduction to Qualitative Research Interviewing.* London: SAGE.

Silverman, D. (2006) *Interpreting Qualitative Data: Methods for Analysing Talk and Text* (3rd edn). London: SAGE.

6

FOCUS GROUPS

OVERVIEW

Focus groups have been described in a number of ways by people who see them from quite different perspectives, most noticeably contrasted in their uses within market research and social science research. Kitzinger, from the latter approach, describes focus groups as 'a form of group interview that capitalises on communication between research participants in order to generate data' (1995: 299). It is important here to note that a distinction is made between a group interview – which, while broadly the same, is perhaps best differentiated as a concurrent sequence of interviews with individuals in a group – and the focus group – which involves much more emphasis upon the group experience, the interaction between the participants and, as noted, the communication between members of the group. Within the realm of market research one finds an emphasis being placed upon attitudes within the group towards products, services, advertising and the like. Of course, these notions are increasingly finding a place within social work with the development of the service user/carer as consumer. Powell and Single deploy the following definition of focus groups which neatly captures the purposeful assembling of focus groups for research that lifts them out from our more usual concept of a 'group':

> A group of individuals selected and assembled by researchers to discuss and comment on, from personal experience, the topic that is the subject of the research. (Powell & Single, 1996: 499)

Given their simplicity, focus groups are a surprisingly under-used method of social research in relative terms. They seldom get a chapter to themselves in the literature of research methodology, perhaps because of their background in market research, and have only relatively recently made inroads into the broader arena of social research (Bryman, 2008). In many ways focus groups are a particularly appropriate method to consider in social work research, being one of the least directive and most empowering forms of data gathering – and therefore broadly in tune with social work values. Furthermore, the practitioner researcher, as a moderator of a focus group, would need to draw on a range of knowledge, skills and sensitivities that typically one could expect social workers (either qualified, or in the process of qualifying) to possess in abundance. Indeed, it may well be that the poor regard held by focus groups in some areas of research literature is due to the relative inadequacies of moderators who don't posses sufficient skills in this area and find them hard to manage well. We would argue that focus groups ought to form part of more research activity in the social work area for all these reasons. Yet, having said that, the use of focus groups as a research method has expanded considerably in recent years and we are now seeing their use across a broad range of social situations, including education, sociology, health, organisations, evaluation, politics, psychotherapy and, of course, marketing (Stewart et al., 2007).

WHY USE FOCUS GROUPS?

- Focus groups are well suited for obtaining several different perspectives on a topic – they are an organised discussion.
- Focus groups can provide insights into shared understandings of people's lives and also the ways in which individuals are influenced by others in a group situation (Gibbs, 1997).
- Focus groups are good for generating information about collective views and the under-standings and meanings that lie behind what groups think.
- Focus groups can have an empowering effect and are congruent with social work values.

National Occupational Standards for Social Work

There are significant close connections with the NOS and Focus Groups where many of the standards relate specifically to working with groups. Key Role 1, Unit 2 looks at working with groups to gather and analyse information (2.2). Key Role 2, Unit 5 looks at how social workers interact with groups 'to achieve change and development and to improve life opportunities'. Key Role 3, Unit 11 is concerned with decision-making in groups and to enable involvement in decision-making forums (11.3).

For social work, as noted, there are clear connections between social work practice and focus group research – and this method will often sit very naturally within a research process. This chapter will consider the practicalities of setting up and conducting focus groups, but first we need to consider some of the broader historical and theoretical background to focus groups.

BACKGROUND AND APPEARANCE

Focus groups are generally acknowledged to have arisen most distinctly in the late 1930s. Most authors seem to believe that the primary push for the growth of focus groups as a research method was a growing concern over the inadequacy of traditional information-gathering methods. Quantitative methods failed to gain sufficient insight into individuals, whilst interviews failed to gain insight into the views of the group and, to a lesser extent, the community. Furthermore, as Rice (1931) argued, interviews were essentially led by the interviewer and were as likely to reveal the interests of the interviewer as much as the interviewee. Focus groups were rightly seen as a valid alternative whose basic starting point was non-directive.

obert Merton is well documented.
responses to various radio pro-
estigate morale in the US military
ior in the development of focus
al to the creation of our current
in do (Merton & Kendall, 1946;
nany social workers, Carl Rogers
i counselling and psychotherapy.
is groups went out of favour for

handedly kept focus groups going
as evolved to support focus group
0s that we have begun to see aca-
search method, emerging from a
is a argument that the needs of
ing nature of focus groups and in
regaining them from the private sector social ......chers have had to revisit Merton's
original work to ensure that first principles – their non-directive beginnings – were
retained within modern usage in the many fields of social research. However, authors
such as Stewart have also traced a lineage from the roots of clinical and social psychological group dynamics analysis (Stewart et al., 2007). This goes some way to explaining why there are quite noticeably different constructions of what a focus group
actually looks like and how their processes are facilitated (Kreuger & Casey, 2000).

More recently, in the modern era focus groups are being utilised within a wide spectrum of activity, e.g. political focus groups and, most commonly, within the private
sector for product evaluation. Within the business community focus groups are
undoubtedly big business and a big influence on research. Wellner (2003) suggests that
around 80 per cent of the $1.1 billion spent by business on qualitative research goes
on focus groups. Practitioner researchers may feel it appropriate, particularly when
working around notions of service users as consumers of the products that agencies
provide, to learn more about the uses of the focus group around market research.

THE SIZE AND COMPOSITION OF A FOCUS GROUP

One of the most difficult tasks in setting up a focus group is deciding on, and arriving
at, the right number of participants. Different authors vary in their advice on the
'right' number. Market research-types of focus groups tend to recruit something in the
region of 10 to 12 members of a group, but within social research this number can
seem too high. Kreuger and Casey (2000) suggest the ideal size is six to eight, numbers
which capture the possibilities of a group discussion where all the participants have
sufficient opportunity to contribute, but does not get too cumbersome and difficult to
manage. Within the field of social work, an awareness of group dynamics and how
they will vary according to the size of the group needs also to be borne in mind.
However, if six to eight is the general rule of thumb, then the best advice that can be
offered is simply to find an optimum size given the characteristics of the participants
and the topic being discussed (Bloor et al., 2001). There is some evidence to suggest,

perhaps not surprisingly, that smaller groups are better at dealing with sensitive, emotionally complex or challenging areas (see for example Maxwell and Boyle, 1995, who used a small focus group process to look at risky patterns of sexual behaviour). Small friendship groups may also be considered appropriate if researchers wish to capture elements of the bonds between group members. An interesting example of this is in the work of Valerie Hey who looked at girls' friendships within small (focus group) clusters and found that:

> The so-called private, marginal realm of schoolgirl friendships is a significant place where the 'social' is indexed. It is between and amongst girls as friends that identities are variously practised, appropriated, resisted and negotiated. (1997: 30)

Activity

Look at this example and reflect on some of the ethical challenges the project will have faced. Also, think about the use of vignettes in focus groups – how might they fit into the topic of your research?

Scourfield et al. (2007) used a focus group methodology to look at how young people's different views of suicide related to the concept of gender. They found that some of the young people associated 'successful' suicides with masculinity and 'failed' attempts with femininity. These views were not specifically related to the gender of the respondents. In the seven different focus groups the participants were known to each other, having been recruited through a FE college and various pre-existing groups including those delivering mental health services – with five of the seven groups from those predisposed to suicide. A total of 33 young people took part in groups of about six or seven – although one group (young mental health service users) was made up of three people only. The focus group process primarily involved reflections on vignettes provided by the researchers. Here is an example of one of the vignettes:

> Cerys is 18 and lives in a flat by herself. She used to have a job in a shoe shop but has recently been laid off. Her relationship with her mother has been poor for some time and now Cerys says that every time they meet they argue. She thinks her mother has never had a good word to say about her. She has recently split up with a boyfriend. She is very depressed, and has started using heroin, which is easily available on the estate where she lives, to help her cope with these feelings. She regularly thinks about 'ending it all' by killing herself, and has been admitted to hospital several times after overdosing.

Clearly, there are significant ethical issues in approaching such a difficult and delicate area of research which had significant potential for causing distress. The project went through a considered process of ethical approval, key members of staff from particular organisations were on hand after each group and the facilitator stayed behind after sessions for debriefing. All respondents were given various contact addresses and numbers.

It may be that the size of a focus group needs to reflect the level of depth that the practitioner researcher is aiming for. If particular insights into the issue being discussed are sought, then the researcher may well choose to limit the numbers in the group (Kreuger & Casey, 2000). Of course, the smaller the group the more problematic it will be to overcome shortfalls in the group discussion – if there are only three people and the conversation fails to flow then the event is in much greater danger of failing than with a larger group. People can be naturally shy or simply not in the mood to discuss particular issues. Similarly, if a group is set up for four people and two fail to turn up then it becomes debatable whether this is a group at all (Bloor et al., 2001). Conversely, larger groups are harder to moderate and it becomes less likely that all the participants will feel they have had an appropriate level of opportunity to contribute to the discussion. Indeed, it may be that the more vocal members of the group are more likely to dominate in the time span of that group.

Perhaps the first question to consider is where there is an existing group of which the researcher is aware that they might approach or 'piggy back' as some authors have called it (Kreuger & Casey, 2000). This is quite a common dilemma in social work where practitioner researchers and students on placements often have access to existing groups or, indeed, already have a role in supporting them. Furthermore, the very existence of a group may have been a motivator in directing the research initiative in the first place. So what are the issues? Far from being concerned about the impact of pre-existing relationships within a group, Kiztinger (1994) has argued forcefully that you are more likely to get a realistic discussion in groups where participants know each other. It is suggested that such groups are more natural as social experiences. After all, how often do we gather together with a group of strangers to discuss something? Where group members know each other they are arguably more likely to challenge statements from participants they know, perhaps reducing the element of 'self presentation' that can distort data unnecessarily. Furthermore, certain existing groups can operate within areas of personal lives that are more difficult to disclose to purposefully formed groups (for example, a support group for people with HIV status). However, one might equally argue the reverse – that people are more likely to talk about certain things more openly amongst strangers who they believe they will never see again, or indeed, might feel more able to challenge something that is said (Bloor et al., 2001). From an ethical point of view the key principle is to ensure that the participants are clear about being part of a focus group and what that entails. The particular ethical issues associated with engaging in research with people we already know (for example, social workers researching a group they have been involved with) are discussed in the chapter on ethics.

Activity

Look at this example and reflect on the challenges of this approach – what might you have to deal with and how would you deal with it?

Roose and John (2003) used focus group methodology to explore children's views about mental health provision for the 10 to 11 age group. They conducted two focus groups with 10 and 11 year old children (Year 6) and involved a mixed sex group of eight in each. Care was taken over ethical approval and children and parents consented to being involved. Selection criteria included: those with no mental health needs, those willing to take part, and those comfortable with talking in a group. The researchers argued that the participants displayed a sophisticated understanding of mental health:

(Continued)

(Continued)

Ten- and 11-year-old children were vocal, articulate participants who were able to express themselves clearly about mental health. They were aware of the issues that can lead to problems in their age group and were aware of the difficulties of peer group pressure particularly for boys. Their level of understanding demonstrates their ability to usefully contribute to discussions on service development for this age group. (Roose & John, 2003: 548)

This is an interesting example which perhaps challenges the assumptions we might have about appropriate age ranges for an involvement in discussions about the shape of service delivery in even complex areas. The children were very clear in expressing a preference for the service being delivered outside of school rather than within.

SELECTION

What general issues should we bear in mind when getting people together for our focus group? Firstly, focus groups are not selected by systematic random sampling: we are not trying to get a group that attempts to reflect a population from which we can make generalisations to the broader population. Focus groups are best thought of as purposively sampled and brought together because of certain characteristics they share. The main point here is that a focus group will only represent the views of a group (for example, particular young offenders) and not the views of all (young offenders). Beyond this point there are certain balances we might wish to bear in mind. We would hope to capture sufficient diversity to encourage a discussion – if everyone is too similar then we might end up with a discussion that consists largely of 'I agree'. Having said that we also need to be aware that heterogeneity may result in conflict, especially around polarising topics (religion, politics, football, etc.) and this can affect depth, so there may be an argument for separate groups. Some researchers have also looked to create a stratified sample of membership within a group so that the members broadly reflect certain characteristics of a broader group. For example, if one wanted to have a focus group of social workers one could stratify the membership to reflect issues of gender, age and race evident in the national population of social workers.

Suffice to say that selecting the composition of a focus group is a complicated process of decision making which needs to take account of many factors. However, the broad rule of six to eight members feels fairly solid ground for most research projects. The decision of whether to use existing groups rests, obviously, on researchers' access to them, but seems a useful avenue to explore if it becomes available.

Activity

You are a social worker working in a children and families team in an urban area. You are looking to research young mothers' views on teenage pregnancy and the appropriateness of services. What factors would you take into account when deciding whether to do either of the following?

- To approach an existing young mothers group in the local Children's Centre to ask if you could use them as your focus group.
- To gather participants through poster adverts in the local area.

PREPARATION AND CONDUCT

Whilst it may seem an obvious point, and little worthy of consideration, researchers need to think carefully about the best place to run the particular focus group they have in mind. Community settings may benefit those that live locally and do not have ready access to transport. Particular times of day are better for those with responsibilities for children of school age. Professional workers might feel the time benefit of engaging with a focus group in their workplace – but this also exposes them to a greater chance of disruption.

Activity

You are doing three focus groups on teenage pregnancy and will involve the following groups of people:

- people who are/have been pregnant as teenagers;
- parents of that group;
- range of community/youth/social workers who have worked with that group.

Suggest a suitable venue for each group and explain the reasons for your choice.

Pre-group questionnaire

It might be useful to prepare a brief questionnaire that covers basic socio-demographic information on the group participants such as their race, gender, age and so forth. This may be useful for providing a brief overview of the profile of the group when you come to write up your research.

Information sheet

An absolute requirement for any research is an information sheet. Some process of signed consent being involved would normally be thought of as good practice, unless a particular rationale can be brought to bear on that issue. As with all social work research the issue of informed consent is absolutely crucial. This is no different in focus group research and the practitioner researcher must ensure that they have done as much as is reasonably possible to ensure that participants know what they are letting themselves in for – and also what happens after the focus group has taken place. Information sheets are central to this and would normally cover the answers to such questions as who the researcher is; what the research is about; who is funding it; why the respondent has been chosen; exactly what will happen to them; how they can opt out; the benefits and disadvantages of taking part; how confidentiality will be managed; what will happen to the results; and how the respondent might complain if they wished to.

Recording

Whilst it is not vital that a focus group is recorded by video or audio means, it certainly makes the process of data analysis far less taxing. Practitioner researchers should reflect on a number of issues here. Clearly if they are dependent on notes taken (either whilst also facilitating the group or by a separate note taker) then the notes will not be a complete record and, most importantly, will inevitably compromise the actual words spoken by the participants – words which are one of the main reasons for setting up the focus group. Thus, audio recording is probably used most, affording playback on all the sessions and access to the memorable quotes that will almost inevitably be generated.

Two points are worth noting here. First is that it is very difficult to ascribe quotes back to individuals unless the researcher is familiar with all the voices in a group. This is not necessarily a bad thing as by its very nature this process is looking at group views rather than individuals. Second, whether audio or video, the sheer volume of data that a group of six people will generate over, for example, an hour, is considerable and practitioner researchers need to think in advance of their approach to transcription and whether it should be in part or full. That leaves the issue of video. The advantages are that one gets to see who says what and, perhaps more importantly, the group interaction. However, whilst this might appear extremely attractive it is particularly hard to create data from the observation of behavioural as opposed to verbal indicators. In either event participants should always know if they are being recorded in any fashion and this should be clear from the information sheet. The nature of focus groups is that they are unique, 'one off' events – all the more reason to ensure that recording devices have sufficient battery power and don't run out half way through. Be absolutely scrupulous in this aspect of preparation and remember that there is no possibility of you asking a group to 'say it all again'. The moment will be lost forever.

Focusing exercises

Whilst by no means a requirement, many focus groups will begin with a 'focusing exercise' – short group activities that will allow the group to relate to general themes connected to the subject matter to be discussed. In this sense they are similar but different to the 'warm up' exercises which many social workers (and group workers of all kinds) will be familiar with. The key difference is that participants are 'warmed up' to the topic at hand instead of, or in addition to, getting to know each other in the group. There are hundreds of possibilities for focusing exercises and the choice will depend on the group characteristics and the subject matter. Typically, there might be vignettes (small case study-type material) where the group will discuss issues emanating from a vignette. Ranking exercises are another example where one might ask participants to place things in order (for example, ranking a list of offences in order of their seriousness, ranking a list of qualities in order of their importance). Other suggestions might be discussions of a particular image or newspaper cutting, or using post-it notes placed on a wall by the participants that showed, say, key words to describe the qualities something should possess.

Activity

Design two focusing exercises suitable for an exploratory study of why young drivers may break the law. Explain the reasons for your choice.

How long should a focus group last?

Again, this is something of a 'how long is a piece of string' question. The most important point to bear in mind here is how comfortable the participants will be, given their particular qualities, with a given amount of time. In any event it is most advisable to ensure that you have a clear idea of how long the group will last and to have conveyed this to the participants. Ninety minutes is probably the upper limit for a focus group for most purposes. One might broadly suggest 30 minutes as a minimum. The more articulate and willing the group are to discuss the issue at hand the more likely we can assume that a productive discussion will result. Could we reasonably anticipate differences, for example, between a group of 15 year old male offenders and a group of the social workers who support them or would that simply be stereotyping these groups?

THE FOCUS GROUP SCHEDULE

Perhaps the single most important aspect of the whole focus group process is the schedule which we can describe as the planned choreography of the focus group. As a picture can often be worth a thousand words, let's simply show you a typical focus group schedule (see Figure 6.1), with this one being prepared for the purposes of looking at practice teacher/assessor and nurse mentor attitudes towards interprofessional learning and whether these may have an effect on their students.

Timings are provided with a note on resources. There is a brief overview of the project for the facilitator, together with the important reminders around confidentiality and consent. The focusing exercise gets the group working together and thinking about the subject matter of the session. The questions are broad, very open ended, and will hopefully allow everyone to contribute. By and large the notion of 'warm up', 'main body' and 'cool down' is to be employed in exactly the same way as in the construction of an interview schedule: being used to introduce the topic in its broader sense before going into the heart of the session and then allowing it to drift back into

Interprofessional Learning: Focus Group Schedule
Overview/Suggested Timings

1 Introduction to project   *5 mins*
2 Focusing exercise   *10 mins*
3 Main topic sequence   *40 mins*
4 Session conclusion   *5 mins*

Required Resources
Venue, flipchart, pens, tape recorder

1 Introduction to project   5 mins

Information sheet. The research project will explore the experiences of interprofessional learning with students and practice staff. There are a number of national drivers that promote the need for interprofessional learning to become inherent in the training of students. The project will consider existing practice and the experiences of nursing and social work students in order to determine current trends and explore future requirements by focusing on attitudes, feelings, beliefs and reactions. The groups will be looking at interprofessional learning. Confidentiality – all participants can be assured of their confidentiality in this process and comments by participants should not be reported outside of the group. The focus groups will be recorded and later transcribed. Tapes will then be disposed of and the material used for no other purpose than the project. Participants are free to leave at any time. Outline of the session – no more than 1.5 hrs. Process – allowing everyone time to speak, important that people don't talk over others, respect for other opinions, etc. Consent Form. Signature.

2 Focusing experience   10mins

Moving into the focus group topic area: Hand out post it notes
   Each participant to individually write down in five separate post-it notes what LEARNING is (e.g. gaining knowledge, change in behaviour, sitting in a classroom, etc). Leader then asks one student to put up first meaning, and then anyone else who has similar/same to make columns on the wall/flipchart. Facilitate a group discussion about the 'learning' to ensure clarity/shared meaning. Conclusion – either general shared view, no shared view, or somewhere in between.

3 Main topic sequence   40mins

1 What is your experience of interprofessional working and learning? (Participants may be more familiar with the term Multidisciplinary/MDT.)
2 What do you think are the differences/similarities between social work and nursing?
3 How do these differences/similarities impact on interprofessional learning for students?
4 What kind of interprofessional learning activities do you deliver for students? How do you rate them? Give examples.
5 How do you know that a student is able to work in an interprofessional manner?
6 What support do you need/get from internal and external sources?
7 Do you believe that interprofessional learning impacts on a service user's experience?
8 How do you think interprofessional learning could be developed for students?

4 Conclusion of Session   5mins

- Is there anything anyone has not had the chance to say?
- Reminder of confidentiality, disposal of tape, etc.
- Thank you for participating.
- Remain available at the end for any questions.
- Ensure tape has recorded and details of exercise are also recorded.

Figure 6.1   An example of a focus group schedule (Dutton & Worsley, 2008)

less taxing generalities towards the end. Of course, the construction of the questions is as vital for the focus group schedule as it is with an individual interview schedule. Practitioner researchers need to take time to ensure that the questions are clear, unambiguous, make sense to all the participants and are informed by a familiarity with the literature. We need to think ahead and anticipate how certain questions are likely to be dealt with by the group. It is important not to launch participants in at the 'deep end' of topics, especially around sensitive areas, and practitioner researchers need to work towards difficult topics through a careful progression using their schedule questions.

Activity

You are a student and want to research either the leisure habits of students on campus, the views of young people about drugs, or social workers' views on child protection legislation. You have decided to set up a focus group. What would be your first few topics for discussion? What difficulties might you anticipate and what would you do about these?

Social workers will be familiar with the different dynamics that can ensue when one adopts distinctive ways of facilitating a group. Each will have their own merits and outcomes. A balance needs to be found between the role of the facilitator – someone who keeps the group conversing and enables all the participants to contribute – and that of the controller – someone whose primary objective is to get through all the topics in the schedule in the time available. Finding that balance requires a sensitivity to group dynamics, an awareness of timings and an appreciation of the ebb and flow of group discussion: there will undoubtedly be some areas of discussion that spark more revealing and stimulating discussions than others. The facilitator needs to ensure that the group can capitalise on these areas and not rigidly stick to a five minutes per topic structure.

Breaking the silence, silencing the vocal

Despite impressive preparations for a focus group there will, almost inevitably, come a time when the conversation dries up and appears to come to a full stop. This is a natural aspect of group discussions and should be anticipated and planned for. Have at least one additional focusing exercise, perhaps of a more physical type (involving movement from a chair), to serve as a break and re-focus for the group. Other strategies might include having a brief video available for playback that could foster more discussion, additional questions in different areas and so forth. Similarly, there is also an inevitability that one or more people will emerge in the group as more vocal than the others. Ground rules on the information sheet might be helpful in ensuring that the group is aware you will intervene if this happens, to ensure everyone gets an opportunity to speak. Group work skills will need to be deployed in order to detect the sensitivity of the group to the dominant voice – is this becoming destabilising in some way? Of course, the obverse here is that it is perfectly acceptable for someone to choose not to speak. Focus groups are not about an enforced discussion.

Debrief and post-group questionnaires

It can be important to ensure that, as participants leave, they are reminded of what happens next. What will happen to the data they have just provided the researcher with, whether they will get a chance to see the final product (the article, the research report) and so forth. It might also be worth talking about the notion of 'What's said within the group, stays within the group'. Of course this won't be policed, but it is a statement of principles that some might find useful. Similarly there may be members of the group who will have found the experience of being in a focus group difficult in some way, especially if it has touched on personal memories and emotionally complex areas. Facilitators need to be willing and able to stay behind afterwards for a debriefing.

Another common technique is to have a brief self-completion questionnaire at the end of the focus group which can cover the areas touched upon or some evaluation aspect of the focus group process.

FOCUS GROUPS AND OTHER METHODS

Focus groups are particularly economical as a research method, enabling the generation of a large amount of data for a relatively little resource outlay – financially as well as time. Focus groups can therefore often provide an acceptable economic alternative to, for example, ethnography in generating data on group meanings, processes and norms. Focus groups are not especially good at finding out detailed information about group members' attitudes since differences within the group will tend to be underreported. In this sense practitioner researchers need to be clear that focus groups are not an alternative to in-depth interviews, although this view is challenged by some in the field in terms of focus groups being a more efficient way of collecting information (Raynes et al., 2001). Many practitioner researchers in social work employ focus groups as a complementary method to others, notably interviews and observation but also to more quantitative data gathering methods: they can form a strong element within a multi-method approach. Focus groups can be particularly effective in certain periods of a research project, for example at the beginning of a study when you might benefit from a discussion about which tack to pursue, or towards the end of the process when you would like to facilitate a discussion about your findings. Fundamentally, focus groups are excellent at extending service user, carer and practitioner involvement in research projects.

ETHICAL ISSUES FOR FOCUS GROUPS

Perhaps the first comment here is that ethical issues for focus groups are little different from other methods. It is vital that all participants have full information about the project, the purpose of the information gathering and the use to which it will be put, and are therefore able to make informed consent decisions about their participation. The fundamental principle of honesty must be applied to all the work concerned with the preparation and conduct of the focus group, and equally, to the analysis, treatment and dissemination of the data and findings. During the actual experience of the group participants should not be pressured to speak although this needs to be balanced with ensuring that every person has an opportunity to say something. Confidentiality, as ever, is a taxing concept. Whilst the facilitator may well talk of 'keeping a protective layer' around the group and encouraging those within it not to talk about what went on in discussions, this is neither likely nor policeable. It might be better to emphasise the anonymity of the research data and encourage confidentiality, whilst ensuring that people only share at a level with which they are comfortable. In social work settings there is often the possibility that the boundaries of confidentiality are tested. What happens if someone discloses an offence? An incidence of abuse? A lot depends on the subject matter of the group and what areas of discussion one *anticipates*. This word is key. It is the facilitator's responsibility to ensure that they have thought through and have clarified with participants where the boundaries of confidentiality lie. It is our belief that boundaries will always exist within research in the practice arena of social work and it is therefore imperative that the facilitator makes those boundaries clear and these are explicit in the information sheet.

THE ANALYSIS OF FOCUS GROUP DATA

Whilst there are methods of employing discursive psychology and conversational analysis in the investigation of focus group data (see for example Puchta & Potter, 2004), by far the most common method is *thematic analysis* which is covered more thoroughly in a later chapter on data analysis. In essence, the session is transcribed and general notes made and then attempts are made to put the data into some form of order by reading and re-reading and trying to delineate some of the themes that emerge: the researcher is thus trying to 'tell a story and paint a full picture' (Hek & Moule, 2006). The themes that emerge can then be applied to all the data, often by cutting and pasting certain sections of the transcription into separate word-processed documents. This creates an 'analytic file' (Robson, 1993) which can then become the basis for a pattern of thinking. This can be seen as a complicated process, but perhaps it will be helpful to unpack it by way of a real example from one of the authors.

Activity

Consider how thematic analysis is achieved in this example and read the corresponding section in the data analysis chapter. Identify some of the strengths and weaknesses of this approach. How might you tackle some of the problems? How might you present this kind of data?

(Continued)

(Continued)

The focus group schedule on inter-professional learning was used with two groups: nurse mentors and social work practice teachers. The sessions were transcribed and the researchers sat down and read the data over a number of times. Six themes appeared to emerge:

- Hierarchies.
- Culture.
- Conflict.
- Role erosion.
- Students.
- Integration.

Both of the transcribed sessions were re-examined with these themes and where someone in the group had spoken of something in relation to the theme then that was copied from the transcription and into one of the six files (hierarchies, etc.). Then each themed file was re-examined and an attempt was made to determine general views (which seem to be shared across the two groups) and particular views (held by one person, but worthy of some comment). (Adapted from Dutton & Worsley, 2008)

CONCLUSION

One of the most rewarding benefits of using focus groups as a research method is the richness of the data that one is able to gather. Because most of us primarily communicate in conversations, the ability of focus groups to generate 'good quotes' is considerable. Respondents in a well-facilitated group will usually be lively, chatty and animated. The focus group practitioner researcher gets to hear, arguably, the clear voice of the researched – neither filtered through a quantitative abstraction, nor unduly influenced by the researcher in a one-to-one interview. Direct quotations are an integral part of qualitative data and focus groups can provide rich seams of these. Whilst we will look later in more detail at the analysis of qualitative data, it is pertinent to note that focus groups, as well as generating high quality data, will also generate large volumes of these. Whilst Wolcott succinctly recommends that we 'save the best and drop the rest' (1990: 67), the practitioner researcher has a difficult role in distinguishing between the many voices they will hear in a focus group because this is an empowering and often collaborative method that encourages involvement. We must remember that we can only really see each focus group as a single observation rather than as several individual voices, because within a group we must conjecture that what people say is influenced by others. We can only make general observations, tentative speculations and neutral descriptions from focus groups. Nevertheless, the 'useful, interesting and actionable results' (Stewart et al., 2007: 166) that focus groups have produced over many years act as a testament to their developing role in social research.

Key points

- Pay close attention to setting up a focus group.
- Using existing groups can save time.
- Pay attention to role and process.
- Anticipate problems.
- Think through the management of data.

Further Reading

Bloor, M., Frankland, J. & Robson, K. (2001) *Focus Groups in Social Research.* London: SAGE.

Kreuger, R. & Casey, M. (2000) *Focus Groups: A Practical Guide for Applied Research* (3rd edn). Thousand Oaks, CA: SAGE.

Puchta, C. & Potter, J. (2004) *Focus Group Practice.* London: SAGE.

Roose, G. & John, A. (2003) 'A focus group investigation into young children's understanding of mental health and their views on appropriate services for their age group', *Child Care, Health and Development*, 29 (6): 545–550.

Scourfield, J. et al. (2007) 'Young people's gendered interpretations of suicide and attempted suicide', *Child and Family Social Work*, 12: 248–257.

Stewart, D., Shamdesani, P. & Rook, D. (2007) *Focus Groups: Theory and Practice.* Thousand Oaks, CA: SAGE.

OBSERVATION, NARRATIVE AND OTHER APPROACHES

OVERVIEW

As with many of the chapters in this book we shall begin with an understanding that research skills around the use of observation and narrative accounts are at the heart of the social worker's professional skill base. It is part of what they do in their everyday working life and, as such, perhaps social workers should appreciate that not only do they possess such skills through this experience but also that those skills are of a high order. This chapter will look at each of these two elements in turn to draw out in what ways it might be useful to consider these methods of research either on their own or as part of a multi-method approach. Observation is simply a process of watching (or sometimes engaging) with a research arena in a structured way or for a particular purpose. Observation is also about looking in a critical way (Clough & Nutbrown, 2002). Its particular interest perhaps lies in the fact that observation affords the practitioner researcher an opportunity to see what people actually do, rather than what they say they do (Wisker, 2001). This is to be contrasted with narrative which, as its title suggests, is concerned with the stories (perhaps the life histories) of individuals. It's about someone's biography as narrated by them to the researcher (Chase, 2008).

> ### National Occupational Standards for Social Work
>
> There are numerous examples of where research skills around observation and narrative might link into the Occupational Standards. Element 2.2 talks of working with others to gather, analyse and understand information. Element 5.1 mentions the need to maintain and develop relationships with individuals and others. Element 7.1 looks at how we examine, with individuals and others, support networks which can be accessed and developed. Element 14.3 asks that we monitor and evaluate the effectiveness of our programmes of work as 15.2 outlines the necessity or our need to contribute to the monitoring of the effectiveness of services in meeting need.

STRUCTURED OBSERVATION

As we noted above, one of the apparently self-evident truths about observation is that, as practitioner researchers, we get to see what people actually do rather than what they say they do. With interviews and questionnaires, the researcher is constantly at the mercy of the respondent. How they choose to present themselves – as saint, sinner, introvert or extrovert – will largely dictate the researcher's view and understanding of that respondent, especially as it is quite rare for the researcher to have a context for previous behaviours and opinions as more often than not they will be meeting the respondent within the interview 'space' for the first time. Looking in more detail, we can reflect upon a range of problems with interviews and questionnaires: how easy it can be to misunderstand the questions one is asked; how difficult it can be to remember certain things, especially those that happened some time ago; and how tempting it is to play with the truth about ourselves. Thus, observation can seem to be an attractive way forward through these problems and yet it has surprisingly not attracted a large following in the research community (Bryman, 2008). Before we arrive at an understanding of why observation doesn't appear to be as popular as its possibilities suggest, let's look in more detail at this research method.

Observation tends to be divided into two main approaches: structured and non-structured. It really depends on what you wish to look at with your research as to which you might choose. Structured observation, as its name suggests, is where the practitioner researcher employs rules and criteria for the observation and recording of behaviour for a set period of time. This, as is the case with interviews, is usually done in accordance with an 'observation schedule'. Let's look at two examples.

Example I

In this example (see Table 7.1) we are using observation methods to try and understand what social workers in an open plan office do in their lunch breaks. It might be interesting to find out particularly if they work during their lunch break or choose not to. An observation schedule could look something like this:

Table 7.1   A completed structured observation schedule of social workers' lunchtime activity

Social worker	Time began lunch	Time finished lunch	Took calls? Yes/No	Talked to colleagues? Yes/No	Left office? Yes/No	Read? Type/No
Julie	12.00	12.15	Y	Y	N	N
Mandy	12.00	12.30	Y	Y	N	Textbook
Tom	12.30	12.55	N	N	N	Magazine
Anne	12.34	12.50	N	Y	N	Textbook
Pauline	1.00	1.10	N	Y	N	Novel
Noreen	1.00	1.15	N	N	N	Novel
Mike	1.15	1.40	N	N	Y	N

We can see what sort of data we are likely to gather with schedules like this one and also how these might help us get past at least one issue of self presentation. Perhaps if we interviewed the social workers we might be told that they have little or no lunch break and that they are constantly working as they eat. They may do this because they wish to give an impression that they are busy professionals and, depending on their perception of why they were being interviewed, might wish to make an indirect case for more resources. Yet perhaps our observation reveals something different?

Activity

Look at the observation schedule in Table 7.1. Make some calculations from the data and reflect on the behaviours of the social workers. Compare the different genders – do you detect any patterns?

Example 2

Let's imagine we wanted to observe certain behaviours within a meeting where social workers and service users discussed proposed new services (see Figure 7.1). We might be especially interested in the amount of time the team leader talks in comparison with the service users and social workers in the meeting. We can construct an observation schedule that requires us to mark exactly what is happening every five seconds which might look something like this:

Five-second intervals ──────────────────────────────────────▶

Minutes passed	5	10	15	20	25	30	35	40	45	50	55	60
1	1	1	1	1	3	3	3	3	2	2	1	1
2	1	4	4	4	1	1	3	3	3	3	3	3
3	2	2	3	3	3	1	1	1	4	4	5	5
4	1	1	5	2	2	2	3	3	4	2	1	1
5	4	4	4	1	1	2	2	2	2	3	3	3

Figure 7.1   A time-based observation schedule

The columns down indicate the five-second intervals whilst the rows across indicate the minutes. We then need to construct codes which will direct what we enter into the relevant box – note that the more complicated the codes the harder it can be to complete. Thus, for our meeting the codes might be:

1 Team leader talking.
2 Service user talking (or perhaps use a code for each person such as their initials).

3 Team member talking.
4 More than one person talking.
5 No one talking.

As we sit in on the team meeting we can work our way through each five-second interval marking either a 1, 2, 3, 4 or 5 in each box – which, when completed, could afford a detailed quantitative analysis of who talks most down to who talks least, how often they talk and in what order people tend to talk. Of course, what it won't do is tell us what anyone actually said. We would need to rely on other ways of recording to do that. Such schedules can provide rich and precise data but clearly also require high levels of concentration from the practitioner researcher.

Activity

Look at the observation schedule in Figure 7.1. Make some calculations from the data and reflect on the balance of the discussions. Try also to look at the sequence of who talks when – do you detect any patterns?

With both these examples we can see the benefits and limitations of fully structured observations. With this approach we can move from simply looking in an open and unguided way to looking for certain things at certain times that are directly relevant to our research topic. This helps us refine our data from the overwhelming range produced under an uncritical gaze into something targeted, manageable and focused. Thus, for approaches where this type of information is key it is invaluable.

However, we could also argue that such an approach can be critiqued as potentially falling prey to the self same issues of self presentation as interviews do. Do people really behave naturally when they are observed? Furthermore, our clear-cut schedule is also open to interpretations just like the questions making up an interview schedule. In our first example, how do we really know when a social worker starts their lunch break? Do they announce it for our benefit or does the observer need to make an assumption? Despite these notes of caution, there is ample scope for the use of structured observation focusing on particular incidents, over certain periods of time. Researchers using this method should give some thought to the issue of sampling here – if we are trying to gain a measure of reliability and rigour we might consider using another observer (do they see what we see?) or observing a number of events. For example, if we were looking, as with Example 1, at social workers' lunches we might either observe a behaviour on a number of lunch breaks (perhaps on different days) or even observe other social work teams' lunch breaks. We need to think through whether such an approach is likely to generate data that are relevant to our research. Whilst seldom used, structured observation can be powerful. The authors once supervised a research project where an observer looked at the behaviour of carers in a day centre for people with severe learning difficulties. It focused on the offering of choices at meal times and its results made a profound impact on the provision of services for that group.

Activity

Consider this example of observation in researching the complex issue of how social workers see women. Could this be done in a structured way?

Scourfield looked at one social work team in the UK using a variety of methods including observed communication, research interviews and case records:

> The main strategies were the analysis of case files, in-depth interviews with social workers and observation of interactions in the office. Almost all data were collected in the social work office and, with the exception of one home visit, I did not observe face-to-face interactions of social workers and their clients ... (2001: 77)

Scourfield suggests that these workers were struggling with participating in a system that simultaneously saw women as victims of oppressive social forces whilst also being expected to act against those self same forces. Women, the mothers of the children under investigation by the team, tended to be seen as either women who were oppressed, women who were responsible for protection, or women making choices.

UNSTRUCTURED AND PARTICIPANT OBSERVATION

As you read the previous section, you might have also considered the problem of participation. When we are observing a dynamic social situation, how far are we engaged with that setting? If we are observing social workers during their lunch breaks (or, as with Scourfield, on a day-to-day basis) we might be doing so 'as' a social worker, a practitioner researcher, a team member and a colleague. How far are the subjects of your research aware of what you are doing, and where might you draw the lines between participation and observation? Are we just looking or are we actually taking part in what is going on around us in the research setting? Gold's (1958) article helps us place the issue of participation and observation into a continuum. He talks of the 'complete participant' (fully emerged in the setting) through to the 'complete observer' (completely removed from the setting). In between are the roles of participant-as-observer and observer-as-participant – where the researcher leans more towards one type of role, but does not either completely become a participant, nor is so detached as to be an observer completely.

Activity

Using Gold's (1958) continuum, reflect on the four different types of roles practitioner researchers could adopt with a piece of participant/observer research that looked at the experience of social work students on placement. Imagine the researcher as a complete participant, participant as observer, observer as a participant and complete observer – what would the difference in the roles be for the researcher?

However, in all these examples we have faced the problem of perhaps being an 'outsider' looking in and, indeed, looking at a very specific aspect of people's lives and behaviour. Unstructured observation attempts to allow *all* information to be included and affords the practitioner researcher an opportunity to take all of it in and make sense of it. But this still leaves the issue of understanding another's world and here we arrive at the other great divide of observation which is participant and non-participant observation. Participant observation allows researchers to live and look alongside the researched: the particular community, gang, group, profession and so forth. Of course, this raises substantial ethical issues which we shall also consider, but participant observation, where we become participants in another person's life is, by far, the most personally overwhelming research method. Lacey describes it as:

> … the transfer of the whole person into an imaginative and emotional experience in which the fieldworker learn(s) to live in and understand the new world. (Lacey, 1976: 65)

There are a few famous examples of participant observation within the broad field of sociology. *Stigma* by Erving Goffman was a (1963) study of mental hospitals based on his work there as an assistant athletic director. The research was mainly covert in that only one or two staff were privy to his research activity, i.e. his attempt to uncover the 'unofficial reality' of life in a mental hospital. Of course, if we are undercover in a setting we can't then also interview those we are researching as that would not be in keeping with our role. This can be contrasted with overt observation where the observed know that a researcher is in their midst. An example of this approach is Whyte's (1955) *Street Corner Society*, a study of life in an Italian neighbourhood in 'Cornerville', USA. Social workers make an appearance in this fascinating book where the researcher was, to a certain extent, protected by a sponsor (named 'Doc'). Interestingly, Whyte talks of how he increasingly came to see himself as one of the gang. Bringing this approach right up to date is *The Hard Sell* by John Bone (2006). This book describes itself as an 'ethnographic study of the double glazing industry' and is based on covert participation techniques as Bone became a double glazing salesman for the length of his research. It is worth noting the connection between ethnography and participant observation as they are closely connected. Ethnography has a long research background, especially within social anthropology, as it relates to the studying of different societies and cultures. Indeed, one could argue that ethnography is a better word as participant observation suggests that the researcher simply observes when in fact they are usually doing much more than that (Bryman, 2008).

Activity

Consider this example and reflect on what the practitioner researcher can discover from things such as bulletin boards and diaries.

Iarskaia-Smirnova and Romanov (2007) looked at the issue of the exclusion of Russian children with disabilities within educational policies and particularly at how such children

(Continued)

(Continued)

were socialised within the educational institution. They used a mixed method ethnographic and qualitative approach to support policy suggestions about mainstream inclusion. This was split into three parts – case studies of children with disabilities in residential and mainstream settings; in-depth interviews with administrators and officials of the Department of Education; and a survey of students, parents and teachers. Here's what they said about the role of the researchers in gathering data for the case studies (see note below) – mixing non-participant, unstructured observation with interviews and general data gathering:

> The researchers spent between three and four hours several days a week at the educational settings. They sat in class, observed various activities during the breaks, talked to students, parents, teachers and administrators, and took part in other activities, such as parents' conferences and school festivals. They studied different texts and artifacts, including bulletin boards and students' performance diaries. Each of the researchers was trying to get into the school life of one group of students. (2007: 6).

Note: In research, when they refer to 'case studies' it tends to refer to the consideration of a single case (such as a school) using multiple methods, but specifically not looking at the case as a sample of a wider population (i.e. not seeing it as representative of all schools) – rather as a case in its own right.

OBSERVATION AND ETHICS

As we link this back to social work perhaps we can begin to think of situations where we might be interested in this type of covert observation and at the same time reflect on the enormous ethical challenges that such an approach might generate. Imagine that we choose to go 'undercover' as a part-time care assistant in a care home to find out what being a care assistant is 'really' like. Imagine that we pretend to be homeless so that we can get the inside story of what it's like to live in a Salvation Army hostel. Whether the research is covert or overt, this still leaves the researcher with many difficult moral dilemmas and role conflicts. More importantly, one has to question how the issue of informed consent operates in such research – would all the residents of the care home or hostel be happy to give their consent? How is confidentiality maintained in these circumstances? Are we able to demonstrate that this will really benefit service users rather than be some form of journalistic exposé? The potential for paternalism in participant observation is neatly captured by Williams, who warns against 'the arrogance of the researcher invading another group's world to get information in order to relay it to the outside world' (1988: 136). Indeed, as practitioner researchers we may be in danger of touching on areas of whistle blowing, for example, that have legal implications.

For these, and many other reasons, it is rare indeed to see participant observation (especially covert) employed in health and social care settings and ethics committees will rightly look closely at such an approach. Nevertheless, overt observation of situations remains an attractive avenue of data collection and, whilst often at its best when combined with other methods is still worthy of close consideration. Our final point here is simply that the problematic nature of ethical debates around overt and covert ethical challenges should not obscure the fact that there are a range of more 'normal' ethical issues that will, as with all primary research, need to be considered (Mason, 2002).

NARRATIVE

Whether as an observer or a participant, the researcher will struggle to 'get inside' the lived experience of those being researched. They will remain an outsider. A narrative approach appears attractive in this regard as it allows researchers an insight into the world of the people being researched. It facilitates someone telling a story – *their* narrative. Observation, semi-structured and unstructured interviewing are closely associated with narrative approaches and can overlap in certain areas. There are a number of differing approaches to gathering and analysing data from narratives, but common to all narrative research is an interest in the temporal nature of the data and the symbolic meaning it offers (Bryman, 2004; David & Sutton, 2010; Elliot, 2005). This places an emphasis on time and the sequencing of events together with a consideration of what these represent. Jane Elliot (2005) suggests a number of other common themes that run through narrative research:

- A desire to empower research participants and allow them to contribute to identifying the relevant themes in an area of research.
- An interest in process and change over time.
- An interest in self and representations of the self.
- An awareness that the researcher him or herself is also a narrator.

Elliott highlights the three key features of narratives as being the chronological (sequential events, their meaning), what is said, and the social aspect (the impact they have on their audience). Chase describes narrative research as 'an interest in biographical particulars as narrated by the one who lives them' (2008: 58). For a social worker this will obviously have some attractive elements as we think about how, as practitioner researchers, we can ask service users for their stories. Indeed, we know that one of the failings of traditional and quantitative approaches to research in the eyes of service users is that it reduces them to ciphers – conditions, offences, opinions, disabilities – and not whole people with their own stories (Beresford, 2007b; Branfield & Beresford, 2006; Evans & Jones, 2004). Narrative accounts can combat this reductive tendency by offering an alternative perspective to professional interpretations and affording a 'narrative of resistance' from the respondent (Mishler, 2005: 432).

What service users will often say is that they want to tell the researchers their stories – to be afforded an opportunity to simply say what they want to say and not be restricted by the questions on an interview schedule. But, as we found with observation, as practitioner researchers we can hear the voice of the researched but whose voice do we use when we communicate someone else's story? The moment we move away from a complete, unedited, verbatim account this thorny problem raises its head. Riessman (1993) emphasises the necessity to gather narrative data through open-ended techniques such as interviews, diaries or biographical material. Others emphasise narrative research as the 'narrative interview' (Mishler, 1986, 2005). As just one example, Mishler (2005) used these interviews to investigate the experience and perspectives of patients with serious health conditions. Of course, as social work researchers we might also wish to look at colleagues' narratives. Imagine how colleagues might respond if they were asked the question in the following activity.

Activity

Reflect on this example.

Gunther and Thomas (2006) looked at 'unforgettable' events linked to the care of patients undertaken by registered nurses (RNs). Using a narrative approach they simply asked nurses, 'Tell me about a time that you provided nursing care to a patient'. The interviewer only spoke to seek clarification or elaboration. This unstructured, individual, in-depth interview allowed the nurse respondents to talk about those events and incidents that had stuck in their minds. Gunther and Thomas found that a sense of moral distress tended to accumulate around things that had 'gone wrong' in practice. Several years after these unforgettable events, practitioners were still trying to understand them, justify their actions and perhaps absolve themselves from blame. A dissonance was detected around problems and events that appeared to have no ready solution.

> Unforgettable care giving episodes, burned into memory by unanswered questions, were described by this sample of American RNs. Moral distress appeared to be inherent in the work life of the RNs. This concept should be clarified and expanded. Nurses have a need to tell their stories because 'stories express our concern and anxieties, they deliver moral judgments' (Rashotte, 2005). Nurses expressed their values in the context of work, and embedded in that work and in their subsequent stories lay the practical wisdom of the profession. (2006: 375)

Now ask one or two colleagues the same question adapted to their profession (i.e. 'Tell me about a time you provided tuition to a student' or 'Tell me about a time you provided social care to a service user', etc.). Reflect on their answer. Does it have the same emotional resonance evoked by Gunther and Thomas?

Narratives can be oral or written and may be elicited or heard during the field work element of research, for instance in an interview or perhaps within a naturally occurring conversation. As we can see from the differing approaches there is an enormous continuum of narratives. At one end they can be brief commentaries on current events or somewhat longer stories about significant aspects of someone's life such as their time in school, their experiences of work, disability and so on. At the other end of the continuum we arrive at the narrative of an entire life. This should not be confused with life histories or life story works, which are essentially different, although they have similar features to narrative research. Indeed, historians use the phrase 'oral history' for this type of approach and they form a useful reminder of the impetus behind much narrative research. Historians seek, through oral history, to place an emphasis not on the major historical events but on the lives of ordinary people who lived through and during those events. However, it is helpful to recall some feminist methodological critiques of this approach which argue that the researcher ought to be interested in the person in their own right and not simply because they exist in some relation to 'grand' events (Hunt & Winegarten, 1983). Ordinary people's everyday oral narratives of their personal experiences are valid in themselves (Labov & Waletzky, 1997). When we think of research in health and social care we can perhaps begin to think – on a smaller scale – of significant changes in the delivery of services, or major legislative innovation and how a narrative approach might afford interesting data and a particular perspective on such events. On a more general level, we can also think of narrative accounts of service users' lives and experiences, perhaps of young people who have been through the care system – which are surely, of themselves, important, fascinating and informative lives that have much to teach others if they are shared?

Activity

Imagine asking your eldest extended family member if you can create a life history about them. How would you go about this? What sort of data would you glean? What would you do with the data you obtained? What do you do think you could achieve with this sort of research approach?

NARRATIVE AND VOICE

When we obtain narratives from those we are researching, where do we fit in as researchers? How authentic is the voice we might use in conveying another person's story? What authority do we have for making interpretations of such a narrative? These are difficult questions because whilst we might quote verbatim everything said by a respondent we still have to represent this material and often we will seek to give it meaning beyond its original intent or perhaps even reduce these accounts 'into brief summaries' (Riessman & Quinney, 2005: 398). On the other hand, it is also worth realising that those who narrate their stories might also assemble them in a way that may bear a variable relation to the actual events. Some of this may be down to self-presentation or simply because it just happens that the story is remembered in that way. The very process of looking back at our lives implies that we reflect on what happened in a way that, of course, we were unable to do as the events unfolded. In this sense it can be seen as a natural process described as 'retrospective meaning making – the shaping or ordering of past experience' (Chase, 2008: 64).

Similarly, we need to understand that the story being told to us as practitioner researchers will simply not be the same story as that told to, say, a journalist or a doctor. Narratives are socially situated interactive performances produced in particular settings for particular purposes. The social worker as researcher, in the same way as the practitioner, needs to be aware of the impact of the professional role on the respondent. We might conjecture that knowledge of the professional role would impact on what the respondent said, what they didn't say, and how they chose to present themselves. It is also important to understand the reason behind the narrative – what might the respondent be seeking to achieve? As Riessman and Quinney argue:

> The persuasive function of narrative is especially relevant for social work. Some clients narrate their experience in ways that engage and convince, while other tellings can leave the audience sceptical, inviting counter-narratives. In case conferences, one speaker can persuade others of a particular clinical formulation, while another fails to convince – a process that can be studied by close analysis of the rhetorical devices each employs to 'story' the case. (2005: 395)

So the practitioner researcher may intend to create an opportunity for the respondent to 'tell it like it is', yet needs to understand that in reality they will be told it 'like it is chosen to be told'. This, we hasten to add, isn't necessarily about deception or omission but rather a natural aspect of all communication as we will create a version of events to suit our audience. This theme takes another step with Loseke (2001), who explored support groups for women who had experienced domestic violence and found that group facilitators appeared to encourage the group members to reshape and reframe their stories – their narratives – into more formulaic stories about spousal abuse. In turn, the women resisted these attempts to be defined as 'battered women'. For Loseke, this was not about a denial of victimisation, but rather a failure of the formulaic stories to encompass the complexities of lived experience: 'as part of everyday lived experiences, narratives themselves are messy and complex' (Chase, 2008: 67). As researchers – and social workers – we need to be aware of the dangers in 'de-privatising' personal experience by reducing it to common stories, familiar narratives, which fail to capture individual differences. Narratives are intimately connected with our identity.

In their critical review of narrative in social work, Riessman and Quinney (2005) concluded that practitioners are more comfortable with using narrative concepts for reflective practice and teaching than they are for research. As an approach it tends to be seen as curtailed by its individuality and the limitations to its applicability – how can we generalise from an individual experience? It might be that narrative approaches earn their place within a mixed methods approach affording, as they do, invaluable insights into the everyday life stories of everyday people and thus providing data that can coexist with dominant perspectives (Mishler, 2005). For example, one of the author's recent research approaches was an evaluation of a SureStart centre. Service delivery quantitative data were analysed together with a sequence of staff interviews and service user narratives which aimed to hear the stories of service users at different stages of their 'career' with the agency (recent recipients of services, a few weeks in, coming to the end, and afterwards). Such an approach can militate against the worst effects of the potentially sterile presentation of statistics by providing a counterbalance via individual perspectives.

UNOBTRUSIVE MEASURES AND DOCUMENTS

To conclude this chapter, it is worth mentioning some research approaches that will not alter the situation under study in the same way that interviews, questionnaires and, as we have just noted, observation and narratives can do (Hall & Hall, 1996) The phrase 'unobtrusive measures' (Webb et al., 1966) refers to researching things that erode through wear and tear or accumulate in some way – thereby creating a physical trace. This can be witnessed in an inconspicuous, discreet manner which will not disturb the people or environment. Webb's famous example is of the floor tiles around a hatching chick exhibition in a museum – the fact that these tiles needed to be replaced far quicker than any others in the museum gave an indication of a particular aspect of human behaviour – 'selective erosion' – the relative popularity of the exhibit was revealed through footfall. In a community setting we might think of things that accrue as opposed to eroding, like graffiti, litter, numbers of derelict properties, satellite dishes and so forth (Hall & Hall, 1996).

You could argue that one might include organisational records in this approach – as something that accumulates and accrues in a similar sense. However, it would probably be better to consider this under a slightly different banner. Documentary, content and archival analysis has some issues of its own, although like unobtrusive measures, we are able, as researchers, to usually consider such documents without disturbing the setting we are researching in the same way that more traditional research methods are prone to do. As some authors have noted, the use of organisational records and such like in some areas of study is fairly commonplace (such as social work), but relatively rare in others (Robson, 1993). Many organisations and professions have accumulated a vast catalogue of archival material dating back many years. Within social work, the sheer volume of policy, procedure, legislation, good practice guidelines (documents of this type are called, most appropriately, 'grey literature' in research circles) and so on forms rich seams of information that will, almost inevitably, find a place in a lot of social work research and in some cases will be the sole focus. But it is important also to think broadly about documentary sources which can include a wide variety of things such as bank statements, company reports, diaries, advertisements and websites. From this point of view biographies and diaries clearly overlap with our discussions of narrative accounts. Especially for grey literature, it is tempting to see those types of documentary data as 'hard' or legitimate evidence, but it is important to retain a criticality about those sorts of data rather than accept them at face value. As with all documents, they were created for someone, for a reason:

> Documents, whether visual or textual, are constructed in particular contexts, by particular people, with particular purposes, and with consequences – intended and unintended. You may wish to investigate why they were prepared, made or displayed, by whom, for whom, under what conditions, according to what rules and conventions. You may wish to know what they have been used for, where they have been kept and so on. (Mason, 2002: 110)

Without this criticality we are in danger of simply reproducing a catalogue of material. So how we look at documents is as important as which of these we look at. Whenever we look at any range of documentary material it is important to be clear about what exactly we are viewing, what the criteria are for the inclusion of certain documents and how we intend to analyse them. Without this 'method' we lack structure and coherence. For example, if we are looking at a range of literature around the mental health of young people in care in a library setting do we simply see what's on the shelves and use that? Perhaps we could develop criteria around geography (national, international, local, regional), the publication date (last ten years, twenty years), type of study (large scale, small scale, user involvement), whether government funded or charity funded, whether peer reviewed journal articles or internal organisational evaluations or even a hierarchy of those sources based on numbers of citations in other articles. By thinking through these sorts of criteria we open up the research to a critical gaze from both ourselves and the eventual reader. We should also be aware that documents are not all equally valid or invalid. Some, such as wikipedia, are simply not comparable to peer reviewed material.

Having approached our documents in a critical but structured way we must also consider how we might analyse them. Many of the same rules apply to the analysis of talk as to text. The basic truth is that much of a document's significance will be revealed when we compare one piece with another:

> We develop our understanding of the ideas, issues and policies with which documents deal, through a comparative analysis. (Blaxter et al., 1998: 187)

Some authors have developed the notion of content analysis to assist this process, which can take many different forms. On a very practical level some research has looked at typographies of content by asking 'What sort of material is this?' and 'How does it relate to other sorts of content?' An example of this might be looking at changes in newspaper content and how many column inches are spent on sport as opposed to scandal, teachers as opposed to the police, etc. This can be reduced to a basic analysis of word frequency within documents, key words, categories or other combinations of criteria (Robson, 1993). Of course, some of the more quantitative approaches will benefit from computer assistance. But this is just a flavour of the different approaches to data analysis within this approach. The separate chapter on analysis should also be read.

Activity

Your next research project involves a comparison of child protection procedures. Think through these questions:

- Will you look at CP procedures from a number of local authorities? What about organisations like the NCH and NSPCC?
- What are the pros and cons of looking beyond national boundaries, such as Scotland, Wales, Europe and wider international data?
- What is realistic given the time you have available?
- How will you gain access to these documents?
- When you have them, what particular aspects might be seen as worthy of attention? What categories of their typical context could you use to compare them with each other?
- Would you be able to critique their authorship, purpose and the organisational pressures behind their production?
- What role would other secondary data such as existing research be able to offer your analysis of these documents?

CONCLUSION

This chapter has pulled together some seemingly disparate approaches to the generation of knowledge. We have considered the observation of social settings in both structured and unstructured ways. The difficult ethical dilemmas of participant observation, especially within social work arenas, suggest caution around covert approaches which tend to appear within broader, sociological research than the field of social care. Following on from the attractiveness of seeing what people actually do, rather than what they say they do, is the use of narratives in research. Their emphasis on the lived experiences of the respondent, relayed to the researcher in a format that suits them and their story, can be an effective counter measure to the sterility of traditional research methods where the less powerful are the people who are researched by the more powerful about things that may bear only a passing relevance to real people's lives. Finally, we have briefly looked at unobtrusive methods and particularly the use of documentary sources. With all these approaches we must recall, using Mason's (2002) notion, that whether we are collecting or 'excavating' data as opposed to generating or 'constructing' data, researchers need to retain a rigour and structure to their approach and an internal and external criticality when looking at what they see, hear and read.

Key points

- Observation can be an illuminating data collection method so don't discount it too readily.
- Observation can often be enhanced by the use of other methods.
- Narrative research has a lot to offer the practitioner researcher.
- Think through the representational issues with your data.
- Retain a criticality with all your data, both primary and secondary.

Further Reading

Bone, J. (2006) *The Hard Sell*. London: Ashgate.

Chase, S.E. (2008) 'Narrative inquiry: multiple lenses, approaches, voices', in N. Denzin & Y. Lincoln, *Collecting and Interpreting Qualitative Materials*. Thousand Oaks, CA: SAGE.

Elliott, J. (2005) *Using Narrative in Social Research: Qualitative and Quantitative Approaches*. London: SAGE.

Mishler, E.G. (1986) *Research Interviewing: Context and Narrative*. Cambridge, MA: Harvard University Press.

Riessman, K.C. & Quinney, L. (2005) 'Narrative in social work: a critical review', *Qualitative Social Work*, 4 (4): 391–412.

Scourfield, J.B. (2001) 'Constructing women in child protection work', *Child and Family Social Work*, (6): 77–87.

ANALYSING DATA

OVERVIEW

The chapters in this book have attempted to take a roughly chronological path through the research process, from the initial idea, past the decisions about method and ethical approval, and onward to the actual gathering of the data. Logically, we now arrive at a chapter that looks at the analysis of the data we have obtained through this journey but that suggests that we will only begin to think about data analysis at the end of the process: the reverse *must* be the case. When we plan our research project an essential ingredient of its design is a consideration of how we intend to analyse the data. It is an intrinsic aspect of the research design in general and the research method in particular that it starts from the outset and is an ongoing process from there.

Some authors have likened the process of data analysis to creating order from chaos (Blaxter et al., 1998). Others think of data analysis in a more conversational tone, as 'the process of making sense of the data and discovering what it has to say' (Holliday, 2007: 89). Whatever our approach, we will engage in a purposive relationship with our data which we must both manage (control) and analyse (understand). Here we might draw a parallel with assessment which is a key social work skill. If we are involved in the assessment of an individual we will clearly be gathering data as we go about that process – talking to the service user, reading existing case notes, talking to previous workers with the family and perhaps broader carers. As we proceed through such a task we are constructing images in our heads of how we might understand the picture that is emerging. We are hopefully not so foolish as to arrive at premature conclusions, but instead allow our accumulating data to 'make sense' and our understanding to emerge. Of course, we are also gathering these assessment data for a clear purpose, perhaps within a procedure so we need to exert some control over the process, and we must realise right from the outset what we are going to 'do' with our assessment. In the same way, our research project must have a notion of its purpose without necessarily prejudging its outcome. We are not arguing that the ability to perform social work assessments is the same as data analysis in research, but we do believe there are parallels in these activities and that skills in the former will assist in the latter. This chapter looks at these ideas and applies them to the analysis of qualitative and quantitative data, focusing particularly on the former. It also looks at the basic ideas of data management, transcribing and dealing with secondary data, and examining frequency counting.

National Occupational Standards for Social Work

There are numerous examples of where research skills around data analysis link into the National Occupational Standards. Unit 1.3 is concerned with the evaluation of data before the initial intervention. Unit 3.2 asks the social worker to assess the needs and risks and options available taking into account legal and other requirements – an analysis of complex data. Unit 13.3 looks at planning, monitoring and reviewing outcomes and actions to minimise stress and risk. Unit 14.3 also asks you to monitor and evaluate the effectiveness of a programme of work, whilst 15.4 is focused on the management of information.

DATA ANALYSIS

Before we go on to some concrete examples and illustrations of data analysis we first need to reflect on the notion of deductive and inductive reasoning. These terms describe, in the broadest, most fundamental manner, a process of analysing data. At its heart, inductive reasoning begins with what we see, allowing us to make generalisations and then, perhaps, a theory or explanation of what we saw. Deductive reasoning is the other way around. It begins with a theory from which we might make some predictions about how something might happen, which we will then explore by looking in detail at an event to see if our theory is correct (see Figure 8.1). Data analysis in

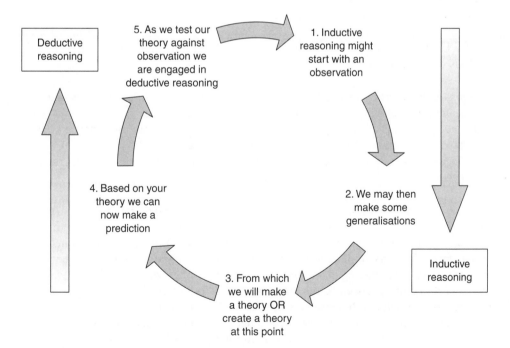

Figure 8.1   Inductive and deductive reasoning

social work research usually involves both inductive and deductive reasoning within the same process of data analysis but, at its heart, tends to begin with an inductive, general approach – open to exploring and understanding the range of activity and complexity that is unfolding before it. Natural and positivist approaches tend to employ a deductive approach. This chapter will follow a broadly inductive route. However, in starting out with this broader canvas it is important when analysing our data that we also think deductively, testing out our theories for understanding our data to see if these really do make sense and are supported by the data. It's important to begin by acknowledging that we can start our process of data analysis both with the data and the theory – with what we see and what we think we might be seeing.

It might be helpful to walk through an illustration of Figure 8.1. Beginning with an inductive reasoning approach at Point 1, we can make an observation by interviewing several service users about money management. By Point 2, we might be able to make some generalisations, e.g. that service users struggle to pay their winter heating bills when on benefits. By Point 3, our theory is that benefits are insufficient to pay for fuel bills throughout the year. Points 1 to 3 are a typical inductive process, but we can now move towards a deductive process – or, of course, start there, at Point 3, with our theory. At Point 4, we can predict with our theory that people on benefits will have insufficient money to pay for fuel bills. At Point 5, we can then interview service users to see if our theory was correct – deductive reasoning.

The reason we start with this is that as researchers we need to know generally how we are going to go about our research and how we are going to find the answer to our question. Our analysis must fit into one of these two processes. But whether inductive or deductive approaches suit us, one of our main challenges will be the management of the data that we gather and we must turn our attention to its analysis. The first problem with data analysis might well be, 'What do I do with all this data?' (Wisker, 2001). There are perhaps three key words to hold in our minds as we approach the analysis of our data:

- *Representativeness* – relates to the concern with which you represent the data in your research. How carefully and honestly do you represent your data?
- *Reliability* – refers to you carrying out your research well enough so that someone following in its footsteps would be likely to find the same outcome as you did.
- *Validity* – means that your methods and approach are congruent with your research question and therefore your findings are likely to be valid.

By bearing these in mind as we consider our research and data analysis in particular, we can begin to provide a firm foundation for a rigorous approach. Our thinking must start at the very beginning. If we intend to gather quantitative, often numerically-based data, that has implications for how we might choose to analyse that data. Similarly, if we are gathering qualitative data, which are often word-based, then we might choose a different approach to our data analysis. More often than not, as practitioner researchers, we will combine aspects of both these approaches.

For many of the reasons we discuss at length throughout this book, it is likely that the social worker engaged in research will adopt a primarily qualitative approach and this will be reflected in our discussion which will focus only briefly on a statistical analysis of data. Just as important as the proactive consideration of analysis before we gather data is the notion of rigour. It is our adherence to this concept that makes the research we undertake valuable and valid. Rigour makes our approach and our analysis transparent and – most importantly – replicable. A key aspect of any research project is simply this: can someone study what you have done and then follow in your wake with their own research? Would they find your route clear and logical? Is your analysis representative, reliable and accurate? This chapter aims to provide an introduction to the central ideas of data analysis and to describe a typical 'thematic' approach, in particular, to the analysis of qualitative data.

ORGANISING YOUR DATA

The first rule of data analysis is *management* of data. If all the data that you gather are organised and kept in good order then their analysis will prove much easier. When we gather secondary data these will usually be in the form of research already conducted that relates to our own studies. Together with organisational policies, government legislation and procedure, journal articles and so on, it may be that we will gather a large range of secondary data. Your first task is to put together a bibliography – a list of all your sources of evidence. This can easily be done using word processing programs such as Microsoft Word (the 2007 version for example has its own bibliography manager). There are a number of software programs that can be used for this task though most universities use Endnote.[1] Several freeware alternatives can be found on the internet and Zotero[2] is recommended for those who use the Firefox web browser as it integrates well into Word. Whatever your choice here do make sure you use a method. Keeping track of your data is vital when you need to ask questions of it later. The second key task is simply to collect your data and collate these appropriately. If all the material you gather is located throughout your home, on a variety of PCs, laptops and USB sticks or in various cupboards and drawers, you aren't controlling your data. Keep the material you accumulate in one place and in order, and do make sure that you back up any digital data.

TRANSCRIBING

When we interview respondents or conduct focus groups in pursuit of our research it is likely that we will be recording what people have said. We will then be faced with the problem of how to manage the data produced. The first, easiest, but perhaps least satisfying way is to summarise (see Table 8.1). This involves sitting down and listening to an audio file and selecting key phrases or particular events, perhaps something like the summary shown in Table 8.1 overleaf.

However, it is generally thought of as good practice to make sure that audio data are transcribed into typewritten scripts of the interview or focus group. This very fact alone may give researchers pause for thought – imagine typing up ten 30-minute interviews or three focus groups that each lasted an hour? This can be a very time-consuming exercise

---

[1]http://www.endnote.com/
[2]http://www.zotero.org/

Table 8.1   Summarising talk data

Time	Description
0:24	Social worker talks of their university training.
1:22	First placement in a SureStart centre.
3:33	Practice assessor and social worker had a good relationship.
7:12	Second placement in local authority, 'Where I really found my feet'.
12:40	'My training was more helpful when I look back than maybe when I was actually doing it, you know … I really think that'.

and researchers will often try to find some money on projects to access the many transcribing services that are out there in order to free up some time to analyse the data. Estimates of how long transcribing can take will vary according to how complex the material is but one can usually allow somewhere between four to six hours for every hour of tape-recorded interview (although it can rise to ten hours for more complex data with more intricate transcription). There are a few rules that researchers follow with transcribing:

- Don't 'correct' respondents' phrasing, language or sentence structure, etc. The transcriber's job is to faithfully type exactly what has been said. We must never put words in a respondent's mouth. A transcription is as accurate a record of what was said as is possible.
- Each one of us speaks in a way that doesn't sit easily on the written page. Our verbal language is littered with 'umms', 'ahhs' and pauses. It is very problematic to depict these when transcribing, but certain pauses – if we listen carefully – can be especially meaningful and we ought to try and capture them.
- Inevitably there will be words and phrases that we can't decipher as we listen. We can insert either [??] or [unclear] (East Midlands Oral History Archive, 2009).
- It is especially difficult to transcribe focus groups because there are repeated opportunities for respondents to talk over each other. Remember this when laying out your ground rules and when facilitating the group discussion. You are unlikely to be able to delineate various members of a group when transcribing.

It is very important when your transcription is completed to make sure that the data are firmly attached in some way to the details of which occasion this was, the profile of the participants and the setting (Winch et al., 2008). When it comes to your analysis a little further on you will need to know which interview or focus group each transcription came from.

Use filing systems to make sure you know where all your data can be accessed. Lofland and Lofland's (1994) advice might be useful as they suggest keeping three different types of files (which they think of as groupings of data rather than, say, an A4 wallet file, although that idea makes sense for many). Mundane files are those which are organised by broader, straightforward categories such as the people you have interviewed or the organisations you have looked at. Analytic files can begin the process of data analysis and involve taking aspects of the data from across the broad files that relate to particular questions or themes. A simple example of this would be when we interview four social workers and ask them the same questions. A mundane file would be a separate file that kept each separate interview on its own. An analytic file might take the four different answers to each question and then assemble them together so that we can more easily compare them (an activity later in this chapter (p. 128) uses an analytic file in this way). A fieldwork file can keep all the information about the process of the research itself, namely on the research project's methodology.

REVIEWING LITERATURE AND SECONDARY DATA

The literature review is a common component of most research reports and, indeed, journal articles. This is because it acts as an anchor and foundation on which to build your own research and a context in which your research can be understood. It is fundamental to the research process that practitioner researchers understand where their own research sits in the canon of existing research in the same and related fields. That knowledge should help shape the nature of one's own research and understanding of how the research community is building answers as it conducts enquiries into particular fields of knowledge. Wisker calls the literature review an account of the 'learning conversations taking place' (2001: 128). As researchers, we are engaged in a dialogue with others, seeing where we fit and what we can contribute. It is not usually our role to simply summarise, but to reflect our findings in the context of the findings of others, thereby avoiding

> The furniture sales catalogue, in which everything merits a one paragraph entry no matter how skilfully it has been conducted: Bloggs (1975) found this, Smith (1976) found that, Jones (1978) found the other, Bloggs, Smith and Jones (1978) found happiness in heaven. (Haywood & Wragg, 1982: 2)

Perhaps most telling in this criticism, when we get past the dullness of such an approach, is the notion that everything is of equal merit. It is tempting to see all knowledge as equally valuable or valid but this is simply not the case. The growth of the internet as a source of knowledge and learning affords us an opportunity to access vast amounts of material and create information – but is it all useful? Clearly we must draw distinctions between well crafted, ethical, research conducted in a rigorous manner with blogs, wikipedia and internet 'thought pieces', even though these may all relate to our topic.

However, beyond the 'contextualisation' element of a literature review, the researcher is also trying to get at what Geertz (1973) called 'thick description'. By this he meant that we, as researchers, need to show the 'different and complex facets of a particular phenomenon' (Holliday, 2007: 74). Let's take an illustrative example of a social worker shaking the hand of a service user at the end of an interview. A 'thin' description would say no more than that. A 'thick' description would look beyond this to try and understand that handshake in a broader context: the relationship, the fact that this was the last meeting, the roles, the policy framework in which the meeting took place, perhaps notions of class, culture, geography, community – all the things that would illuminate one's understanding of that action. As we look at different elements of the range of secondary data we need to think about 'thick' descriptions and how the material we are gathering fits together to create a fuller picture.

The analysis of data, especially qualitative data, is a subjective process. With our 'thick' descriptions we need to think how we can immerse ourselves in situations and see beyond that which is presented to us. Interpreting the data in this way, however, must not mean that we somehow lose a critical perspective. Some authors talk of a reflexive relationship with the range of data that we gather as we research, where we read 'through or beyond' that which is immediately presented to us (Mason, 2002). Why might something have been said in a certain way? Why might a letter have been written in a certain style? What might the impact have been of a particular group's funding of a research project? Indeed, how do we understand ourselves in relation to the data – what does the material mean to us personally or, as Mason's neat turn of phrase enquires, how do we locate ourselves as part of the data? If, for example, you are researching into the professional identity of social workers, the fact that you are a social worker yourself is a fundamental issue for the research project that will affect your view of the data gathered.

We must therefore use our research skills actively to critique the material we may wish to include in our literature review. Tools have been devised that are particularly helpful in this process, such as the Critical Appraisal Skills Programme[3] devised by the Public Health Resources Unit (2006). This tool simply provides us with pertinent questions with which to interrogate any piece of research we happen to come across – a yardstick. These questions can include:

- Is there a clear statement of the aims of the research?
- Was the research design appropriate to addressing the aims of the research?
- Were the data collected in a way that addressed the research issue?
- Have ethical issues been taken into consideration?
- Was the data analysis sufficiently rigorous? (Public Health Resources Unit, 2006)

All of these can help us not only to interrogate this research, this new knowledge, but they can also help structure our interrogation so that we can apply similar tests against the other secondary data we are considering. This tool could perhaps be guilty of a slight bias towards a 'health' understanding of qualitative research and as we must always critique that which we read, so must we also critique the tools that help us to critique! Thus, for example, we might take a view from a social work standpoint that the CASP tool leaves out service user involvement as a key indicator, a vital component, of good quality research in our area.

Activity

Select two qualitative research-based journal articles where each has a section on methodology. Compare the two articles' methods using the CASP tool.

- What does this tell us about the quality of the research?
- What have you found out about the quality of the article?

---

[3]The Qualitative CASP tool can be accessed at http://www.phru.nhs.uk/Doc_Links/ Qualitative%20Appraisal%20Tool.pdf

BEGINNING QUANTITATIVE ANALYSIS

When we involve people in our research we will normally understand and keep a record of some key demographic aspects of their profile: their age, gender, race and so on. These are a grounding sort of data that help anchor and contextualise the interview, questionnaires, observations or the focus group that follows. Indeed, it might be that we wish to consider these particular indices as things to compare against the rest of the data. For example, we might want to see whether the female respondents said something similar or different to the males, the younger to the older, the employed to the unemployed and so forth. When we are simply 'adding up' we are presenting *frequency counts*. This type of data is very easy to present by using Word or similar word processing packages. Below is a bar chart (see Figure 8.2) from an article that looked in general at the changes within the qualifying social work degree across four universities in the North West of England over four years and with this bar chart looked particularly at the ages of incoming students.

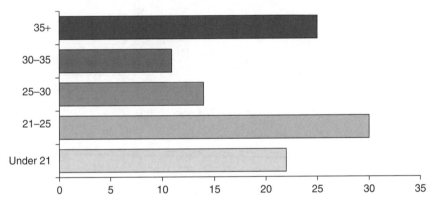

Figure 8.2   Age profile at entry by percentage of student population (Worsley et al., 2009)

This simply shows that 25 per cent of the entrants onto the social work programmes in these four universities were over 35 and that 22 per cent were under 21. The biggest single group of students were 21–25. We should remember that percentages magnify the actual differences between data more as the total numbers get smaller. A general rule of thumb is to use actual numbers below incidences of 20 or less (Hall & Hall, 1996) .

We can also present similar information in a pie chart which, if we separate out each slice of the pie, is charmingly known as an 'exploding' pie (see Figure 8.3, overleaf). This particular one looks at the data from several interviews with social workers that asked them what they thought about a post-qualifying programme they had attended and if they felt the aims of the programme had been met.

Figure 8.4 is another example of a bar chart with a three dimensional feel from the same research project mentioned above and shows what respondents felt overall about whether the curriculum they were being taught on the post-qualifying course reflected the sort of work they were doing.

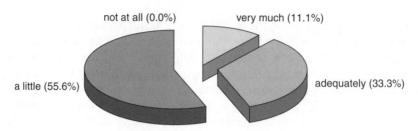

Figure 8.3 An exploding pie diagram (Worsley, 2000)

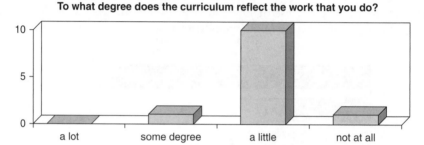

Figure 8.4 A three dimensional bar chart (Worsley, 2000)

Activity

Let's use some basic data to create our own diagram with Word. Look at the table below which conveys data about four social workers and how many clients they see each month. Convert these data into a chart by going to Word > Insert > Picture> Chart and then editing these data into the table. Using the tools, try out different shapes and styles for the table.

Social worker/month	Jan	Feb	March	April
Ian	5	12	30	25
Janice	10	12	30	12
Karen	7	11	23	24
Phil	6	25	6	30

The activity outlined above uses a key tool for the analysis and presentation of data – a matrix. To all intents and purposes (indeed, as it is used in the activity) it is simply a table. But a matrix is an extremely efficient method of presenting all kinds of data, not just numbers. In the example above we can see that it enables us to compare changing data over time from four individuals. This is known as a time-ordered matrix as the columns are arranged in a time sequence. We could also, for example, have produced a role ordered matrix where the rows, instead of being all social workers, could have been a broader variety of professional roles. Other matrix variants include an effects matrix and checklist matrix (Robson, 2002). With qualitative data the matrix can be used to abstract smaller, significant phrases or quotes from people who have been interviewed on different themes that have emerged. In the example below (Figure 8.5), a thematic matrix has been produced which outlines what each of the three social workers interviewed felt on a range of issues. The practitioner researcher's task, and the function of data analysis, is to try and capture the essence of their responses and reduce this down to a manageable size. This can abstract the data to a very small bite-sized chunk: here this is merely a few words about what social workers feel about four key issues.

SW/Issue	IT	Admin	Supervision	Income
Rhiannon	Just another pain	Fabulous	Never happens	Not enough
Stephen	No good here	Excellent	Always cancelled	I live like a tramp
Rachel	Makes me angry	Great	Poor	No comment

Figure 8.5   Data presentation by matrix

CONTENT ANALYSIS

Of course, what the above matrix (Figure 8.5) fails to do is give quantitative, numerical overviews of what the social workers thought. A typical method of doing this is with content analysis. At its most basic, we can simply do a frequency analysis of certain words – such as how many times did the team leader say 'procedure', how often did the social work say 'workload', and so on? But this is unlikely to be very revealing in most circumstances. More common is to ascribe codes to responses to enable quantitative analysis. For example, if we ask the question '*Why did you want to become a social worker?*' we might get a range of responses, but some of them may be saying more or less the same thing and we can therefore code them as the same. Let's look at six responses to the question '*Why did you want to become a social worker?*':

A. I wanted to help people.
B. To improve the lives of the vulnerable.
C. To earn a living.
D. Because of the salary.
E. It seemed like a good career move.
F. To help others.

We could argue that A, B and F are similar and so could be coded as, say 1 (perhaps giving it the name 'Helpers'). Similarly, C, D and E are alike and could be coded as

2 ('Earners'). This enables us to make simple frequency counts and perhaps percentages where appropriate. However, this is also a subjective process which we must keep under review – do our codes make sense? Are they comprehensive and do they discriminate sufficiently between responses (Hall & Hall, 1996)? In relation to the last of these questions we could look again at the six responses above and ask ourselves: is B really the same as A and F because it seems more specific? Doesn't E portray a sense of disillusion whilst C suggests ready cash was a motivator and the 'salary' of D conveys something more akin to the notion of career? We need to be careful with content analysis as its subjectivity can sometimes be hidden behind its numerical basis.

Statistics and generalisability

When we are broadly involved in this kind of frequency counting analysis of quantitative data we must remember to be modest about the claims we are making for our data, especially with regard to its 'generalisability'. Just because we interview six social work students and they all agree on a particular topic does not mean that all social work students think the same: it only means that those we interviewed thought this way, nothing more and nothing less. The statistics we derive from frequency counting are only *descriptive*. For the small-scale practitioner researcher using this book, it is unlikely that the scale of the research will be sufficient to afford us the opportunity of engaging with rigorous statistical methods of analysing quantitative data which rely on much bigger numbers of people. *Inferential* statistics and the laws of probability can work with representative sampling techniques to allow reasonable generalisations to be made from the data. There are also certain software packages, especially the Statistical Package for Social Sciences (commonly known as SPSS)[4], which can help practitioner researchers manage this task. Our advice is to seek appropriate support right at the very beginning of your research from a statistician if your work is likely to employ these types of approaches to analysis.

NARRATIVE ANALYSIS: CONTENT AND STRUCTURE

We looked closely, in an earlier chapter, at the issue of narrative in research, demonstrating the emphasis such an approach places upon the real stories of real people. A definition of narrative analysis is offered below:

> An approach to the elicitation and analysis of data that is sensitive to the sense of temporal sequence that people, as tellers of stories about their lives or events around them, detect in their lives and surrounding episodes and inject into their accounts. (Bryman, 2004: 541)

This definition emphasises the temporal element but still leaves us with the crucial question as practitioner researchers, committed to allowing a narrator's perspective to be revealed, of how do we stay true to the meaning intended? How do we tell

---

[4]SPSS is also known as Predicative Analysis Software (PASW).

someone else's story as they wished it to be told? The literature in this area suggests a number of ways of going about this, the first of which proposes a simple focus on *content* where the researcher focuses on the content of the single, whole narrative – often the person's life story (Elliott, 2005). The practitioner researcher sets out to present the content of the narrative. This approach is evidenced in a range of research that we have already considered (Bone, 2006; Hunt & Winegarten, 1983; Whyte, 1955) which, although focusing on individuals, is also able to locate them in the context of the community and society. Just because the practitioner researcher's focus is on the narrative, it doesn't mean that the way we might present it should be without wider context. Shaw (1966), for example, in his look at a 'delinquent boy's story', argued that he presented the views of the boy in question as well as the social and cultural situation in which he played a part. This could be obtained from the boy as well as from other secondary data sources.

For narrative content analysis, in addition to looking at each individual story and giving it a broader context, we can also look at a number of stories (perhaps, for example, of a group of children who have been looked after). We can look at the 'common elements in the(ir) trajectories' (Elliott, 2005: 40). With this method we can analyse and present the data as a form of collective story with common features and make connections between the individual experiences and the structural elements that have influenced them. In our example, we might focus on particular aspects of the stories that are shared – such as the entry into care, friendships and relationships with staff – and see how different narratives compare. We can then place these comparisons into the broader context of the delivery of social care and provision for looked after children, perhaps illustrating these broader points with comments from the children given to us, as practitioner researchers, in the context of their narrative.

Another approach to the analysis of narrative is to include a focus on the structure. In this approach, a researcher will not just look at 'what' is said, but will also be interested in 'how' it is said and how the person telling the narrative shapes, constructs and structures their story, including their use of language. In this fashion, Labov and Waletzky [1967/1997] believed, narratives will have a set form that can be used to analyse and discover patterns. However, there is a danger that this type of approach will lose some of the symbolic meaning offered and thus can be viewed as a rather reductionist technique that quantifies and measures complex nuanced accounts (Riesmann and Quinney, 2005) and is therefore probably unsuitable for the purposes of practitioner research. David and Sutton (2010) summarised an alternative approach to narrative analysis from that of Riessman (1993) with her three qualitative areas for analysis: the life story told, the critical events described, and the poetry revealed in the telling. However, Riessman argued that the crucial phase lay with a careful interpretation of the gathered data:

> ... they do not speak for themselves. Narrative excerpts require interpretation, expansion, and analysis – 'unpacking' to uncover and interpret the inevitable ambiguities contained in any form of language. (2001: 81)

Chase (2008) offered helpful insights into how we might deal with some of the particular problems that may emerge when looking at the data that can be generated with a narrative approach.

- Think through the differences that are inherent to being an interviewer who asks questions to being a person who has a story to tell.
- Don't focus too closely on narrative themes such as work, disability, services, family – look at connections among the stories.
- What voice will you (the researcher) adopt? Will it be an 'authoritative' voice that presents a story and then comments on it? Or a 'supportive' voice where you step back and let the story take the lead? Or an 'interactive' voice where you analyse both the narrator's voice and your own?

Although the literature in this area can be complex and contested, the central themes are straightforward. We can aim to retell the story, focus on its content, or analyse its structural form. We can also consider the patterns and themes that emerge and, for example, the temporal organisation of the narrative (what happened when within the narrative).

THEMATIC ANALYSIS

Without doubt the most important method of data analysis for the majority of typical social work and social care-based research projects is likely to be thematic analysis. For this reason we will dwell on this subject in some detail. It is surprising that relatively little has been written about the process of thematic analysis given its central place in qualitative analysis:

> It is the first qualitative method of analysis that researchers should learn, as it provides core skills that will be useful for conducting many other forms of qualitative analysis. (Braun & Clarke, 2006: 78)

What a review of the literature in this area will find is that there is relatively broad agreement about the process of getting to grips with thematic analysis. For the purposes of this book we have constructed a model (see Figure 8.6) that draws on various writers, including Braun and Clarke (2006) and presents a clear sequence of events:

1 *Knowing* (know your data)   This will usually involve transcribing your data and reading these through more than once. The sheer volume of material that can be generated by a small number of interviews will quickly become apparent. This potentially laborious dimension must not be skimped on. The key task is to 'know' your data and become very familiar with who said what in your interviews.

2 *Coding* (code and memo your data)   When you have become familiar with your data you must begin the process of analysis. It is unfortunate that 'coding' is a word that is used in slightly different ways in research methodology. Its meaning in the general quantitative area is the ascribing of numerical codes to groupings of data (e.g. male is 1, female is 2). This is not what your job should be here. Coding in the general qualitative area refers to the process of categorising your data, engaging with what these might mean and beginning the process of organising these data into more meaningful, inter-connected pieces. If the themes are the key divisions in your data, these themes will emerge from your coding of the data. This builds on a process of 'memoing' which can simply be a commentary or annotation of the data: your thoughts on what was being said, hunches or sparks of

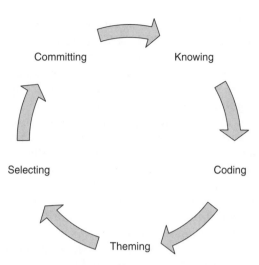

Figure 8.6   A route map for thematic analysis

imagination and thought that come to you, helping you draw together findings from different sources (Wisker, 2001). We will look at an example of this later.

3   *Theming* (generating themes from your data)   In many ways this is an extension of your coding process as it looks to the generation of broader themes that are emerging from your data analysis – over-arching themes that will connect all aspects of the data and make sense of it. It usually entails the drawing together of the codes you have created into groups (themes) which will then become your substantive structure for data analysis. For example, a small-scale, focus group-based piece of research has looked at nurse and social worker practice educators in multi-disciplinary settings. It has found evidence to suggest that two broad groups could be identified that crossed the professional divide: a group who taught their students more about how to maintain professional boundaries and were worried about losing their distinctive role, and another group who taught their students more about working with other professions in a more blurred but joined-up way. The authors' overarching thematic analysis reduced these groups down to doves and hawks (Dutton & Worsley, 2008).

4   *Selecting* (choosing which pieces of data best illustrate your themes)   Having reviewed the themes you have selected you will now face the task of illustrating the themes you have chosen. As a researcher you need to choose wisely and honestly. Some quotes from respondents will typify the general themes that many within the group will have given in their interviews. Others, whilst perhaps not typical, will nevertheless be either representative of a significant or interesting sub set or be simply interesting in their own right. As Holliday says 'selected fragments contain the elements that have been recognized during analysis which generate the thematic organisation' (2007: 106).

5   *Committing* (writing this down in the research report)   Whilst the process of analysing data is ongoing, the memos, codes and themes that emerge have, at some point, to be decided upon and committed to paper, either in the research report or in the dissertation. 'Letting go' of data can be surprisingly hard to do in our experience. The richness of qualitative data and the sheer volume of secondary data are such that these may afford endless opportunities for connection. But you must not allow the process to continue indefinitely and so must prepare and adhere to clear time boundaries on how long you can let this process go on for.

Let's walk through the following example taken from a piece of research conducted with probation officers which broadly looked at their views on the status of their profession (Worsley, 2004). The pressures of space here mean that we can only present a few individual responses to a single question. Clearly, when looking at the transcribed data from several interviews these would cover many more pages and so this activity should therefore be viewed as an introduction to some of the skills and possibilities that thematic analysis can offer. The question posed was in relation to National Standards – government requirements outlining the prescribed levels of contact between offenders and their probation officer – although these also apply to youth justice workers. At the time of the data collection this was quite an issue for the service as a whole. Broadly speaking, some felt the National Standards to be a good thing, providing a clear, no-nonsense framework for contact, and some saw them as a bureaucratic expression of managerialist changes in the service, whilst others saw them more as a challenge to professional autonomy. Here's what five officers said. We have added boxed memos with possible codes (reduced to single words) in capitals. Read through the extracts from the interviews and then the memos and codes. Don't forget, these are (basic) transcriptions, so will be presented as faithfully as possible to the way these were spoken in the interview.

How do National Standards affect the way in which you work?

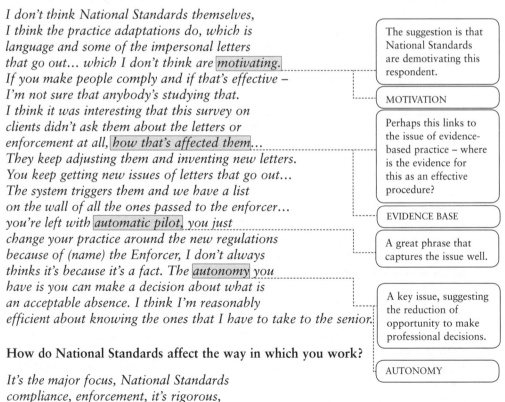

I don't think National Standards themselves,
I think the practice adaptations do, which is
language and some of the impersonal letters
that go out... which I don't think are motivating.
If you make people comply and if that's effective –
I'm not sure that anybody's studying that.
I think it was interesting that this survey on
clients didn't ask them about the letters or
enforcement at all, how that's affected them...
They keep adjusting them and inventing new letters.
You keep getting new issues of letters that go out...
The system triggers them and we have a list
on the wall of all the ones passed to the enforcer...
you're left with automatic pilot, *you just*
change your practice around the new regulations
because of (name) the Enforcer, I don't always
thinks it's because it's a fact. The autonomy *you*
have is you can make a decision about what is
an acceptable absence. I think I'm reasonably
efficient about knowing the ones that I have to take to the senior.

The suggestion is that National Standards are demotivating this respondent.

MOTIVATION

Perhaps this links to the issue of evidence-based practice – where is the evidence for this as an effective procedure?

EVIDENCE BASE

A great phrase that captures the issue well.

A key issue, suggesting the reduction of opportunity to make professional decisions.

AUTONOMY

How do National Standards affect the way in which you work?

It's the major focus, National Standards
compliance, enforcement, it's rigorous,
it's got to be. It's about the view of the

general public and the Home Office,
if you don't deliver on that agenda,
you're not going to exist in the future ...
there are other agencies just waiting
there that can do some of the things that
the probation service ... I think it's survival,
but I also link it to good practice.
National Standards has meant that we
deliver a better service *but we are also*
more effective, you can't get them to
come to these programmes without enforcement
and practice is just all centred around it *and*
increasingly for managers, that's the
bread and butter of the job ... we get
regular read outs on caseloads, officers feel
its like Big Brother constantly *and it is I can't*
get away from that, but I see it positively as
well and its about improving practice really.
Gone are the days when you'd have somebody
on probation and you'd decide oh this person
really isn't a problem and you'd see them
once a month from the offing. That used to
happen quite a lot when I started. It's good
that it's gone and we are much more into
assessment, needs and risk and national
standards comes in there.
So the autonomy has gone, there are still
rooms for creativity in terms of how you
deliver your work, but that's increasingly
prescribed *but I think it had to go because*
we were just... I think we were benevolent
aunties and uncles really, *we weren't doing*
much good for anybody ... we had to change.
I think some people would still like to be a
benevolent aunty and uncle, we can't we've
got to focus on risk and reducing that risk
and at times, to do that you have to be really firm.

Sees this matter tied to the future of the profession and the organisation.
THE FUTURE
It becomes an issue of quality.
QUALITY
Are National Standards at the heart of this?
Managers are aware of the bureaucratic burden as perceived by Officers.
Suggests a context for National Standards with risk and assessment.
CONTEXT
A definite statement with little room for creativity.
The past being described.
THE PAST

How do National Standards affect the way in which you work?

I think if you've got a high caseload and you
know that's one of the things that needs doing,
it's easy to fall into 'doing'. In some respects,
what I have tried to do is use National Standards
constructively *and look at rights and responsibilities.*
In this service, you have a right to expect ... –
it's setting those boundaries and working within them.
I think you can be creative within them,

Losing the space for reflection.
WORKLOAD
Being positive.

but it takes effort. It takes effort and it takes thought,
it means that you have to think very carefully
about how you communicate enforcement to clients.
Thinking very carefully about how you
inform clients about things like risk assessments
and how you positively frame that so it's
something constructive for them
as well as something accountable to the service ...

> Development of new skills? The pressures of workload inhibiting creativity and promoting 'doing'.

> WORKLOAD

How do National Standards affect the way in which you work?

Horrendous. I was working there when
National Standards were getting
absolutely ridiculous in my view –
impossible to meet and I felt that
I was so glad that I left when I did.
I *did not feel like a probation officer,*
I felt that I was an admin officer.
I came into work and sat at that desk –
eight forms to complete to do a PSR, to me that is outrageous.
It took me longer to write them friggin' forms
than it did to write the report! I was going to work
and all I was doing was moving papers and writing –
have I ticked the box? Oh God that needs a review,
oh I need to do a risk assessment, oh, that's due.
And that was all that I was doing. There was no *quality.*
When clients used to turn up I was irritated,
I thought, oh I'm not going to get the paperwork done.
And all they were interested in was
whether your files were bang up to date...
it really riles me... there was an officer
who was disciplined because he hadn't
breached[5] a client two weeks ago and he'd
gone out and committed a serious offence and
because he hadn't done all the paperwork, he was disciplined.

> The impossibility of meeting National Standards – an interesting thought.

> Clearly felt very strongly around this area and possibly linked to decision to leave the service.

> A great expression: how should a probation officer feel?

> A clear suggestion that bureaucracy is swamping the role, in this person's view.

> BUREAUCRACY

> The other side of the quality issue mentioned above.

> QUALITY

How do National Standards affect the way in which you work?

To some extent I *have been slightly out on a*
limb about this because I have always
believed that if the court makes an order
and ask the Probation Service to supervise
it then that's what should be done and that
within that there should be constraints about

> Suggests the respondent is/believes himself to be isolated in this perspective.

> Do probation officers not do this? Or do they fudge the issue in some way?

---

[5]'breached' is a term that normally relates to an offender being returned to court for a failure to abide by the conditions of their probation order. The conditions have therefore been 'breached'.

whether someone is coming in making
contact with the service or not. I suppose
there could be issues about whether two
failures warrants breach or not or whether
there's another system of doing it. But the
principle behind it, that there is a requirement to be supervised,
I can't disagree with.

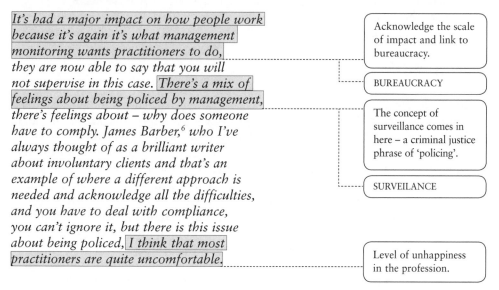

It's had a major impact on how people work
because it's again it's what management
monitoring wants practitioners to do,
they are now able to say that you will
not supervise in this case. There's a mix of
feelings about being policed by management,
there's feelings about – why does someone
have to comply. James Barber,[6] who I've
always thought of as a brilliant writer
about involuntary clients and that's an
example of where a different approach is
needed and acknowledge all the difficulties,
and you have to deal with compliance,
you can't ignore it, but there is this issue
about being policed, I think that most
practitioners are quite uncomfortable.

Acknowledge the scale of impact and link to bureaucracy.

BUREAUCRACY

The concept of surveillance comes in here – a criminal justice phrase of 'policing'.

SURVEILANCE

Level of unhappiness in the profession.

The themes of autonomy, workload and bureaucracy, one could argue, seem to characterise significant messages in the data. But clearly, as we can see, the processes of memoing, coding, theming and selecting are all subjective and for valid reasons you might disagree with these suggestions. We must not pretend that we are engaged in anything other than a subjective process. Holliday emphasises particular aspects of data analysis, arguing that the researcher:

> … must submit herself to emerging patterns of data and be free to engage strategically and creatively with the complexities of realities that go beyond her initial design. (2007: 93)

Yet within that process of analysis we can operate honestly and transparently with our data and ensure we represent the respondents openly. Here we can begin to see some of the responsibility we must take on as practitioner researchers. We must be grateful to our respondents for their interview data, but the power we can wield over how we choose to represent them is enormous and, of course, if those who are interviewed are also vulnerable then the *ethics* of our analysis are every bit as important as the ethics of our methods and general approach.

---

[6]Barber (1991) *Beyond Casework*. This book tried to offer practical steps to achieving change with clients who had no choice but to attend for appointments with their social worker/probation officer.

Activity

Take another look at the data outlined above. What memos, codes and themes might you have derived from it?

- Select three themes that seem significant to you.
- Select no more than five key quotes that either a) relate to your themes or b) are in some other way relevant.

CONCLUSION

Analysing data can seem a difficult task when first approached – rather like climbing too high a mountain. Hopefully this chapter will have helped you arrive at a good initial understanding of the things that can be done with the data you gather. Whether this is through forms of frequency counting, basic statistical analysis, a narrative and thematic analysis of qualitative data or a combination of these approaches, it is vital that as a researcher you begin to consider your approach to data analysis from the outset. Whilst we feel we have offered good advice about where to begin your analysis, our best would be to simply engage with a research project and experience the reality of data collection and analysis, for it is probably only through this process that you can arrive at an understanding of the techniques of analysis. It may also help to reflect, as you pursue your research project, that 'all research strives to reduce reality to a tellable story' – albeit that the more we look at things the more complicated they tend to get (Cronbach et al., 1980: 184).

Key points

- Always think about analysis at the beginning and throughout your research.
- Never stint on time as analysis takes time.
- Give consideration to how you can present your data.
- Think carefully about how you are going to represent the voices of those who have given you the data.
- Be honest and transparent in your approach.

Further Reading

Hall, D. & Hall, I. (1996) *Practical Social Research: Project Work In The Community.* Basingstoke: Macmillan.

Holliday, A. (2007) *Doing and Writing Qualitative Research* (2nd edn). London: SAGE.

Lofland, J. & Lofland, L. (1994) *Analyzing Qualitative Data: A Guide to Qualitative Observation and Analysis* (3rd edn). London: Wadsworth.

Mason, J. (2002) *Qualitative Researching.* London: SAGE.

Silverman, D. (1998) *Qualitative Research: Theory, Method and Practice.* London: SAGE.

Silverman, D. (2006) *Interpreting Qualitative Data: Methods for Analysing Talk and Text* (3rd edn). London: SAGE.

DEVELOPING A RESEARCH PROPOSAL AND WRITING A RESEARCH REPORT

OVERVIEW

This chapter will explore the process of both planning a research project and writing a research report. These initial and final stages of the research process are then brought together to demonstrate the correlation between these two activities. Planning a research project is broken down into eight stages that can lead to a robust and systematic research proposal. Figure 9.1 takes us through the different stages of a research process. Consideration of these stages will show how it is possible to advance from an initial research idea through to gaining a greater understanding of the topic in the context of relevant literature, research and policy, and the assessment of the kind of data that will be required to advance understanding on the subject. Deciding on the nature of the data that should be gathered leads to a consideration of the most appropriate methods for the task and how the gathered data will be analysed to ensure the findings can be collated into a meaningful report that has the potential to impact on and influence social work for the better.

The second part of this chapter will discuss writing a research report with the emphasis placed on this report as a tool for communicating findings to an identified audience. Inevitably this chapter can only cover some of the choices open to you as a researcher both in planning and writing up your research and has therefore focused on your likely needs as a social work student or practitioner.

National Occupational Standards for Social Work

There are numerous opportunities to link the Standards in with proposal and report writing. Element 1.3 asks that one looks at a range of information to plan initial involvement. Element 5.3 notes the need to apply and justify models of social work to achieve change. Element 11.1 concerns the preparation of reports and documents. Element 14.3 focuses on the evaluation of the effectiveness of practice. Finally, Element 15.3 centres on the practitioner's contribution to the monitoring of the quality of services provided.

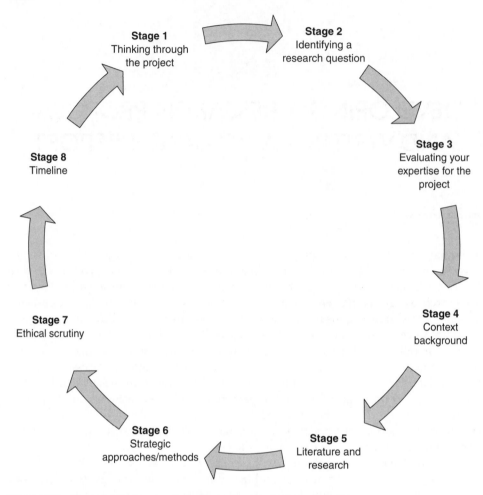

Figure 9.1 The eight stages of a research plan and proposal

STAGE 1 – THINKING THROUGH THE WHOLE PROJECT FROM BEGINNING TO END

Before you reach the point where you need to formulate a research plan you will need to have identified a topic for investigation and decided whether this is a feasible subject for a research project. This entails identifying a topic that you could broadly visualise investigating from the beginning through to the completion of a research report. Reardon (2006) describes this process as a research life cycle. To do this you need to consider the amount of time you can dedicate to the task, the resources you have available to you, and whether it is a topic that can be narrowed down to a manageable and focused question.

Thinking through the research process from beginning to end is similar to the planning involved when inviting friends round for a meal. If your overall purpose is to have a convivial, relaxed evening you will need to plan meticulously to achieve this objective. This involves more than just a matter of sending out invitations. You will need to decide what you would like cook. Which ingredients are required and will they all be available in the supermarket? Will your recipe meet the dietary requirements of your guests? Will you have the time, equipment, skills, and finances to ensure your meal is successful? Will everyone know how to reach your place and, when they do, will they get along together? As with the planning that goes into significant events in everyday life, when conducting research you need to think though the process carefully. This way you will ensure a focused, rigorous and ethically sound investigation. This is not to say that all well planned projects are plain sailing: on the contrary, there will always be unexpected circumstances and obstacles, but these may prove insurmountable if the groundwork of planning has failed to take place.

Nobody engages in this process without bringing their unique professional repertoire and preferred theoretical perspectives to it. Awareness and transparency in relation to influences and sources of knowledge and any resulting bias are all important in ensuring the validity of research. The most important thing is that the conceptual approach and methods chosen fit the purpose of the investigation and not only a researcher's conscious or unconscious preferences. For instance, a personal phobia of working with statistics should not divert a researcher's choice of methods away from quantitative scientific methods if the type of data sought are within a large-scale enquiry into the attitudes of residents in a specified geographical area to the local services offered. The greater our understanding of the range, choice and appropriateness of the approaches and methods available is, the better integrated and credible our study will be.

Preparing and writing a research proposal offers one of the most important opportunities for testing out whether your research question can translate into a feasible and desirable project and provides you with a map for doing your research (McNiff & Whitehead, 2009). This process provides the means to explain to others clearly and concisely what it is you intend to do, how you intend to do it, and what it is you hope to discover (Reardon, 2006). For students a research proposal will often be an assessed piece of work in itself, which may or may not provide the basis for a future research project. For practitioners a proposal will provide an opportunity to explain ideas to interested parties, colleagues, managers, institutions and/or funding bodies, as well as ethics committees. In addition, it will usually be a determining factor in gaining support for a project. Support can take the form of resources, supervision, and access to participants, secondary data and/or sponsorship.

Supervision

Consulting with your supervisor should begin at this planning stage of your research and continue through your writing-up of the research report. If you are doing research as part of an undergraduate or postgraduate degree then you will invariably be allocated a supervisor. Each academic institution is likely to have its own practices and guidelines for this important relationship (i.e. the number of contact hours and expectations of both the student and supervisor). To some extent the onus will lie with the student to check out these guidelines and ensure that they use these arrangements to the best effect. Bryman urges supervisees to 'use your supervisor to the fullest extent that you are allowed and follow the pointers you are given by him or her' (2004: 524).

If you are not a student then we would strongly advise that you engage a supervisor who should be someone with both the knowledge and experience of the research process and preferably also have some knowledge of the research subject. An obvious supply source will be found in interested academics, or someone in your practice setting who has research experience. Alternatively you could engage a steering group of interested individuals who can bring their differing skills and perspectives to the supervisory relationship. Wherever the supervision comes from it is always helpful to complete a learning contract to give clarity to the arrangements and expectations (Hall & Hall, 2004; Wisker, 2005).

STAGE 2 – IDENTIFYING A RESEARCH QUESTION

Before you begin to write-up your research proposal you will need to have identified a question for investigation which can become the basis for developing a workable research strategy or plan. This question or statement needs to consist of few sentences that sum up the central thrust of your project and provide a succinct and precise summary of what the focus of the investigation will be (Reardon, 2006). Inevitably some areas of interest are going to be easier to pursue than others and some will lend themselves better to the rigours required in doing research (Reardon, 2006). A test of this is whether your research question can be placed in the context of relevant literature, research and policy. If this is a problematic process then your project might also be problematic as you may not be able to place it in a sound contextual background or relate your findings to credible sources for their verification or comparison. When you arrive at preparing a proposal you will only need a working title for your project. This may be refined through the process and by the final report stage.

Your research should be underpinned by social work values and seek to empower service users and carers. While this may coincide with your personal interests, you will need to make transparent how your project will seek to make a difference for the better and add to the profession's knowledge base. Your research question or statement might be framed as a hypothesis where you are seeking to test out an idea, or as a hunch or observation against a variable, or it might seek to evaluate, measure or explore a specific subject (Bell, 2001; Hall & Hall, 2004; Kumar, 1999).

STAGE 3 – EVALUATING YOUR EXPERTISE FOR THE PROJECT

You will need to examine whether you have the skills and expertise to do justice to the investigation. Inevitably you will learn this while doing your research, but you need to be confident beforehand that you have a sufficient foundational knowledge of the research methods and the topic itself, as well as the ability and opportunity to learn while engaged in the research process. Only if you can match up to these requirements will you do credit to the subject as well as yourself. It is important to be realistic about this if you are to avoid raising expectations from participants, sponsors and partners that will remain unmet. Not all credible knowledge has to come from research and if you do not have the required skills you might consider other ways of facilitating insight and a new perspective. SCIE acknowledges that relevant knowledge can also come from the views of service users and practitioners and these may be presented using diverse means of communication such as videos, commentaries and discussion groups (SCIE, 2007).

Basic skills required to do research

1 The ability to recognise and investigate problems.
2 The ability to undertake original and critical thinking.
3 A knowledge of recent advances within one's field and related areas.
4 An understanding of relevant research methodologies and techniques and their application within one's project.
5 The ability to analyse critically and evaluate one's findings and those of others.
6 The ability to summarise, document, report and reflect on progress. (Joint Research Councils' skills training requirements)

STAGE 4 – SITUATING YOUR PROJECT IN A CONTEXTUAL BACKGROUND

Social work takes place in a fast-changing social and demographic context and this makes continuous demands on the social work community to update its knowledge base and engage in reflexive enquiry. The demand for services across the welfare sector is under a constant pressure, at the same time as being increasingly subject to a variety of marketing processes that inhibit access to services for those least educated and able bodied (Taylor-Gooby, 2008). There are greater numbers of older people, single people, and people living alone, more lone parents and an ever-growing number of carers (see *Social Trends* 39 (2009) at www.statistics.gov.uk/statbase).

The day-to-day experiences of services users and carers and the working lives of practitioners are all in a state of continuous transformation. In this changing world there are major challenges to service provision emerging within a welfare system that is struggling to adjust to the trends (Taylor-Gooby, 2008) and the social work community also has to keep pace with these trends. Engaging in our own research provides a helpful way of feeding back information to this community to enable considered change and review. It is impossible to conceive of any social work research that would not, in some way, be connected to this contextual background.

Activity

Begin to think through the contextual background to your project and identify:

- local, organisational or national policies;
- community issues;
- organisational issues;
- professional issues;
- personal issues.

How has this affected your understanding of your project?

STAGE 5 – SITUATING YOUR PROJECT IN RELEVANT LITERATURE AND RESEARCH

To begin to get to grips with your project you'll need to review relevant literature relating to the topic (for more in-depth guidance see the chapter on analysing data). This will help to bring clarity and focus to your research question and broaden your knowledge base of the research topic. Literature that is relevant to your study may deal with universal trends or ones specific to a local circumstance. There may be a general consensus on the subject or widely disparate views and accounts. Through reviewing the most pertinent literature you will be able to develop an overview of what is currently being said about the subject and how your investigation might add to this knowledge. You may be filling a gap, adding a new perspective, or endorsing existing ideas.

To decide whether your chosen sources have credibility and can bring relevant knowledge and understanding to the subject it is important to evaluate their worth. Is a source written from a particular perspective that may make it biased or one-sided? This involves thinking about why the document was written and by whom. Who commissioned/sponsored/ proposed the research and what are the implications of this in relation to the methods used and findings shown?

Here you will need to draw on the experiences of others who have undertaken similar research before you. In other words, it is very helpful to evaluate methodological approaches that have been tried and tested. Familiarising yourself with some of the numerous research methods texts available and a variety of research methods used in peer reviewed articles on completed research will help you to make the right choices in the research process.

Your literature review can also form the basis for interpreting your findings (Bryman, 2004). Your data may be confirmed by the literature, challenge previous understandings or deepen understanding of existing knowledge.

STAGE 6 – CHOOSING THE MOST APPROPRIATE STRATEGIC APPROACHES AND METHODS

The most appropriate strategy for your research will depend on the type of data you wish to gather. If you are looking for measurable quantifiable data you are approaching aspects of reality that are existing independent of interpretation and are just out there waiting to be measured or quantified. This approach has developed from scientific enquiry and is associated with quantitative research methods. On the other hand, if you are looking for data that are contingent and open to interpretation and concerned with meaning more than facts then you will have to adopt an approach that is more interpretive and likely to be associated with qualitative methods (Denscombe, 1998).

As has been explored earlier, qualitative methods lend themselves to small-scale projects where the interpreted meaning provides the data (Denscombe, 1998) – the type of projects that students and practitioners might have the inclination and resources to engage in. This type of project requires reflexivity on the part of the researcher where they need to be very self aware and take into account their own values and biases and the impact of these on the information gathered. Typical qualitative methods are unstructured or semi-structured interviews, focus groups and ethnographic participatory approaches such as observation, videoing, photography, community picnics, mural painting and community theatre.

Quantitative approaches lend themselves to larger-scale studies. This is where the researcher is often forced by the scale of the study to adopt an independent and distant approach to gathering and analysing the data. This type of data lends itself to quantification into numbers (Denscombe, 1998) – the type of investigation recognised as credible by the scientific community. Typical quantitative methods are surveys, questionnaires, and structured interviews.

A fundamental choice here will be deciding which methods will be most appropriate to your project and whether you intend to use more than one method to gather data. Using a variety of methods (such as in 'triangulation' – checking out your findings from three different perspectives that could relate to methods chosen, and/or participants and/or analysis of findings) the data will be open to greater scrutiny which will lend it greater credibility (Flick, 2007). The type of triangulation you adopt will depend on the underlying questions/problems you have identified.

As there is a strong connection between the types of data you wish to gather and the strategic approach and methods you choose, it is important to provide a rationale for these choices to make them explicit to yourself or to those you wish to convince of the merit of the project. It is also important to think through the methods you are going to use as this will not only determine the kind of data you gather but also how you will analyse those data. This type of planning can overcome later practical problems. For instance, if you are planning to process your data through a computer program like SPSS then your questionnaire questions should be characterised by closed questions where the answers can be listed, ranked, categorised or scaled, and coded at the outset. Also, this would be an inappropriate approach with a very small-scale study as SPSS is designed for a minimum of 30 responses. Open questions leading to qualitative responses with a verbal emphasis will be difficult to process using this type of software. Also, when planning your methods, you will have to consider the resource and skills implications. For instance, if you are running a focus group you may require an assistant to take notes or observe the session or to assist you if you lack experience in facilitating groups.

STAGE 7 – ETHICALLY SCRUTINISING ALL ASPECTS OF THE RESEARCH PROCESS

Even at the planning stage, as with every other stage of the research process, an ethical review is required. This involves thinking about the implications of the investigation for participants, partners, practitioners, and policy makers. An ethical review also involves a consideration of the contribution the investigation hopes to make to existing knowledge and its potential for facilitating change for the better. (This is discussed more fully in the ethics chapter where attention is paid to the JUCSWEC codes of ethics.)

The Association for Research in the Voluntary and Community Sector (2001) has summarised much of the broad concerns identified earlier under the four headings that follow:

- *Equal opportunities* – Implicit in equal opportunities is a recognition of difference both in terms of sexuality, race, disability and class and in relation to need and opportunities in life. A good research strategy should aim to be as inclusive as possible. This involves thinking about whether the approach to and methods for collecting data are inclusive and appropriate enough for the various participants involved throughout the research process. For example, if you are trying to gather data concerning the views of young children about a particular service and decide to interview them, this might not only be intimidating but also might elicit poor data and fail to give them a credible voice in the project.
- *Participation and consent* – This involves making sure that everyone involved in whatever way is fully aware that they are participating in a project. This becomes very pertinent with observational methods when the researcher is not always clear at the outset which situation and which person might elicit significant data.
- *Confidentiality* – This relates to whether participants have given their informed consent not only as regards participating in the study but also as regards consenting to how the information relating to them may be used in the future. To be transparent about this with participants the researcher must decide at the outset how information will be made available on an ongoing basis and how it will be used in the future.
- *Data protection* – The Data Protection Act 1998 lays down expectations of how data should be obtained, secured and disposed of. Your research should comply with this. For instance, this applies to how your data are to be stored and how these will be disposed of in the future.

Other considerations

In addition, as a practitioner researcher you will want your research to make a difference to some aspect of social work and add in some way to existing knowledge. To this end you will need to start thinking through the potential implications of your investigation and the gaps it might seek to fill. Before you do this you will need to recognise how the key values associated with different research approaches and methods might impact in various different ways on your investigation.

Associated with this is a consideration of how you plan to disseminate your findings. Research reports that gather dust on office shelves or on dissertation racks in university libraries are not likely to effect change for the better. It is good practice for all participants in a project to receive feedback about findings. This may take the form of an executive summary or the whole report, but there are also more creative ways of feeding back. You might run a forum or day conference or perhaps a focus group. Where appropriate there will also be a need to filter findings through to the larger social work community. Again this could be via a poster presentation, a workshop, a paper at a conference, or writing up the findings for a journal article.

STAGE 8 – PRODUCING A TIMELINE OF THE PROJECT

At each stage of the research process it will be helpful to identify the length of time you estimate each activity will take and whereabouts on your calendar you expect each activity to occur. There will usually be a rhythm to the research process that can be broken down into quadrants of time. This rhythm falls into four phases: planning the research and preparing a research proposal (*planning*), carrying out the research or revising it in the light of experience (*fieldwork*), analysing the results (*analysis*), and finally writing the report in a clear and accessible style (*report*) (Hall & Hall, 2004). These phases relate to Reardon's (2006) four stages in the research life cycle. Time management is a very important element in this process, especially if your research is a relatively small part of your overall roles and responsibilities.

Following a strict timeline (see Table 9.1) can also be a helpful way of tackling aspects of the research process that you might prefer to delay or are ambivalent about. Doing social work research can sometimes be politically sensitive, or may involve what might appear to be individuals or groups who are hostile to the investigation, or might demand that you engage in an activity in which you lack confidence and experience. In these circumstances difficult tasks can easily be delayed and become overwhelming if not sequentially mapped out.

Table 9.1 Example of a research timeline

Stages of the research	Starting date	Completion date
Planning the research	Early October	Late October
Carrying out the research	November	January
Analysing	February	March
Writing report	Late March	Late April

THE CORRELATION BETWEEN A RESEARCH PROPOSAL AND THE FINAL REPORT

There will be a direct correlation between your research proposal and the final report because the structure of the proposal offers a broad template for developing the structure of that report (Reardon, 2006). A report is a very specific way of communicating research findings to an identified audience and as such it should be written in a style that is appropriate to that audience and be as straightforward, readable and accessible as possible. It is also a way of transposing a private road of discovery into the public domain (McNiff & Whitehead, 2009). Good reports should enable a reader to understand something they did not know before, in a way that is persuasive and potentially influences future decision making and action.

Key to producing an effective report is to plan and prepare a well-structured, logical framework for your information. The findings will need to be presented in a succinct fashion that is quickly digestible for the reader. This is not only dependent on your use of language but also on your choice of visual materials, diagrams and the influence of design. A skilled use of these aids will enhance your communication of your findings and increase the potential of the report to persuade the reader (Hall & Hall, 2004).

Williams (1994) identified a number of key principles involved in thinking about the overall design of a research report. By looking through reports yourself you will have noticed the importance of a contrast between different aspects of the reports such as headings and the body text or differing data, etc. This is usually achieved by adopting different fonts and sizes so that a reader can immediately identify the difference between various aspects. It is important when using contrast that there is a consistency in usage and that it enhances understanding rather than acting as an unnecessary diversion. For example, such good use of contrast would usually be evident between the normal text, quotations, paragraph headings and chapter headings.

Williams (1994) also identified the use of repetition so that each page of the report has a similar character, look, shape and texture and is identifiable as a part of the overall design. He also drew attention to the use of alignment. This entails ensuring that every page and section of the report has some kind of a visual connection. Alignment relates to margins, paragraph spacing, tables, graphs, quotations and photographs. These features should not be placed randomly but follow an identified system. Finally, Williams highlighted a use of proximity to ensure there is a distinction between items that are similar to each other and those that are not. This entails deciding what should go in each chapter or section and in the subheadings within these. It can be confusing to a reader if, for example, the contextual background is mixed in with items that relate to the research findings or if the introduction pre-empts some of the report's recommendations.

Another very important feature of reports is the use of language. This should be appropriate to the audience for whom the report is written. It is no good including terms or jargon that will not be understood by this target audience. This aspect also relates to how various social groups, communities and individuals are described. This needs to be sensitive to the language participants use about themselves and should always avoid stereotyping, judging or labelling (Hall & Hall, 2004).

Another important consideration is deciding the audibility and presence of the researcher in the report. This relates to deciding whether the researcher's voice will be present in the text, explaining the part they played and the impact of this on the findings, and will depend on the strategic approach that has been adopted. For example, if the report contains predominantly quantitative findings it might be expected that 'the researcher is typically absent from the report as the passive voice is used' (Hall & Hall, 2004: 167). However, if the research has taken a participatory, action research orientation which involves a reflexive interrogation of the process and findings then one might expect that the researcher's voice will be active and apparent. It is also important to avoid assertions that are not backed up by evidence and to ensure that, even if the researcher's voice is active, their opinions and interpretation are separate from other findings.

Whichever strategic approach you adopt you will have to make decisions about which data to include and which to discard as it would be impossible for you to include everything. This represents an ethical decision because it should be driven by the desire to make the report as representative and authentic as possible. This may not necessarily be your own or a sponsor's preferred emphasis. Research reports should have the 'Brighton Rock' effect where, metaphorically speaking, relevant words run through the middle of the candy. This is to say that the central thesis should recurrently re-centre on the core question/problem and that this is integrated into every aspect, be it the context, choice of methods, findings or discussion.

STRUCTURE OF THE REPORT

Cover

This is important as it must detail important information about the report such as the name of the researcher, the title of the project, the contact details and the name of the organisation, community group, university, sponsor, or partners in the project.

Contents page

This is important to the reader as it enables them to locate differing chapters or items rapidly. It also helps them understand the systematic process that the report represents.

Preface

This gives a researcher the opportunity to acknowledge the contributions of those supervisors, sponsors and participants who have directly or indirectly assisted with the project. With research participants this is particularly important as it would be completely unprofessional not to recognise that without their contribution there would be no project. It also provides an opportunity for researchers to offer 'a sense of the personal' (Hall & Hall, 2004: 176) at the outset of the report, even if the rest of it is very impersonal and formal.

Abstract/Executive Summary

This is usually a relatively short item and provides a succinct overview of the whole project. This should cover the research problem, the contextual background to the investigation, any methods adopted and key findings, and also the conclusion and recommendations. Some readers may only ever look at the summary as it should be able to provide an effective 'briefing tool'. As such it is best written with this in mind (Reardon, 2006).

Introduction and background to the research

The introduction should explain clearly the aims and objects of the project. Much of the background can be incorporated from stages 4 and 5 of the research plan.

Literature review

Depending on the nature of the report it might be advisable to explore key contextual material to help 'create the need' for the research and locate it within existing data.

Findings

This section can include both the findings and discussion or can separate the findings from the discussion with the former preceding the latter. Whichever kind of data you have you will want to present these in a clear, logical and straightforward way. One of the most difficult tasks at this stage is deciding which data to include and which to abandon. You cannot include everything otherwise you will have an unfocused, over-lengthy dossier that fails to communicate the pertinent messages. This decision should be determined by whether or not the data directly relate to the original research question and its related themes.

Quantitative data are likely to be presented as numerals with the use of tables and graphs. These should be clearly headed and introduced and be followed by a short commentary that does not repeat the findings in the table (why bother having a table if this is the case?) but instead highlights the salient message it offers (Bryman, 2004). Qualitative data are likely to be presented predominantly in prose or in a matrix and may include quotes from participants. This type of data can be particularly challenging when deciding what to include because it can easily become over-descriptive.

Conclusions and recommendation

The conclusion should begin with a brief overview of the context, purpose and methods of gathering the data. It should then provide an opportunity for a discussion of the findings and explain and interpret the salient points if this has not already happened in the findings section. If this is so, then the findings should be briefly summarised. This is a chance to highlight how the findings relate to the research question, the literature and the context of the investigation. Findings may confirm, challenge or deepen understanding of existing knowledge of the subject. This part of the report should not introduce any new ideas or sources. It has to be a logical culmination of all that has gone before.

In addition a researcher will want to draw attention to the implications of their research for social work and any limitations on the scope of the enquiry that might have existed. Out of the findings there may be key recommendations. These need to be achievable and should emerge directly from the investigation and should not represent a wish-list for future action.

References and appendices

Whether a research report is for academic assessment or other purposes, it should provide full references to all the texts cited in the script. This is not only good scholarship but also lends credibility to the investigation. There is nothing more frustrating than an interesting citation in the text that proves to be untraceable because it is not properly referenced in the bibliography.

An appendix should include material such as information sheets for participants, consent forms, questionnaire or interview schedules, ethical approval letters, etc.

CONCLUSION

The overall emphasis of this chapter has been that doing research should lead to an outcome that communicates a new perspective to an audience in the wider community in order to make a difference for the better. To achieve this any enquiry needs to plan the research process meticulously from beginning to end so as to provide a map that guides the researcher through the research process and provides a credible and transparent proposal for partners, sponsors, participants and others. On completion of the research the process should be written up in a report that will clearly and concisely communicate its findings and any new perspectives that have emerged from the investigation.

Key points

To plan the research and prepare a research proposal:

- Initially, you will need to identify a feasible subject for your research project and broadly visualise how you might investigate this from the beginning through to the completion of a research report. This planning can then form the basis of a research proposal that will provide both a plan for action and an opportunity to communicate the feasibility of the project to interested parties.
- The subject for investigation then needs to be summarised by you into a clear research question that neatly encompasses the central thrust of the project.
- Having thought through what might be involved in the investigation you must assess whether you have the skills and expertise to do justice to the investigation.
- You will need to situate your research question in relevant policy, literature and research to bring clarity and focus to the subject.
- You will need to think through the methods you are going to use to gather the data to ensure you choose those most appropriate for your research question.

- At each stage of the process you must identify the activities required and the expected length of time each will take.
- Throughout the planning, doing and writing-up phases of the research you will have to continuously review any ethical implications of the project.

Writing the report:

- After doing the research remember that you can be assisted in writing it up as a report by recognising the correlation between the research proposal and the report's structure.
- Remember that an effective research report is one that clearly and concisely communicates its findings to an identified audience in order to enable them to understand something they were unaware of and to influence their future decision making and action.

Further Reading

Bell, J. (2001) *Doing Your Research Project: A Guide for First-Time Researchers in Education and Social Science* (3rd edn). Buckingham: Open University Press.

Flick, U. (2007) *The SAGE Qualitative Research Kit.* London: SAGE.

McNiff, J. & Whitehead, J. (2009) *Doing and Writing Action Research.* London: SAGE.

Reardon, D.F. (2006) *Doing Your Undergraduate Project.* Thousand Oaks, CA: SAGE.

Wisker, G. (2001) *The Postgraduate Research Handbook.* Basingstoke: Palgrave.

Wolcott, H. (1990) *Writing up Qualitative Research.* Newbury Park, CA: SAGE.

CONCLUSION

This book has attempted to demystify research for practitioners and encourage an active engagement in the research process, highlighting the part this has to play in social work's multi-dimensional roles. It has been argued that conducting research should be an integral part of practice, offering the opportunity for a knowledge exchange whereby practice informs research and research knowledge informs practice. Practitioners should no longer allow others to have a monopoly on knowledge production because social work requires research that both arises from, and reflects, the complexities of the practice context. It requires knowledge of the specific contextual situation found in practice settings. It is time for practitioners to use this situated knowledge to communicate an evidenced understanding to a wider audience and influence future practice and policy initiatives from this perspective. We hope that in pursuing these objectives practitioner researchers will work in partnership with service users, carers and colleagues in academic settings.

Throughout we have focused on the social work practitioner and student undertaking research because, as with service user-led research, practitioner research is an undervalued perspective both within the social work and academic community and the broader welfare sector – indeed not just undervalued but almost invisible. There are numerous reasons for this, ranging from the lack of infrastructure support provided by employers, funding bodies, academics and policy makers, to the traditionally low academic expectations of qualifying and post-qualifying courses that have given cursory consideration to practitioners doing research. All of this has contributed to a lack of confidence in the practitioner contribution. Social work requires research from multiple perspectives and this should include both the practitioner and the service user since each provides a unique 'coal face' insight which complements 'top-down' inductive knowledge.

The challenge for practitioners is to develop an attitude of reflexive destabilisation and 'research mindedness', a state of mind that can open up the possibility of exploring the interface between individuals and communities to seek further understanding and allow critical questions to emerge that relate to social work. This is a process that questions and challenges taken-for-granted assumptions to facilitate a better understanding of the experiences and forces that impact on practitioners, service users and communities. This endeavour can be seen as the starting point on a research continuum, with an awareness of the situated knowledge of the 'here and now' leading to the investigation of relevant research and literature to confirm and deepen this everyday understanding. From this stage of the enquiry a number of possibilities may emerge, ranging from endorsing and giving legitimacy to what is already known to acknowledging challenging aspects of that understanding and re-evaluating the situation. All practitioners should engage at this level of the research continuum to inform their practice and where appropriate should be encouraged and supported to move beyond this towards an active enquiry that identifies those areas that demand further investigation.

To achieve this transition to active researchers, practitioners will also need the support of the broader infrastructure of social work (for example, GSCC, DoH, JUCSWEC) and social work organisations (both statutory and third sector), as well as research institutions (universities and research funders like the ESRC). All these macro learning environments should encourage cultures of both individual and organisational learning.

Social work draws on specific values that predispose it towards 'relationship-based practice' to achieve social change for the better for individuals, groups, and communities. For the practitioner the service user is not just an individual in a social situation who is the subject of engagement but in fact also a unique individual in complex and uncertain circumstances. This means that any engagement must always seek to facilitate a relationship which can enhance well-being. This 'caring relationship' can provide practitioners with the opportunity for 'bottom-up' knowledge that is specific to the situation and context of practice – and it is from this perspective that practitioners can situate their research and sustain social work values in the enquiry process.

This is not about reducing the research scope by only looking inward to the individual circumstance. It is about looking upwards, inwards and outwards to explore the specific in the broader context, allowing the possibility of research that can address social injustice for disadvantaged individuals, groups and communities. To achieve these goals practitioners will need to work together *with* and *for* disempowered individuals, groups and communities in collaborative partnerships using methods that are appropriate to the task.

The type of approach and methods used will depend on the kind of data being sought. For instance, professional researchers might seek and have the capacity for large-scale quantitative surveys that will use frameworks for large amounts of data which can be analysed quickly and have the potential to inform national statistics. However, practitioners are unlikely to have the capacity to undertake this type of investigation and are likely to be concerned with small-scale enquires that relate to their specific situation – the service users and carers, the organisations and communities they work with.

This is why we have focused on methods that are appropriate to this type of small-scale investigation. We have explored those that are appropriate for applied social research such as interviews and questionnaires, observation and narrative and focus groups. With any method the most important thing is that the conceptual approach and methods chosen fit the purpose of the investigation and not just researchers' conscious or unconscious preferences. It has been argued that the requirements of this type of data gathering correspond very closely to features of an action and empowerment research orientation that assumes a participatory/collaborative approach, informed by a reflexive problematisation that involves a cyclical process of action, reflection and review. Also, this type of research endeavour is predicated on the assumption that it will seek to change things for the better thereby empowering the individuals and communities involved. Doing research is not in itself enough – it needs to be communicated to an identified audience. Therefore a dissemination of findings is a crucial element for successfully effecting change for the better and should be a central consideration for practitioner researchers. Thus they can make a difference: doing research, involving and telling others, achieving change.

Key points

- Doing research should be an integral part of social work practice.
- Practitioner research is presently an undervalued perspective. However, social work requires multiple perspectives including the 'bottom-up' knowledge coming from practitioners.
- The challenge for practitioners is to incorporate 'research mindedness' into their everyday reflexive approach to practice and to become research active.
- The transition from practice alone to active researcher requires the support of a broader infrastructure, including social work settings, regulatory bodies and research institutions.
- 'Relationship-based practice' can be applied to research as well as practice. It can sustain core social work values in the enquiry process and emphasise the imperative of working together *with* and *for* disempowered individuals, groups and communities in collaborative partnerships.
- Ethical considerations run throughout all aspects of the research process. Practitioners need to adopt an approach of reflexive deliberation to ensure they are 'open' and 'listen' to what is the most appropriate course of action.

BIBLIOGRAPHY

Alderson, P. (2000) 'Children as researchers: the effects of participation rights on research methodology', in P.H. Christensen and A. James (eds), *Research with Children: Perspectives and Practices*. London: Routledge Falmer. pp. 241–245.

Allen, G. & Langford, D. (2008) *Effective Interviewing in Social Work and Social Care*. Basingstoke: Palgrave Macmillan.

Anglia Ruskin University (2009) *Narrative Analysis*. Available at http://web.anglia.ac.uk/narratives/basics1.phtml (last accessed 25 November 2009).

Argyris, C. & Schön, D. (1974) *Theory in Practice: Increasing Professional Effectiveness*. San Francisco, CA: Jossey-Bass.

Argyris, C. & Schön, D. (1978) *Organisational Leaning: Theory of Action Perspective*. San Francisco, CA: Jossey-Bass.

Backett, K. & Alexander, H. (1991) 'Talking to young children about health: methods and findings', *Health Education Journal*, 50 (1): 34–38.

Baldock, J., Manning, N. & Vickerstaff, S. (eds) (2003) *Social Policy* (2nd edn). Oxford: Oxford University Press.

Barbara, A., Chaim, G. & Doctor, F. (2007) *Asking the Right Questions 2*. Canada: Centre for addiction and mental health. Available at http://www.camh.net/Publications/Resources_for_Professionals/ARQ2/arq2.pdf (last accessed 21 May 2009).

Barber, J. (1991) *Beyond Casework*. London: Palgrave Macmillan.

Becker, H. (1953) 'Becoming a marihuana user', *American Journal of Sociology*, 59 (November): 235–243.

Becker, H. (1967) 'Whose side are we on?', *Social Problems*, 14 (Winter): 239–247.

Bell, J. (2001) *Doing Your Research Project: A Guide for First-Time Researchers in Education and Social Science* (3rd edn). Buckingham: Open University Press.

Beresford, P. (2007a) *The Changing Roles and Tasks of Social Work from Service Users Perspectives*. London: Shaping Our Lives.

Beresford, P. (2007b) 'The role of service user research in generating knowledge-based health and social care: from conflict to contribution', *Evidence and Policy*, 3 (3): 329–341.

Beresford, P., Croft, S. & Adshead, L. (2008) 'We don't see her as a social worker: a service user care study of the importance of the social worker's relationship and humanity', *British Journal of Social Work*, 38 (7): 1388–1407.

Biklen, S. & Moseley, C. (1988) '"Are you retarded?" "No, I'm Catholic": qualitative methods in the study of people with severe handicaps', *Journal of the Association for People with Severe Handicaps*, 13 (3): 155–162.

Bisman, C. (2004) 'The moral core of the profession', *British Journal of Social Work*, 34 (1): 109–23.

Blaxter, L., Hughes, C. & Tight, M. (1998) *How to Research*. Buckingham: Open University Press.

Bloor, M., Frankland, J. & Robson, K. (2001) *Focus Groups in Social Research*. London: SAGE.

Bone, J. (2006) *The Hard Sell*. London: Ashgate.

Booth, T. & Booth, W. (1994a) *Parenting Under Pressure: Mothers and Fathers with Learning Difficulties*. Buckingham: Open University Press.

Booth, W. & Booth, T. (1994b) 'The use of depth interviewing with vulnerable subjects: lessons from a research study of parents with learning difficulties', *Disability and Society*, 11 (1): 55–69.

Boud, D., Keogh, R. & Walker, D. (eds) (1985) *Reflection: Turning Experience into Learning*. London: Kogan Page.

Bouma, G.D. & Atkinson, G.B.J. (1995) *A Handbook of Social Science Research*. Oxford: Oxford University Press.

Bowlby, J. (1982) *Attachment and Loss (Vol 1) Attachment*. London: The Hogarth Press.

Branfield, F. (2007) *User Involvement in Social Work Education: Report of Regional Consultations with Service Users to Develop a Strategy to Support the Participation of Service Users in Social Work Education*. Swindon: Shaping Our Lives National User Network.

Branfield, F. & Beresford, P. (2006) *Making User Involvement Work: Supporting Service User Networking and Knowledge*. York: Joseph Rowntree Foundation.

Branfield, F., Beresford, P. & Levin, E. (2007) *Common Aims: A Strategy to Support Service User Involvement in Social Work Education*. London: SCIE. Available at http://www.scie.org.uk/publications/positionpapers/pp07.asp (last accessed 15 March 2009).

Braun, V. & Clarke, V. (2006) 'Using thematic analysis in psychology', *Qualitative Research in Psychology*, 3: 77–101.

British Broadcasting Corporation (2001) *BBC News UK* (internet) 'Jedi makes the census list'. Available at http://news.bbc.co.uk/1/hi/uk/1589133.stm (last accessed 6 July 2008).

Bryman, A. (2004) *Social Research Methods* (2nd edn). Oxford: Oxford University Press.

Bryman, A. (2008) *Social Research Methods* (3rd end). Oxford: Oxford University Press.

Burchardt, T., Le Grand, J. & Piachaud, D. (2002) 'Degrees of exclusion: developing a dynamic, multi-dimensional measure', in J. Hills, J. Le Grand and D. Piachau (eds), *Understanding Social Exclusion*. London: Oxford University Press. pp. 30–44.

Butler, I. (2003) 'Doing good research and doing it well: ethical awareness and the production of social work research', *Social Work Education*, 22 (1): 19–30.

Cave, E. & Holm, S. (2002) 'New governance arrangements for research ethics committees: is facilitating research achieved at the cost of participants' interests?', *Journal of Medical Ethics*, 28 (3): 318–321.

Charity Commission (2007) *Stand and Deliver: The Future for Charities Providing Public Services*. London: Charity Commission.

Chase, S.E. (2008) 'Narrative inquiry: multiple lenses, approaches, voices', in N. Denzin and Y. Lincoln (eds), *Collecting and Interpreting Qualitative Materials*. Thousand Oaks, CA: SAGE.

Clough, P. & Nutbrown, C. (2002) *A Student's Guide to Methodology*. London: SAGE.

Cohen, L. & Manion, L. (1989) *Research Methods in Education* (3rd edn). London: Routledge.

Cooksey, D. (2006) *A Review of UK Health Research Funding*. Norwich: HMSO.

Corby, B., Doig, A. & Roberts, V. (1998) *Public Inquiries into Residential Abuse of Children*. London: Jessica Kingsley.

Corcoran, K. & Vandiver, V. L. (2004) 'Implementing best practice and expert consensus procedures', in A.R. Roberts and K.R. Yeager (eds), *Evidence-Based Practice Manual: Research and Outcomes in Health and Human Services*. New York: Oxford University Press. pp. 15–19.

Cornes, M.L. & Clough, R. (2001) 'The continuum of care: older people's experiences of intermediate care', *Education & Aging*, 16 (2): 179–202.

Crigger, N.J., Holcomb, L. & Weiss, J. (2001) 'Fundamentalism, multiculturalism and problems conducting research with populations in developing nations', *Nursing Ethics*, 8 (5): 459–469.

Cronbach, L., Robinson A.S., Dornbusch, S.M., Hess, R., Hornik, R., Philips, D.C., Walker, D.F. and Weiner, S.S. (1980) *Toward Reform of Programme Evaluation*. San Francisco, CA: Jossey-Bass.

Dana, J. (1999) 'Ways of listening to women in qualitative research: interview techniques and analysis', *Canadian Psychology* (May). Available at http://findarticles.com/p/articles/mi_qa3711/is_199905/ai_n8844178/pg_1?tag=artBody;col1 (last accessed 15 July 2008).

Darlington, Y. & Scott, D. (2002) *Qualitative Research in Practice: Stories from the Field*. Maidenhead: Open University Press.

Darou, W., Kurtness, J. & Hum, A. (1993) 'An investigation of the impact of psychological research on a native population', *Professional Psychology: Research and Practice*, 24: 325–329.

David, M. & Sutton, C.D. (2010) *Social Research: An Introduction* (2nd edn). London: SAGE.

Davidoff, F., Haynes, B., Sackett, D. & Smith, R. (1995) 'Evidence based medicine', *British Medical Journal*, 310: 1085.

Davies, H. T. & Nutley, S. (2002) 'The role of evidence in "modernised policy making" in the United Kingdom', *Academy for Health Services Research & Health Policy*, 19: 19.

Deakin, N. (1998) 'The voluntary sector', in P. Alcock, A. Ershire and M. May, *The Student's Companion to Social Policy*. Oxford: Blackwell.

Defilippis, J., Fisher, R. & Shragge, E. (2006) 'Neither romance nor regulation: re-evaluating community', *International Journal of Urban and Regional Research*, 30 (3): 673–689.

Denscombe, M. (1998) *The Good Research Guide for Small-scale Social Research Projects*. London: Open University Press.

Denzin, N.K. (1970) *The Research Act in Sociology: A Theoretical Introduction to Sociological Methods*. London: Butterworth. Available at http://www.getcited.org/pub/101658559 (last accessed 6 July 2008).

Department of Health (DoH) (1994) *A Wider Strategy for Research and Development Relating to Personal Social Services*. London: HMSO.

Department of Health (DoH) (1998a) *Quality Protects: Framework For Action*. London: DoH.

Department of Health (DoH) (1998b) *Modernising Social Services: The White Paper*. London: The Stationery Office.

Department of Health (DoH) (2001) *Seeking Consent: Working with People with Learning Disabilities*. London: DoH.

Department of Health (DoH) (2005) *Research Governance Framework for Health and Social Care* (2nd edition). London: DoH.

Dutton, A. & Worsley, A. (2008) 'Doves and hawks: practice educators attitudes towards inter-professional learning', *Learning in Health and Social Care*, 7 (3): 145–153.

East Midlands Oral History Archive (2009) *Transcribing and Summarising Oral History Recordings*. Available at http://www.le.ac.uk/emoha/training/no15.pdf (last accessed 24 April 2009).

Elliott, J. (2005) *Using Narrative in Social Research*. London: SAGE.

Engster, D. (2004) 'Care ethics and natural law theory: toward an institutional political theory of caring', *The Journal of Politics*, 66 (1): 113–135.

Erikson, E. (1977) *Childhood and Society* (2nd edn). St. Albans: Triad/Paladin.

Evans, C. & Jones, R. (2004) 'Engagement and empowerment, research and relevance: comments on user-controlled research', *Research Policy and Planning*, 22 (2): 5–14.

Faulkner , A. (2006) *We Need User-led Research More Now Than Ever Before ...* 5th Involve National Conference, Hatfield, 25 September.

Fletcher, J. (1966) *Situation Ethics: The New Morality*. London: SCM.

Flick, U. (2007) *The SAGE Qualitative Research Kit*. London: SAGE.

FOCUS & University of Chester (2008) *Walk This Way: Service User and Carer Led Research into Post Qualifying Training*. Chester: University of Chester.

Fook, F. (2002) 'Theorizing from practice. towards an inclusive approach for social work research', *Qualitative Social Work*, 1 (1): 79–95.

Fraser, S., Lewis, V., Ding, S., Kellett, M. and Robinson, C. (eds) (2004) *Doing Research with Children and Young People*. London: SAGE.

Friar, J. (1998) 'A vacuum in a minefield? Ethical dilemmas in research with learning disabled people', *Management Issues in Social Care*, 7 (1): 19–26.

Geertz, C. (1973) 'Thick description: toward an interpretive theory of culture', in *The Interpretation of Cultures: Selected Essays*. New York: Basic Books. pp. 3–30.

General Social Care Council (2004) *Code of Practice for Social Care Workers*. Available at http://www.gscc.org.uk/codes/Get+copies+of+our+codes/ (last accessed 20 May 2009).

Gibbs, A. (1997) 'Focus groups', *Social Research Update*, 19. Available at http://sru.soc.surrey.ac.uk/SRU19.html (last accessed 25 May 2008).

Gilchrist, A. (2003) 'Community development in the UK – possibilities and paradoxes', *Community Development Journal*, 38 (1): 16–25.

Gilchrist, R. & Jeffs, T. (eds) (2001) *Settlements, Social Change and Community Action*. London: Jessica Kingsley.

Glasby, J. & Beresford, P. (2006) 'Who knows best? Evidence-based practice and the service user contribution', *Critical Social Policy*, 26 (1): 268–284.

Glasby, J. & Beresford, P. (2007) 'In whose interests? Local research ethics committees and service user research', *Ethics and Social Welfare*, 1 (3): 282–292.

Goffman, E. (1963) *Stigma: Notes on the Management of Spoiled Identity*. New York: Prentice-Hall.

Gold, R. (1958) 'Roles in sociological field observation', *Social Forces*, 36 (3): 217–223.

Guardian Unlimited (2001) 'Alder Hey organs scandal: the issue explained', Available at http://society.guardian.co.uk/alderhey/story/0,,450736,00.html (last accessed 21 January 2009).

Gunther, M. & Thomas, S.P. (2006) 'Nurses' narratives of unforgettable patient care events', *Journal of Nursing Scholarship*, 38 (4): 370–377.

Gutch, R. (1992) *Contracting Lessons from the US*. London: NCVO.

Hall, D. & Hall, I. (1996) *Practical Social Research: Project Work In The Community*. Basingstoke: Macmillan.

Hall, I. & Hall, D. (2004) *Evaluation and Social Research*. Basingstoke: Palgrave.

Halliday, M. & Sherwood, L. (2003) 'Mental health user/survivor research in the UK', *Mental Health Foundation Update*, 5 (2): 1–6.

Hardwick, L. (2000) 'Older people with dementia and social work: lessons learned from an evaluative study', *Practice: A Journal of the British Association of Social Work*, 12 (2): 33–44.

Hardwick, L. & Hardwick, C. (2007) 'Social work research: "every moment is a new and shocking valuation of all we have been"', *Qualitative Social Work*, 6 (3): 301–314.

Hardwick, L. & Worsley, A. (2007) 'Bridging the gap between social work practice and community based welfare agencies', *European Journal of Social Work*, 10 (2): 245–258.

Harvey, L. (1990) *Critical Social Research*. London: Unwin Hyman.

Haywood, K. & Wragg, T. (1982) *Reviewing The Literature*. Nottingham: University of Nottingham School of Education.

Hek, G. & Moule, P. (2006) *Making Sense of Research: An Introduction for Health and Social Care Practitioners* (3rd edn). London: SAGE.

Hey, V. (1997) *The Company She Keeps: An Ethnography of Girls' Friendship*. Buckingham: Open University Press.

Holliday, A. (2007) *Doing and Writing Qualitative Research* (2nd edn). London: SAGE.

Hunt, A. & Winegarten, R. (1983) *I Am Annie Marie: An Extraordinary Black Texas Woman in Her Own Words*. Austin: University of Texas Press.

Iarskaia-Smirnova, E. & Romanov, P. (2007) 'Perspectives of inclusive education in Russia', *European Journal of Social Work*, 10 (1): 89–105.

INVOLVE (2008) *Deliberative Public Engagement: Nine Principles*. London: National Consumer Council.

Joint University Council Social Work Education Committee (2008) *JUCSWEC's Code of Ethics for Social Work and Social Care Research*. Available at http://www.juc.ac.uk/swec-res-code. aspx (last accessed 18 November 2008).

Jones, C. & Novak, T. (1999) *Poverty, Welfare and the Disciplinary State*. London: Routledge.

Jones, K., Cooper, B. & Ferguson, H. (eds) (2008) *Best Practice in Social Work: Critical Perspectives*. Basingstoke: Palgrave Macmillan.

Jordan, B. (2001) 'Tough love: social work, social exclusion and the third way', *British Journal of Social Work*, 31: 527–546.

Jordan, B. (2004) 'Emancipatory social work: opportunity or oxymoron?', *British Journal of Social Work*, 34 (1): 5–19.

Kadushin, A. & Kadushin, G. (1997) *The Social Work Interview: A Guide for Human Service Professionals*. New York: Columbia University Press.

Kapborg, I. & Bertero, C. (2002) 'Using an interpreter in qualitative interviews: does it threaten validity?', *Nursing Inquiry*, 9 (1): 52–56.

Kellett, M. & Ding, S. (2004) 'Middle childhood', in S. Fraser et al. (eds), *Doing Research With Children and Young People*. London: SAGE.

Kemmis, S. & McTaggart, R. (1988) *The Action Research Planner* (3rd edn). Geelong: Deakin University.

Kemshall, H. & Littlechild, R. (2000) *User Involvement and Participation in Social Care*. London: Jessica Kingsley.

Kendall, J. (2003) *The Voluntary Sector: Comparative Perspectives in the UK*. London: Routledge.

Kendall, J. & Knapp, M. (1996) *The Voluntary Sector in the UK*. Manchester: Manchester University Press.

King, M. (1997) *A Better World for Children: Explorations in Morality and Authority*. London: Routledge.

Kitzinger, J. (1994) 'The methodology of focus groups: the importance of interaction between research participants', *Sociology of Health and Illness*, 16 (1): 103–121.

Kitzinger, J. (1995) 'Qualitative research: introducing focus groups', *British Medical Journal*, 311: 299–302.

Kreuger, R. & Casey, M. (2000) *Focus Groups: A Practical Guide for Applied Research* (3rd edn). Thousand Oaks, CA: SAGE.

Kumar, R. (1999) *Research Methodology: A Step-by-step Guide for Beginners* (2nd edn). London: SAGE.

Kvale, S. (1996) *Interviews: An Introduction to Qualitative Research Interviewing*. London: SAGE.

Labov, W. & Waletzky, J. ([1967]1997) 'Narrative analysis: oral versions of personal experience', *Journal of Narrative and Life History*, 7: 3–38.

Lacey, C. (1976) 'Problems of sociological fieldwork: a review of the methodology of "Hightown Grammar"', in M. Shipman (ed.), *The Organisation and Impact of Social Research*. London: Routledge and Kegan Paul.

Lee, R.L. (1999) *Doing Research on Sensitive Topics*. London: SAGE.

Likert, R. (1932) 'A technique for the measurement of attitudes', *Archives of Psychology*, 140: 1–55.

Lofland, J. & Lofland, L. (1994) *Analyzing Qualitative Data: A Guide to Qualitative Observation and Analysis* (3rd edn). London: Wadsworth.

Lorenz, W. (2003) 'European experiences in teaching social work research', *Social Work Education*, 22 (1): 7–18.

Lorenz, W. (2006) *Perspectives on European Social Work*. Leverkusen: Verlag Barbara Budrich.

Loseke, D. (2001) 'Lived realities and formula stories of "battered women"', in J. Gubrium and J. Holstein (eds), *Institutional Selves: Troubled Identities in a Post Modern World*. New York: Oxford University Press.

Lukes, S. (1972) *Emile Durkheim: His Life and Work*. London: Penguin.

Lyons, K. & Lawrence, S. (eds) (2006) *Social Work in Europe: Educating For Change*. Birmingham: Venture.

Maddock, J., Lineham, D. and Shears, J. (2004) 'Empowering mental health research: user led research into the care programme approach', *Research Policy and Planning*, 22 (2): 15–22.

Marsh, P. & Fisher, M. (2005) *Developing the Evidence Base for Social Work and Social Care Practice Using Knowledge in Social Care Report No.10*. Bristol: SCIE /Policy Press. Available at http://www.scie.org.uk/publications/reports/report10.pdf (last accessed 22 June 2009).

Marshall, A. & Batten, S. (2004) 'Researching across cultures: issues of ethics and power', *Forum: Qualitative Social Research*, 5 (3): Art.39.

Mason, J. (2002) *Qualitative Researching*. London: SAGE.

Masson, J. (2004) 'The legal context', in S. Fraser et al. (eds), *Doing Research with Children and Young People*. London: SAGE.

Maxwell, C. & Boyle, M. (1995) 'Risky heterosexual practices amongst women over 30: gender, power and long term relationships', *Aids Care*, 7 (3): 277–293.

McCabe, H. (1968) *Law, Love and Language*. London: Sheed & Ward.

McCarthy, M. (1999) *Sexuality and Women with Learning Disabilities*. London: Jessica Kingsley.

McCrove, P., Dhanasiri, D., Patel, A., Knapp, M. & Lawton-Smith, S. (2008) *Paying the Price: The Cost of Mental Health Care in England to 2026*. London: King's Fund Publication.

McLaughlin, H. (2007) *Understanding Social Work Research*. London: SAGE.

McNally, D. & Hardwick, L. (2000) 'Barriers to making rehabilitation happen', *Managing Community Care, The Journal for Social Care, Health and Housing*, 8 (3): 28–37.

McNiff, J. & Whitehead, J. (2009) *Doing and Writing Action Research*. London: SAGE.

Merton, R. (1987) 'Focussed interviews and focus groups: continuities and discontinuities', *Public Opinion Quarterly*, 51: 550–566.

Merton, R. & Kendall, P. (1946) 'The focused interview', *American Journal of Sociology*, 51: 541–557.

Merton, R., Fiske, M. & Kendall, P. (1956) *The Focused Interview*. Glencoe, IL: Free Press.

Mier, N., Medina, A.A., Bocanegra-Alonso, A., Castillo-Ruiz, O., Acosta-Gonzalez, R. I. & Ramirez, J.A. (2006) 'Finding respondents from minority groups', *Journal of Research Practice*, 2 (2), Article D2. Available at http://jrp.icaap.org/index.php/jrp/article/view/74/74 (last accessed 22 November 2009).

Mills, C. (1959) *The Sociological Imagination*. London: Oxford University Press.

Mishler, E.G.(1986) *Research Interviewing: Context and Narrative*. Cambridge, MA: Harvard University Press.

Mishler, E.G. (2005) 'Patient stories, narratives of resistance and the ethics of humane care: à la recherche du temps perdu', *An Interdisciplinary Journal for the Social Study of Health Illness and Medicine*, 9 (4): 431–451.

Morrison, F., Stewart, C. & Okroj, L. (2008) *Children and Young People as Partners in the Design and Commissioning of Research*. Edinburgh: Scottish Womens Aid.

Munson, C.E. (2004) 'Evidence-based treatment for traumatised and abused children', in A.R. Roberts and K.R. Yeager (eds), *Evidence-Based Practice Manual: Research and Outcomes in Health and Human Services*. New York: Oxford University Press. pp. 252–263.

National Association of Social Workers (2001) *Code of Ethics*. Available at http://www.social-workers.org/pubs/code/default.asp (last accessed 21 November: 2009).

Noddings, N. (1984) *Caring: A Feminine Approach to Ethics and Moral Education*. Berkeley: University of California Press.

Office of National Statistics (2009) *Social Trends 39*. Newport: Palgrave Macmillan.

Oliver, M. (1992) 'Changing the social relations of research production?', *Disability & Society*, 7 (2): 101–114.

Orme, J. & Powell, J. (2008) 'Building research capacity in social work: process and issues', *British Journal of Social Work*, 38 (5): 988–1008.

Padgett, D. (1998) cited in Shaw, I. (2005) 'Practitioner research: evidence or critique?', *British Journal of Social Work*, 55: 1231–1248.

Pahl, J. (2004) *Ethics Review in Social Care Research: Option Appraisal and Guidelines*. London: Department of Health.

Parton, N. (2003) 'Rethinking professional practice: the contribution of social constructionism and the feminist "ethics of care"', *British Journal of Social Work*, 33 (1): 1–6.

Payne, M. (1981) 'Implementing community social work from a social services department: some issues', *British Journal of Social Work*, 13 (1): 435–442.

Powell, J. (2002) 'The changing conditions of social work research', *British Journal of Social Work*, 32 (1): 35–49.

Powell, R. & Single, H. (1996) 'Focus groups', *International Journal of Quality in Health Care*, 8 (5): 499–504.

Preece, D. (2009) 'Effective short breaks services for families with children with autism spectrum disorders: how one local authority in the United Kingdom is working to meet the challenge', *Practice: Social Work in Action*, 21 (3): 159–174.

Preston-Shoot, M. (2007) 'Whose lives and whose learning? Whose narratives and whose writing? Taking the next research and literature steps with experts by experience', *Evidence and Policy*, 3 (3): 343–359.

Public Health Resources Unit (2006) *Qualitative Appraisal Tool*. England: Public Health Resource Unit. Available at http://www.phru.nhs.uk/Doc_Links/Qualitative%20Appraisal%20Tool.pdf (last accessed 26 April 2009).

Puchta, C. & Potter, J. (2004) *Focus Group Practice*. London: SAGE.

Punch, K.F. (2005) *Introduction to Social Research: Quantitative and Qualitative Approaches*. London: SAGE.

Putnam, R. D. (1995) 'Bowling alone: America's declining social capital', *The Journal of Democracy*, 6 (1): 65–78.

Ranganathan, M. & Bhopal, R. (2006) 'Exclusion and inclusion of non-white ethnic minority groups in 72 North American and European cardiovascular cohort studies', *PLoS Med*, 3 (3): e44.

Rashotte, J. (2005) 'Dwelling with stories that haunt us: building a meaningful nursing practice', *Nursing Inquiry*, 12: 34–42.

Raynes, N., Temple, B., Glenister, C. and Coulthard, L. (2004) *Quality at Home for Older People: Involving Service Users in Defining Home Care Specifications*. Basingstoke: Palgrave.

Reardon, D.F. (2006) *Doing Your Undergraduate Project*. Thousand Oaks, CA: SAGE.

Reason, P. & Bradbury, H. (eds) (2004) 'Handbook of Action Research London', in S. Becker and A. Bryman (eds), *Understanding Research for Social Policy & Practice: Themes, Methods & Approaches*. London: Policy.

Reason, P. & Bradbury, H. (2003) 'Action research: an opportunity for revitalizing research purpose and practices', *Qualitative Social Work*, 2 (2): 155–175.

Rice, S. (ed.) (1931) *Methods in Social Science*. Chicago: University of Chicago Press.

Riessman, C. (1993) *Narrative Analysis*. London: SAGE.

Riessman, K.C. (2001) 'Personal troubles as social issues: a narrative of infertility in context', in I. Shaw and N. Gould (eds), *Qualitative Research in Social Work: Introducing Qualitative Methods*. London: SAGE.

Riessman, K.C. & Quinney, L. (2005) 'Narrative in social work: a critical review', *Qualitative Social Work*, 4 (4): 391–412.

Robson, C. (1993) *Real World Research*. Oxford: Wiley Blackwell.

Robson, C. (2002) *Real World Research* (2nd edn). Oxford: Wiley Blackwell.

Rogers, C. (1942) *Counseling and Psychotherapy*. New York: Houghton Mifflin.

Roose, G. & John, A. (2003) 'A focus group investigation into young children's understanding of mental health and their views on appropriate services for their age group', *Child Care, Health and Development*, 29 (6): 545–550.

Rowan, J. (1981) 'A dialectical paradigm for research', in P. Reason and J. Rowan (eds), *Human Inquiry: A Sourcebook of New Paradigm Research*. Chichester: Wiley.

Ruch, G. (2005) 'Relationship-based and reflective practice: holistic approaches to contemporary child care social work', *Child and Family Social Work*, 10: 111–123.

Ruckdeschel, R. & Shaw, I. (2008) 'Teaching as practice: issues, questions and reflections', *Qualitative Social Work*, 1 (2): 229–244.

Rutter, M. (2001) *Conduct Disorder, Future Directions: An Afterword*. Cambridge: Cambridge University Press.

Sackett, D.L., Rosenberg, W.C., Gray, J.A.M., Haynes, R.B. & Richardson, W.S. (1996) 'Evidence based medicine: what it is and what it isn't', *British Medical Journal*, 312: 71–72.

Schön, D. (1983) *The Reflective Practitioner*. London: Basic Books.

SCIE (2007) *Practice Guide: The Participation of Adult Service Users Including Older People in Developing Social Care*. Social Care Institute for Excellence. Available at http://www.scie.org.uk/publications/guides/guide17/files/guide17.pdf (last accessed 21 November 2009).

Scourfield, J., Jacob, N., Smalley, N., Prior, L. & Greenland, K. (2007) 'Young people's gendered interpretations of suicide and attempted suicide', *Child and Family Social Work*, 12: 248–257.

Scott, D., Alcock, P., Russell, L. & Macmillan, R. (2000) *Moving Pictures: Realities of Voluntary Action*. London: Policy Press.

Scourfield, J.B. (2001) 'Constructing women in child protection work', *Child and Family Social Work*, 6: 77–87.

Seebohm, F. (1968) *Report of the Committee on Local Authority and Allied Personal Social Services* (The Seebohm Report). London: HMSO.

Senge, P.M. (1990) *The Fifth Discipline: The Art and Practice of the Learning Organization*. London: Random House.

Sevenhuijsen, S. (1998) *Citizenship and the Ethics of Care: Feminist Considerations on Justice, Morality and Politics*. London: Routledge.

Shaping Our Lives & University of Leeds Centre for Disability Studies (2007) *Developing Social Care: Service Users Driving Culture Change*. London: SCIE.

Shaw, C. (1966) *The Jack Roller: A Delinquent Boy's Own Story*. Chicago: University of Chicago Press.

Shaw, C. & Palattiyil, G. (2008) 'Issues of alcohol misuse among older people: attitudes and experiences of social work practitioners', *Practice: Social Work in Action*, 20 (3): 181–193.

Shaw, I. (2005) 'Practitioner research: evidence or critique?', *British Journal of Social Work*, 35 (8): 1231–1248.

Shaw, I. (2007) 'Is social work research distinctive?', *Social Work Education*, 26 (7): 659–669.

Shaw I. & Gould, N. (eds) (2001) *Qualitative Research in Social Work*. London: SAGE.

Shaw, I. Arksey, H. & Mullender, A. (2004) *ESRC Research, Social Work and Social Care*. London: SCIE.

Sheppard, M. and Ryan, K. (2003) 'Practitioners as rule using analysts: a further development of process knowledge in social work', *British Journal of Social Work*, 33 (2): 157–176.

Silverman, D. (1998) *Qualitative Research: Theory, Method and Practice*. London: SAGE.

Silverman, D. (2006) *Interpreting Qualitative Data: Methods for Analysing Talk and Text* (3rd edn). London: SAGE.

Simey, M. & Bingham, D. (eds) (2005) *From Rhetoric to Reality: A Study of the Work of F.G. D'Aeth, Social Administrator*. Liverpool: Liverpool University Press.

Social Research Association (2003) *Ethical Guidelines*. Available at http://www.the-sra.org.uk/documents/pdfs/ethics03.pdf (last accessed 30 November 2009).

Stanley, N., Manthorpe, J. & Penhale, J. (1999) *Institutional Abuse: Perspectives Across the Life Course*. London: Routledge.

Stapleton, N., Whitehead, E. & Worsley, A. (2008) *Research Methods for Health and Social Care Practitioners*. Chester: University of Chester.

Starkey, P. (2000) *Families and Social Workers*. Liverpool: The University of Liverpool Press.

Stewart, D., Shamdesani, P. & Rook, D. (2007) *Focus Groups: Theory and Practice*. Thousand Oaks, CA: SAGE.

Stoecker, R. (2003) *Research Methods for Community Change*. London: SAGE.

Strauss, A. & Corbin, J. (1989) *Qualitative Research Methods*. Newbury Park, CA: SAGE.

Tammivara, J. & Enright, D. (1986) 'On eliciting information: dialogues with child informants', *Anthropology and Education Quarterly*, 17 (1): 218–238.

Taylor, J., Williams, J., Johnson, R., Hiscut, I. & Brennan, M. (2008) *We Are Not Stupid*. London: People First Lambeth and Shaping Our Lives. Available at http://www.shapingourlives.org.uk/documents/wansweb.pdf

Taylor-Gooby, P. (2008) *Reframing Social Citizenship*. Oxford: Oxford University Press.

The Association for Research in the Voluntary and Community Sector (2001) *Community Research, Getting Started: A Resource Pack for Community Groups*. London: ARVCS.

Thompson, S. (1996) *Paying Respondents and Informants*. Social Research Update Issue 14 Autumn. Available at http://sru.soc.surrey.ac.uk/SRU14.html (last accessed 1 November 2009).

Training Organisation for Social Services (TOPPS) (2004) *National Occupational Standards for Social Work*. London: TOPPS.

Trevithick, P. (2005) *Social Work Skills: A Practice Handbook* (2nd edn). Maidenhead: Open University Press.

Tronto, J. (1993) *Moral Boundaries: A Political Argument for an Ethic of Care*. New York: Routledge.

Turner, M. & Beresford, P. (2005) *User Controlled Research: Its Meaning and Potential*. Brunel University: Shaping Our Lives.

Virkki, T. (2008) 'Habitual trust in encountering violence at work: attitudes towards client violence among Finnish social workers and nurses', *Journal of Social Work*, 8 (3): 247 –267.

Vonk, E.M., Tripodi, T. & Epstein, I. (2007) *Research Techniques for Clinical Social Workers*. New York: Columbia University Press.

Walter, I., Nutley, S., Percey-Smith, J., Mcneish, D. & Frost, S. (2004) 'Improving the use of research on social care practice', *Knowledge Review 7*. London: SCIE/The Policy Press.

Warren, J. (2007) *Service User and Carer Participation in Social Work*. Exeter: Learning Matters.

Watson, T. (2006) *Organising and Managing Work* (2nd edn). London: Pearson Longman.

Webb, E., Campbell, D.T., Schwartz, R.D. and Sechrest, L. (1966) *Unobtrusive Measures: Non-Reactive Research in the Social Sciences*. Chicago, IL: Rand McNally.

Webb, S.A. (2001) 'Some considerations on the validity of evidence based practice in social work', *British Journal of Social Work*, 31: 57–79.

Wellner, A. (2003) 'The new science of focus groups', *American Demographics*, March (1): 29–33.

Wheeler, R. (2006) 'Gillick or Fraser? A plea for consistency over competence in children: Gillick and Fraser are not interchangeable', *British Medical Journal*, 332: 93–108.

White, S. (2001) 'Auto-ethnography as reflexive inquiry: the research act as self-surveillance', in I. Shaw and N. Gould (eds), *Qualitative Research in Social Work*. London: SAGE.

Whyte, W.F. (1955) *Street Corner Society: The Social Structure of an Italian Slum*. Chicago: University of Chicago Press.

Wiles, R., Crow, G., Charles, V. & Heath, S. (2007) 'Informed consent and the research process: following rules or striking balances', *Sociological Research Online*, 12 (2). Available at http://www.socresonline.org.uk/12/2/wiles.html (last accessed 5 November 2009).

Williams, L. (1988) *Partial Surrender: Race and Resistance in the Youth Service*. London: Falmer.

Williams, R. (1994) *The Non-Designer's Design Book: Design & Typographic Principles for the Visual Novice*. London: Peachpit.

Wilson, K., Ruch, G., Lynberry, M. & Cooper, A. (2008) *Social Work: An Introduction to Contemporary Practice*. Harlow: Pearson Education.

Winch, S., Henderson, A. & Shields, L. (2008) *Doing Clinical Healthcare Research*. Basingstoke: Palgrave Macmillan.

Winnicott, D.W. (1964) *The Child, The Family, and the Outside World*. London: Penguin.

Wisker, G. (2001) *The Postgraduate Research Handbook*. Basingstoke: Palgrave.

Wisker, G. (2005) *The Good Supervisor: Supervising Postgraduate and Undergraduate Research for Doctoral Theses and Dissertation*. Basingstoke: Palgrave.

Wolcott, H. (1990). *Writing up Qualitative Research*. Newbury Park, CA: SAGE.

Woodcock, J. & Dixon, J. (2005) 'Professional ideologies and preferences in social work: a British study in global perspective', *British Journal of Social Work*, 35: 953–973.

World Medical Association (1964) 'World Medical Association Declaration of Helsinki – ethical principles for medical research involving human subjects', cited in E. Cave and S. Holm, 'New governance arrangements for research ethics committees: facilitating research achievement at the cost of participants' interest', *Journal of Medical Ethics*, 28 (5): 318–321.

Worsley, A. (2000) *Halton Social Workers Experience of PQ1: A Research Report*. Liverpool: Liverpool John Moores University.

Worsley, A. (2004) 'Probation as profession' (M.Phil thesis, University of Manchester).

Worsley, A., Stanley, N., O'Hare, P., Keeler, A., Cooper, L. and Hollowell, C. (2009) 'Great expectations: the growing divide between students and social work educators', *Social Work Education*, 1 (13). Available at http://www.informaworld.com/10.1080/02615470802512697 (last accessed 24 April 2009).

INDEX